ROCKIN' YOUR STAGE SOUND

A Musician's Guide to Professional Live Audio

ROB GAINEY

HAL•LEONARD®

Hal Leonard Books
An Imprint of Hal Leonard Corporation

Published in 2010 by Hal Leonard Books
An Imprint of Hal Leonard Corporation
7777 West Bluemound Road
Milwaukee, WI 53213

Trade Book Division Editorial Offices
33 Plymouth Street, Montclair, NJ 07042

Book design by Adam Fulrath.
Graphics and illustrations by Rob Gainey.
Additional graphics pages 7, 45, 83, 125, 153, 171, 197, and 211 by Justin Bond.

Printed in U.S.A.

Library of Congress Cataloging-in-Publication Data is available upon request.

ISBN 978-1-4234-9278-8

www.halleonard.com

Dedicated to the loving memory of my grandparents,

R. H. Sr. and Marie T. Gainey, and George B. and Maddie Horne

CONTENTS

Chapter 6: Soundchecking
A Systematic Approach to Consistency

FOREWORD

GEORG VOROS

From my experience as a musician who has played in many different venues of all types and sizes, I have learned (the hard way) that there is no one ideal solution for achieving a great sound on or off stage. It is dependent on so many variables that to use one set of rules would be senseless and extremely foolish. That being said, there are certain solid principles and guidelines that, if taken into account and adhered to, will without a doubt lead to a better-sounding show—whatever the situation or venue.

Rob Gainey's book greatly helps to achieve this end result. By asking so many fine musicians, techs, engineers, and producers for their invaluable advice and suggestions, Rob has managed to cover an astounding number of areas and solutions regarding live sound. I believe that no self-respecting musician or engineer can afford to ignore the good advice offered here. There is something to be learned by all musicians, even those like me who have been performing for over 30 years.

This book also reminded me of situations I experienced where if I had had more insight into and knowledge of sound in general, I would definitely have avoided some sound-related issues. It also hammered home the obvious truth that what works for one person may not necessarily work for another. After all, you're not going to take a high-tuned jazz-sounding kit to audition for a metal or heavy rock band, are you?

Naturally, most things in life are much easier if you apply good old common sense, but a lot of the time this common sense needs to be guided. I enjoyed this book immensely, not only because it contains these commonsense solutions we sometimes fail to discover, but also because it provides new insight into existing questions concerning our immediate live sound environment. Most important, it offers one of the most valuable pieces of advice for musicians reading this book, which is simply to be nice to the people responsible for your sound. Let's face it; they can (and will) make or break your show. On the other hand, if you are an FOH or monitor engineer, and have received more than your fair share of criticism for your inability to deliver whatever standard of sound your job requires, then I truly hope you take in the relevant advice offered here to raise your game—to everyone's benefit.

Rob Gainey needs to be commended on tackling an often misunderstood "can of worms" subject—live sound! Anybody with any notable live (and studio) experience will undoubtedly agree that this subject is not for the fainthearted. Whether you are responsible for sound in front of an instrument or behind it, this book is for you. It will give you fresh, gainful insight into many sound-related issues and make you much more aware of how to achieve your very best personal sound and other sound-related goals.

Enjoy and learn!

Georg Voros
LRSL (Perf) Trinity College-London
Drums/Percussion/Author/Instructor/Clinician
www.georgvoros.com

PREFACE

For as long as I can remember, there's always been somewhat of a love-hate relationship between musicians and sound engineers. When things don't go well, each blames the other, but very little is ever resolved in the heat of the moment. Since I'm also a musician, I understand what it's like to deal with stage problems, regardless of whose fault they may be. Nobody likes a bad show, not even sound engineers!

Having sat behind the console for four to five bands a night, five to six nights a week for long periods of time, I have seen many amazing performances and more than my share of train wrecks. Some of these occurrences were back to back, and I was dead set on figuring out why. How could one band sound so great and the next band sound so bad? Being the house engineer made me the prime suspect, so my first evaluation was of myself: Did I do this? It was from this moment that the basic concept of this book was born.

Was it my fault? In some cases, yes. There were times when human error was inevitable, and not being one to walk on water, I accepted that responsibility and learned as much as I could. There's not an engineer among us who wouldn't tell you the same thing, but the ability to shake it off and get right back in the saddle allowed me to make sure it didn't happen again. Other times it was simply a misunderstanding or a complete lack of familiarity with what a band was trying to accomplish onstage that led to some mishaps; this would have been avoidable had the communication been better between the bands and myself.

Was it the band's fault? In some cases, yes. I became keenly aware of common mistakes that many bands were making onstage and made every effort to inform them of a problem, but many times my words evaporated into thin air; showtime adrenaline can very intoxicating! Other times it was, once again, a lack of communication or preconceived misconceptions that led to otherwise avoidable mishaps onstage. Young bands often spend much more time in rehearsals than actually onstage, so it's understandable that they would not be familiar with what works onstage . . . and what doesn't.

What's the real problem? While there can be no doubt that both engineers and bands have their share of responsibility, the real problem lies in the communication gap between them. There seems to be a "sound barrier," especially in the terminology used by both. Engineers seem to speak one language, and bands speak another. And while each of them knows what they're talking about and they both know exactly what they're doing, they don't always know or understand each other's situation. This is a direct result of people not communicating, and even when they're willing to work together; they don't know how to break the pane of glass that separates them.

What's the real solution? The first part of the answer lies in providing musicians with solutions to the things they alone are in control of: their equipment, their stage setup, their performance, and how well it's all organized. These elements are completely out of the reach of a sound engineer, so if these aspects are addressed properly, your band should sound consistently great every time you play. If they are not addressed, you can't possibly expect an engineer to organize them in the brief time they will be working with your band; it's not going to happen. It takes great communication to coordinate a show. I'm not only willing to put the cards on the table and tell you what many engineers would tell bands if they could, but also listen to as many successful musicians as I can to get their perspectives as well. I've probably learned more about the stage by doing this than I could ever learn sitting behind a console, and it's all here in this book!

The second part of the solution lies in providing engineers with a "bird's-eye view" of what many professional musicians look for in a great performance: their equipment, their stage setup, their monitors, and their goals at soundcheck. While many engineers will have a band play at a minimal stage level in order to have the most control over the FOH (front-of-house) sound, this doesn't always work for those players who need to feel what's happening onstage; monitors are not always the solution to everything. I think that once you see what these players have to say about their performances, you'll understand that one perspective doesn't always work for every band.

I invite you to read this book and learn as much as you can from it. You'll find great advice from musicians of all types and styles, as well as solid advice from sound engineers. I don't believe that any one person has all the answers, so I tried to bring as many people together as I could to get as many solutions as possible. I'm sure you'll find a lot to consider in here!

Rob Gainey

ACKNOWLEDGMENTS

I would to thank the following people for their help and encouragement during the process of writing this book; to the people who have inspired me and helped focus certain elements; and to others who have always been by my side, in spirit if not in person: Mr. and Mrs. R. H. Gainey, Sammy Gainey and family, Daylene, Paul and Brett Michael Horn, Terry and Jan Horne, Michael Gunderson, Sean Topham, Matt Clark, Scott Freak, Rob Escher, Matt Beal, Willie Basse, Clint Savage Bryant, Maya Henderson, Danny Rusak, Scott Stratton, Ron Tropp, Terry Davis, Ronnie Malpass, The Reedys, Justin Bond, Julliette Klanchar, Reuben and Diane Aguirre, Mike and Erin Grote, Brian Tracy, Tyler and Wayne Crook, Louis Mitchell, Chris Post, Bobby Koch, Tom Le Blanc, Michael Miller, Brian Buster, Bob and Lisa Marlette, Dale Turner, Darwin and Sandy DiVitis, Greg Birribaure, Damon and Mike Wilson, Len Fagan, Rob Harper, Audrey Marpol, Dennis Mancini, Matt Smyrnos, Lance Hubp and Zach Zallen, Alicia Mundy, Tommy and Glen Culbertson, Ricky Arnold, Bobby Suit, Robby Leak, Kyle Harrison, Ricky Hill, Sonny Lothridge, Tony Kennedy, Johnny Rampage, Dave Costner, Mike White, Matt Mahaffey, Bob and Alan Smithy, Ross Stern, Lionel Barton, Kevin and Dana Campbell, James Floyd, Tommy Scott (RIP), Howard Smith, and the many others too numerous to count who have helped and inspired me in some way.

Very special thanks to Scott Stratton and Markus Erren Pardinas, who dragged me kicking and screaming into the light of truth. You made this a much better book!

Special thanks to Lori Brake, Denny Gerard and West Coast Sound & Light for the use of their amazing photos in the graphics work. Thanks also to Paul and Leslie Doty and Tim Nesbitt of West Coast Sound & Light, Lori Brake, Randall Aiken, Jeffrey Kelly, Hillorie Rudolph and Brian Stewart of *Music Connection* magazine, and Bobby Kimball for the introduction to Tim!

Extra special thanks to Maya Dawn Henderson, Joy Sumida, Neil Zlozower, Lori Brake, John Payne, and Joe Petro, who have gone far beyond the call of duty to help me in every way possible. You're the best!

My most sincere thanks go to the many awesome professionals who have given their heart and soul to their music and this book to inspire us all! Atma Anur, Ed Roth, Willie Basse, Maurice "MO" Rodgers, Jerry "Wyzard" Seay, Sean McNabb, Ralph Saenz (Michael Starr), Doug Doppler, Bobby Rondinelli, Francis Ruiz, Geoff Nichols, Glen Sobel, Jaime St. James, Trevor Thornton, Pawel Maciwoda, Scott Honsberger, Louis Metoyer, Ira Black, Earle Dumler, Bjorn Englen, Georg Voros, Burleigh Drummond, Bruce Bouillet, Frankie Banali, Nick Menza, Rob Marcello, Dave Foreman, Paul Doty, Jon Butcher, Mitch Perry, Bryan Bassett, Mindi Abair, Alex DePue, Tollak Ollestad, Erik Norlander, Todd and Troy Garner, James Kottak, Mike Hansen, David Garfield, dUg Pinnick, and Tim Franquist.

Thank you all. *You rock*!
Rob Gainey

INTRODUCTION

Welcome to *Rockin' Your Stage Sound*. The book you are about to read is not just a book, but also a Web-interactive blueprint that will forever change the way musicians perceive stage sound. The website for this publication is www.rockinyourstagesound.com.

This book combines a solid foundation of basic principles with advanced techniques and radical concepts. It transcends the ordinary bag of tricks and reaches for a new level of understanding in live performance. While many of the ideas in this book will be familiar to most of you, never before have they been assembled in a way that reveals their true nature and underlying denominators. Based on common sense and the laws of physics, you will find this book fast-paced, easy to read, and surprisingly devoid of technical gibberish. While there have been many changes in both PA and stage equipment, the physics and logic that apply to using them has not. A solid understanding of the basics and a creative approach will always be the key to making any system work to its fullest potential. The primary objective of this book is to show you what you need to know about stage equipment and stage sound so that you can make the best use of both.

Sound is an invisible force that has its own set of rules, most of which are fairly easy to comprehend once you learn to visualize sound with your mind and imagine that it is visible. Learning how to listen is one of the most important aspects of sound to master. Listen to an instrument from all angles and distances; observe how it changes from point to point; change its location in the room; even change environments. As you do this, you will find out just how much *location, focus,* and *balance* can help to overcome obstacles in your stage setup.

Many people think that the sound engineer controls the sound of the band, but that is a misconception. The band provides the sound for the engineer to control and mix. Therefore, it is extremely important for your band to sound great onstage. Your tones, your balances, and your level of comfort are the most important objectives for you as a performer. There are many variables in live performance—the room, the PA system, the monitor system, the bands, and the engineers that run these systems—and every show you play will be different in some way. There will be some things you won't be able to control, but there are quite a few things that you can. In this book you will learn the fundamentals of your equipment, techniques for setting it up, basic PA and monitor usage, input sources, and organizational skills. It is a flexible system that will meet the needs of any band, not just a handful of tricks that will only work in some situations. While it is not the purpose of this book to teach you how to operate a PA system, you do need some idea of how it works to avoid creating problems for yourself onstage. This is crucial to good onstage communication.

It is important to read this entire book, in the order it was written. While the parts that are specific to your instrument will be of special interest to you, even the parts that don't apply to you will illustrate the logic that applies to all instruments and sound sources. In the beginning of each chapter, I establish its objective and introduce the wholesale logic that is applied to it. As each individual point is introduced, it is followed by a full explanation and in many cases illustrations. After all points are made, a logical conclusion presents a final look at how they tie together. The chapter ends with a summary of all the individual points made during the chapter. Once you have thoroughly read a chapter, these points will serve as a checklist before rehearsals and shows. They are listed in order so that you may find the entire explanation when you need more than just a "point line." Some points are made more than once, and some appear in other chapters.

You will see some terms and definitions in this book that you may never have seen before. I needed some way to describe what was in my head, so I took the liberty of creating a few of them. Don't be surprised if you get the "deer in the headlights" look when using them with other people—it just means they haven't read this book yet! There can be other names for some of these terms, but the idea will often be the same. I have included a glossary to define the majority of the audio terms used in the book, as well as a chapter on technical aspects that will help you with some of the more challenging issues you will face as a musician. The technical aspects are a bit more detailed than most of the individual points, and I felt they would slow down your reading if they were included in the middle of the book. To keep things moving, I saved them for last, when you will have a better idea of what you want to accomplish.

I have tried to include everything that I think is important to stage sound, without an abundance of superfluous information. Because I believe this book should be the beginning of a new direction in stage sound, I have created a website that continues the ideas and principles set forth in *Rockin' Your Stage Sound*. Anyone can access the chapter forums and specific topics at www.rockinyourstagesound.com, and I am sure that there will be many interesting discussions on the site.

For those of you who are hungry for more, there will be a second book to supplement this one called *Rockin' Your Stage Sound: Pro Tips*. It will contain even more professional tips from established players with a few surprises.

If you are tired of feeling helpless onstage, then it's time to turn the page and find out how you can finally "break the sound barrier" and take control of your stage sound once and for all. Let's rock!

CHAPTER PRIMER

Before we get into the chapters of this book, it is a good idea to have a look not only at what you will be seeing, but why it is important. Some of you may be tempted to skip around or skim through this book, but it is essential to work your way through from beginning to end in order to get the most from what you will be reading. Everything ties together and in a specific order that will make sense as you move along. But just so you know what to expect, let's take a closer look.

CHAPTER 1—YOUR TONE

This chapter covers getting the best possible sound before you even begin to think about rehearsing or performing. This is the very first part of your stage sound, and it should be as good as it possibly can. You will see how to eliminate common mistakes, prepare for future necessities, and find the tone that suits you best. Be sure to go through *all* of the instruments, not just the ones you are playing. By examining other instruments, you may find principles that apply to your instrument or save someone else the trouble of learning the hard way! After all, you will be onstage with some of these other instruments; don't let their problems become yours. It all begins with your tone.

CHAPTER 2—SETTING UP

This chapter deals with the very first step of rehearsing: setting up properly. The many options that are presented will give you more than just a handful of tricks; they will teach you the logic that is needed to understand what may work best for your band. When you have more than one instrument in an area, you need to coordinate everyone's tone without adversely compromising anyone. In this chapter, you will learn the basics of Location, Focus, and Balance. These principles apply to everything onstage. You need to set up in a manner that will allow your stage monitors to work their best. Put the right sound in the right place.

CHAPTER 3—MONITOR SYSTEMS

In this chapter you'll get to see the many different aspects of the monitor systems you will be rehearsing and performing with. If you have a good stage setup, your monitors will be much more effective. You will learn the limitations of each type of monitor system and how to make the best use of each one. The numerous examples will provide options and emphasize the importance of Location, Focus, and Balance. These first three chapters will be very important to productive rehearsals. Without productive rehearsals, there can be no productive performances! Put the right monitor in the right place.

CHAPTER 4—INPUT SOURCES

Now is the time to look at what you will need to make your band sound its best in the PA system. Choosing the right input sources for each instrument will not only give you the best sound in the mix, but also in the monitors. Most bands believe that the sound engineer should decide on and supply these elements, but when you see the advantages of your band providing the options that give you a decisive edge; it's a no-brainer. Not all of these options require spending money; some are simply considerations in your setup. Location, Focus, and Balance will again be very important to your input sources. Put the right source on the right sound.

CHAPTER 5—GETTING ORGANIZED

Your band is unique, even if it's a common five-piece rock band. The instruments and amps that you use, how you set up, the levels that you use in your playing, your monitor assignments, the input sources you prefer, your set list, mix cues, and lighting scenes will set you apart from everyone else. It would be absurd to think that someone outside of your band would *just know* what you need. Even if you took the time to verbalize all of these elements, it would be next to impossible for anyone to remember them all. By organizing the information that shows venue personnel what you need, you can increase your chances of having a consistently successful gig. Put the right information in the right hands.

CHAPTER 6—SOUNDCHECKING

Soundchecking and line checking are very important to the success of any live performance. Unfortunately, these checks are usually rushed through and can create an uncomfortable environment for everyone. By being prepared and having a solid plan, you can make the best use of this time to work on your sound, not just your load-in. All of the previous steps have brought you to a point where you should have a very good idea of what you need, and the less time you spend setting up, the more time you have to actually soundcheck. How you handle soundcheck determines how you will handle showtime. Make the best use of your time.

CHAPTER 7—MAKING IT WORK

Each individual chapter has been assembled with specific elements in mind, but this chapter puts them all together with a single perspective. Recapping the primary objectives of each chapter in succession brings continuity to all of them and shows how they work together. While this chapter is more philosophical than instructional, it covers the entire spectrum of taking control of your stage sound from start to finish and provides a logical conclusion to a practical system. Put everything into perspective.

CHAPTER 8—TECHNICAL ASPECTS

There are many technical aspects to musical equipment in general, but each can be specific to a particular application. This chapter provides a deeper explanation of stage equipment that can save you hundreds of dollars in repairs and many hours of frustration. It also covers specs and terminology that will increase your understanding of why something will or won't work. While these aspects aren't actually part of controlling your stage sound, they are definitely part of taking control of your stage equipment. Go the extra mile.

EXTRA CHAPTER (WEBSITE ONLY)— UNUSUAL STAGES
WWW.ROCKINYOURSTAGE SOUND.COM

This chapter, available only on the www.rockinyourstagesound.com website, looks at unusual stages and other oddities using the solid, basic understanding outlined in chapters 2 and 3. It is important to get a firm grasp of how conventional setups and monitors work before introducing these enigmas, since most of the techniques in this chapter are derived from combinations of those two chapters. You will see many of these strange stage environments before you get to the arena level. Once again, Location, Focus, and Balance will be your best friends onstage. Learn to be flexible and creative.

AUDIO GLOSSARY

This section provides definitions for some of the technical terms and acronyms used in this book and in the audio world. While most of the terms are discernable from the context, this chapter provides a quick reference when needed. Some of the terms used in the book were adopted to illustrate distinctions that have not been classified as of yet, but are clearly needed when discussing specific stage applications. Others are part of the language of engineers. Good communication will help you *Rock Your Stage Sound*!

Getting the Most from Your Tone Before You Get Onstage

YOUR TONE

Forging your tone is the most important thing you can do for your stage sound. It all begins right here. If you're not happy with your tone, you will never be comfortable with any subsequent adjustments you make. It is here where you will have the most control of your stage sound, and you need to make the best of any advantage you can muster. Even if you are confident about your tone, take the time to read this chapter thoroughly and see how all of the instruments work together. You may be able to help someone else who is struggling with their tone.

The logic is quite simple here: *You need to sound as good as you can before someone puts a mic in front of you.* Your instrument needs to play in tune with no squeaks or squeals, no buzzes or rattles, no hum or hiss, and no shorts or crackles, and it needs to do so in a consistent manner. In a perfect world, you would be able to eliminate all of these problems, but in reality you may only be able to reduce them to a tolerable level. Often it's a matter of getting it as good as you can and continually searching for ways to improve your tone. You will have the tools you need to shape your sound once you have finished this book.

Beyond simply having a great tone is the ability to project that sound into a PA system properly. It may sound great from where you are listening, but you want the audience to hear what you are hearing. This requires understanding the best means of getting that sound into the PA system, where it can be most effective in both the PA and the monitors. While the majority of this is covered in Chapter 4: Input Sources, this chapter will introduce the concepts of what you need to have and what to expect when you get onstage. There are some simple tools that will make the transition much easier.

Always listen to your instrument—that means actually listening to the sound of it. Ask yourself where the tone is coming from and why it sounds like it does. Then, consider all the elements of your particular instrument. Once you have done this, you are on your way to the "Zen" that is required to make intelligent decisions about your tone. When you can visualize the sound your instrument is making, you can understand it much better.

ELECTRIC GUITARS/ BASSES

1. ALWAYS USE FRESH STRINGS

This is something I can't place enough importance on. Strings go dead long before you notice them being dead. There is a temper to fresh strings that gives them the tone we all love. All those nice overtones and singing notes come from fresh strings. That temper is what makes them feel right. Your bends sound correct, your tuning sounds on, your action feels right. When strings lose their temper and go dead, they get rubbery. It takes more pick travel to pluck them, and that pulls the string sharp. Once picked, the sharp note now returns to its original pitch. That gives you a smeared reading on your tuner. How do you tune something like that?! Cheap tuners aren't fast enough to show this, but a good strobe tuner will.

When your strings are dead, you have to bend them further than normal because they're rubbery. Your finger motion has a memory, so chances are you will bend the string up to its normal bend position and may not notice that you're flat.

Crud buildup and kinks in your strings that develop near the frets also have a detrimental effect on your overtones and sustain. The crud will dampen your sustain, so wiping your strings down is very important to the life of your strings. The slight kinks that happen at the frets prevent your strings from developing the complex harmonics that make your instrument sing. Next time you change a worn set of strings, take a good look at what happens near the frets, and you'll see that your string is no longer perfectly straight.

Now, back to the rubbery string effect: your picking is really going to suffer. Your picking hand remembers what it takes to play a certain part, but if the string tension has changed, you will sound sloppy and out of time. You'll need a longer pick travel to pluck the string, and that will slow down any fast picking you have worked on. Since strings go dead gradually, it will be up to you to decide when to change them. If you can hear or feel the deadness in your strings, you have probably waited too long. Do yourself a favor and don't get accustomed to dead strings. Wiping them down every day along with cleaning the entire guitar will allow your strings to last a little bit longer. This will also help your frets. The bottom line is that you will sound better and play better with fresh strings. Use them!

2. LISTEN IN A QUIET ROOM

Your physical inspection should start with your guitar or bass unplugged in a quiet room. Tune it up to the correct pitch and play some of your songs, carefully listening to your sound. Look down the neck to see if it is straight, examine the body for cracks and loose parts. Shake your instrument to find rattles and buzzes. These small noises can really be a problem at loud volumes when the entire stage is a "vibration zone."

3. ELIMINATE BUZZES AND NOISES

Tighten loose parts or pad them to stop noises. Some of the trouble spots for guitars and basses are scratchy pots, crackling input jacks, and loose hardware. Even the untrimmed length of string that hangs from the headstock can create some strange noises. The portion of the string that runs from the nut to the tuners, from the bridge to the tailpiece, and the springs of a tremolo can introduce odd frequencies and dissonant harmonics to your tone. If you're hearing something you don't like in your tone, try dampening one of these areas to see if this may be the problem, but by all means trim your strings at the tuners! I've heard some ridiculous superstitions regarding not cutting them, but don't fall for that nonsense.

Bruce Bouillet—Guitar
Racer X/The Scream/DC 10 Epidemic/Bottom Dwellerz
Grammy-Winning Producer/Engineer
www.myspace.com/brucebouillet

"I put a chunk of foam under the pickups of my guitar, and I can almost face my amp directly without it feeding back. This is a crucial aspect in my sound; I have a lot of stops and breaks in my songs, and there's just no time to keep rolling the volume back and forth. I also recommend using graphite in your nut; it'll save you a lot of grief. There's always a temperature change when you go from an air-conditioned dressing room to a hot stage, and this will be the first place it shows up! I always have my guitars set up and intonated by a pro. If you aren't good at this, take it to someone who is, because they'll get it right. And if you do this once, it should last you a while.

I change my strings every time I play. I used to break them in for a day, but I found out that I'd get used to playing new strings if I changed them every time. I'll get a clean tone from my amp, and use an old-school Boss DS-1. It's a cool setup for me because I can go anywhere and my guitar tone is consistent.

Your instrument is like a car: if you don't change the oil and take care of the maintenance, you're going to have problems when you don't want them—onstage. At the end of the day, everybody just wants a good show; walk out there with your stuff in top condition."

COURTESY OF BRUCE BOUILLET

Hardware should be tightened enough to stop any rattles, the input jack can be replaced or bent with pliers to hold the plug tighter. Scratchy pots are difficult to clean and replacement is generally a good idea. Once you have your guitar/bass in a noise-free acoustic condition, you'll be ready to check out your amp in a similar fashion. This is covered later in this chapter.

4. INTONATE YOUR INSTRUMENT

Adjust your string height and intonate your guitar/bass for perfect pitch *in the key it is to be played in.* If you use several different tunings, it would be smart to have several instruments pretuned and intonated to the correct pitches. When that isn't possible, a compromise in the intonation is risky, but don't push that very far. If you can do intonation yourself, it is a good idea to do it every two to three months, or when you change string gauges. If you don't know how to do this, you should pick a string gauge you can live with and have your intonation set for the gauge and key you prefer to play in; a qualified tech will certainly ask you these questions. You may even want to stay with a particular brand as well. It's important that you set the action and pickup height before intonating. It's also wise to have your guitar or bass tightened up as best you can before taking it to a technician, so get it as close to being right as you can. The tech may be able to see something you've missed and correct it if it's a problem. In any case, your tech will have a better idea of what you are going for if you have your guitar or bass as close as it can be. If you've never had this done to your instrument, it's not a bad idea even if you think you know what you are doing.

5. CHECK ALL BATTERIES AND KEEP SPARES

Active Electronics. Another item that is often missed is the active electronics on some guitars; they require batteries. Even when the guitar is not using active pickups, sometimes there will be preamps or sustainers built in. Truthfully, I'm not a fan of these battery-powered devices; even when they do sound good, they always seem to lose their tone over any significant period of time.

Battery-powered devices can leave you open to problems, but they can also solve a few as well. If you decide to use them, just be aware of what you may run into down the road. It's nice to have all that tone at your fingertips, but it's much more reliable to create it at the amp than in your guitar or bass. Fresh batteries are very important to good tone, but *especially* so on bass guitar. It seems that the lower and higher frequencies are the ones that suffer the most with a weak battery, and the larger magnets used in bass guitars really like to chew through batteries. Keep the instrument unplugged from the input jack when not in use. This actually turns off the battery of the device. Always keep a spare battery in the guitar case of any guitar that has active pickups.

6. USE A QUALITY GUITAR STRAP AND FASTENER

While there's no need to spend a lot of money on a strap for your guitar or bass, it docs need to be strong enough to support your instrument while you're putting on a show. Using old, worn-out straps that could break during a performance is not a good idea. I'm sure your vintage leather strap may look really cool, but if it is starting to get thin near the strap buttons, it could let go, and it could cost you a considerable amount of money to replace a broken guitar. It's also an inconvenience to your show—if you really want break a guitar onstage, do it with style! You also need to examine how your strap connects to your guitar, as this is the most common failure in straps. Usually it's not the button itself, but the screw that holds it to the guitar. This can loosen up over time and eventually strip out. The two things you are looking for are:

> ***Is the button large enough to prevent the strap from coming unhooked?***
> This is easy to check. Remove the strap from the button; if it comes off easily, it's probably not big enough. This end is the part that wears out first on guitar straps, right where it hooks on to the button. Strap locks are very common and come in several choices; they are a wise investment for any guitar you would like to keep.

> ***Is the button attached to the guitar properly?*** Wiggle it, try to spin it, and even pull on it lightly; if you can feel it moving around, it may be a problem. There's a lot of movement happening at that point on your guitar, and even the most secure attachment can loosen up over time.

It would be better to check the button every month than grind it in and risk stripping it. Tighten it just to where it stops moving around; a loose button wear the fastest. Occasionally, the hole can become stripped out and the screw that holds your strap button won't stay in. This can be repaired with a toothpick and some water-soluble glue. Insert a small, flat toothpick and mark the depth, then cut the toothpick slightly shorter than the mark with a sharp knife. Cover the toothpick with an Elmer's-type glue and drop it in the stripped hole. Install your strap button and wait a while for it to dry. Use a water-soluble glue or you may not be able to remove it when you need to. For a quick fix at a gig, the glue isn't really needed.

7. SECURE YOUR INSTRUMENT CABLE

This is one of the small things that experienced players know very well. Run your instrument cable through the bottom of your strap at the point just before it plugs into your input jack. About 4 to 6 inches of slack is all you need. It doesn't take much to create a short in the plug, and running it through your strap gives it some strain relief. Otherwise not only can you damage the end of the cable, but you could also damage the input jack of your guitar or bass. You will occasionally stretch out the cable at some point, and if your cable is secured through the strap, it won't damage the instrument jack, the end, or come unplugged during rehearsals and shows. It will simply tighten up the slack you leave when you run it through the strap.

Jon Butcher—Vocals/Guitar
Jon Butcher Axis
Barefoot Servants/Johanna Wild
www.jonbutcher.com

COURTESY OF JON BUTCHER

"I'm primarily a Fender player, so I'm used to having to work for my tone. Unlike humbuckers, the single coils are translators; they have a different range of frequency response and touch sensitivity, so if you've got big hands like I do, it's a marriage made in heaven. I find that I can use any amp and get my tone with any of the Strats in my rotation; the tone is really between my hands and the fretboard. Taking it a step further, there's something so distinctive about the guitar that it seems to adapt to the personality of the player. I'll use Jeff Beck as an example—his tone has changed tremendously since he went from the old Les Paul to the Strat.

I prefer the sound of tube amps, specifically a small combo like a Deluxe, but I also use a Fender Blues Jr. It can go from a 4×12 to the softest jazz tone you can imagine, and people would never guess which amp I was using. My amps don't have to be boutique; I'm an "off the rack" guy. I can go pick one out at a Guitar Center and do a show with it that night. I see guys that feel naked without their fancy toys, and I'm exactly the opposite. It's just another link to go wrong. I've seen the huge pedalboards, and thought it was just too much to focus on; it takes away from playing.

Like most guys, I'll do a light warm-up before the show, but I don't have a pregame ritual. Some guys do. My last show was with an amp, cord, and an old '63 Strat, and I felt completely free. It's confirmed—I don't need anything! If you ever use a backline that isn't yours, what do you do? Do you cry, or do you plug in and make the guitar do the work? The audience doesn't care what you're playing."

8. ADJUST YOUR ACTION PROPERLY

Set your string height as low as you can comfortably play without buzzing. A lower action will have less tuning error than one that has to be pulled down further to fret. This becomes apparent when playing fretted notes along with open strings; the instrument never seems to sound in tune, even when it's set correctly. Keep in mind that there is some margin to work with, but a really high action will pose more of a problem than a moderate action. This is a compromise on any guitar, but especially so on bass. They aren't the easiest instruments to play, so you will want to drop that action, but at some point it will start to buzz and fret out. This is where truss rod adjustments and neck angles can really help.

If you are experienced, or have a good idea of what you want, you can go after this yourself. If not, it's time to go to the repair shop, and have a good idea of what you want for your action. Try to get the guitar as close as you can to where you like it when you take it in. It is important to set your action before moving on to intonation and adjusting pickups.

9. ADJUST YOUR PICKUPS PROPERLY

A common mistake made by a lot of people is adjusting the pickups too close to the strings. Since bass guitars are often played with your fingers, there is much more string travel, and that will sometimes take the string right into the pickup covers. This will give you a nasty kind of clink or clicking sound that gets worse with audio compression. Having the pickups very close to the strings may sound just fine for the smooth stuff, but will sound like garbage on the more dynamic playing. You may be playing so hard that you don't even notice it, but it will show up in recordings and live shows.

It will also show up acoustically when you play in a quiet room without an amp. It is most noticeable with metal pickup covers. Another problem with having your pickups very close to the strings is the fact that strong magnets will pull the strings slightly and kill your sustain. It's difficult for the string to vibrate freely when it is being pulled by the magnet. Totally eliminating this will be impossible, but there is a fine margin where your pickup will sound its best and the string will sound its best. It may take some experimenting to find the spot where you are most happy.

COURTESY OF CINDI CRAMER

Mitch Perry—Guitar
MSG/Cher/Edgar Winter Group
Asia Featuring John Payne
www.mitchperry.com

"Make sure your stuff's working correctly. You don't need to have everything hot-rodded and the latest mod and all that; it seems like less is more. I put graphite in the nut to keep the string slipping through, use one wind on the post, and lock the string onto itself to keep the guitar in tune. Your hands get the sound out of the instrument much more than the amp, but the amp shapes what you can or can't do, obviously. *Ultimately it's who plays the instrument; that's where your sound comes from.* I use a wah to shape the tone a bit and a tube screamer for sustain, not so much distortion. What I'm looking for in my tone is some body and width, not thin and "transistor-y." If you listen to Eddie Van Halen warming up backstage through a small amp, it still sounds like his Marshalls and 5150s, and it's not because he found the one amp that magically sounds like "Eddie"—it's because *he* sounds like Eddie!

Don't oversaturate or distort your sound; many of us are often guilty of this, but the more you distort it, the more you compress it, and that makes it sound small. It's why AC/DC sound as big as they do. You want a nice ballsy sound, and I don't like twangy guitars, but you have to get it to twang and then add with discretion. I see guitarists playing too many notes, using too many effects and gimmicks, worrying about too many scales and modes, and they forget to play *music*."

10. KEEP STRONG MAGNETS AWAY FROM PICKUPS

Avoid *any* contact with a magnet and your pickups: This will ruin your tone!! Even small magnets can be a problem, but very strong ones can damage a pickup permanently. This isn't a common problem, and it's one that most musicians may not even think about, but small children can find the most unusual places for magnets. This problem also exists for the degaussers used to demagnetize tape heads in recording studios. These devices can be permanently damaging to other magnetic devices if used improperly. Keep guitars at least five feet away from degaussers.

Bjorn Englen—Bass
Soul Sign/Yngwie Malmsteen
Robin McAuley/Quiet Riot
http://bjornenglen.com

COURTESY OF CARVIN; USED WITH PERMISSION

"The first link in your sound is of course your brain, but next is your hands; how you're attacking the notes is how you control your sound. *You should be able to get an even tone with both a pick and your fingers!* Practice with both, because it's not about the speed; it's about the tone, and you should be able to play fast with both. Then you need to have a good instrument; something that's solid, reliable, and well-crafted. I love the Carvin basses for that; plus they have a very even sound all over the neck, with all the notes on all of the strings retaining punch as you move up the neck.

I like my four-string basses to be passive and organic, but an active system seems to work great on five- and six-string basses. And who doesn't love the sound of a tube amp, but for traveling around they aren't the greatest for dependability. They're fragile and heavy. There are so many new amps that sound great, maybe a couple tubes in the preamp, but they've come a long way with solid state.

Marcus Miller said something interesting. I think it was, 'Find your tone and you'll find your amp, then move on and go back to the music! Don't spend your life looking for your sound!' Find a tone that works well for many situations where you don't have to adjust it too much and it will give you a lot of consistency."

DRUM SETS

11. ELIMINATE SQUEAKS AND RATTLES
Squeaky foot pedals are the most obvious source of noise, and some WD-40 will often take care of that, but rattles from loose hardware are more difficult to hear. Sometimes there will be a rattle when the kick or tom is played, but if you're not in the right spot, you won't hear it. However, that doesn't mean that the mic won't! You will want someone to help you with this and walk around your kit carefully as you play, and vice-versa. Both of you will probably hear something different as you do this. Always bear in mind that the room you are listening in will have some effect on your sound. You may often tune your drums very loose in a dead room and very tight in an ambient room to get your desired tone. In each case, your kit will sound different, and you may hear noises in one room that you don't hear in others.

12. USE FRESH DRUM HEADS
I can't stress this enough. Nobody likes the sound of cardboard! If you can see uneven spots in the heads, it's probably time to change them.

They should have some sustain to them, but not a constant ringing. It's very easy for other instruments to resonate in a badly tuned drum head. If your drums have a lot of sustain, some dampening may be a good idea. The "moon gel" that is sold in music stores can be found in a computer wrist pad for much cheaper. A cloth strip placed toward the edge underneath the drum head will give you some dampening, but may effect your bearing edge. Some drums have a felt pad on a spring arm that will dampen the heads when its adjustment is tightened. "Richie Rings" and "tone rings" are placed on the outside of drum heads to stop them from ringing, but can flap around when the drum is struck hard. Regardless of how it's done, some slight dampening will help keep heads from vibrating to every sound onstage. Just be careful not to go too far, or they will completely lose their tone; you still want to be able to hear the pitch of the drum. A little bit of reverb can open them up without having them ring.

Drums aren't like guitars and basses where you have specific pitches you need to tune to, but pitch is something that should be taken into consideration. I can remember producers and engineers tuning the drum set to the pitch of the songs or to complementary pitches in the band's overall sound. This art has long since been overlooked and is quite subjective, but it probably deserves a entire chapter unto itself. Whatever tuning you choose, there are some things that will apply to just about everything.

COURTESY OF ALEX SOLCA

Mike Hansen—Drums
Tribe After Tribe/George Lynch
Souls of We/Leif Garrett
The Pointer Sisters/Paula Abdul
www.myspace.com/cymbalcrasher1

"How I approach my tuning is that I start with the shell. I tune the drum up with the new shells to hear what they sound like, and then I send them off to be re-edged. They're beveled on both sides, but the angle has a lot to do with the tone of the drum. Depending on how you edge them, you can change the way they sound. The sharper the bearing-edge angle, the more attack you get. You also want to make sure that your edge is flat. It's similar to a gasket: if the gasket's not on straight, it'll leak tone and won't resonate properly. Take your drum and set the bearing edge on a flat surface; if you can shine a flashlight inside the drum and see any gaps, you need to have it trued and re-edged. You want this to be perfectly flat.

Always crack the seal on your heads before you put them on; otherwise you'll be tuning them twice as long. I love die-cast hoops for all my drums, but the snare is an absolute must. I don't always have them for the toms, but I prefer them. I usually have Ambassadors for the bottom heads because they're thinner, and Emperors for the top in live situations. If I want a warmer tone, I'll use a coated head, but for attack, I use the clear heads. I like my heads fairly loose. I finger-tighten all my heads, top and bottom, and I use my bottom head for 'threshold' more than tuning the shell. I use it for resonation, 'expanding the shell.' The tension of the bottom head will open up the drum or choke it. The top head gets tuned for tone, not technique. I sacrifice my technique for my tone. I'll finger-tighten it, and then I'll key it for a full turn, which is just enough to get the wrinkles out of it."

13. TUNE DRUMS EVENLY
Tune *evenly*, which means checking the tension at each lug. This will give you a more consistent sound when you strike different places on the drum head (yes, you will!).

Another thing you'll notice if you don't tune your heads evenly is that your stick response will change slightly in different places. It also helps the drum head last longer by not distorting or warping it. Not only will an uneven tune warp your heads but this phenomenon is exaggerated by the force of the sticks striking it over a significant period of time. By lightly tapping the head near each lug and carefully listening to each area, you can get an idea of how close they are in tension. This is a lot easier to do in a quiet place; not on a busy stage! They make a tension meter specifically for this purpose, but it's quite expensive and doesn't really make that much difference to the naked ear. Even if you don't have one, you can still do a good job without it.

Francis Ruiz—Drums/Tech
Great White/Samantha 7
40-Cycle Hum
Scorpions/Thin Lizzy/Motörhead tech
www.myspace.com/francisruiz

COURTESY OF NIKKI CORY

"The snare is one of the backbones of a great-sounding kit, as is the kick drum. Learn how to tune your snare drum. Whether you're into the 'wet paper bag' sound, or you like the high 'ping' sound, there's not much a soundman can do with either. In fact, a lot of times, the soundman won't put much of the high 'ping' in the mix because it's too obnoxious of a sound. Spend a few bucks and get a decent snare head. I've seen guys try to get a great sound using a beat-up old double-ply head on their snare—not gonna happen. If you loosen your snare head and it starts to resemble a soup bowl, it's time to change it. I've never been one for the muffled-to-death kick drum sound myself, but if you use the right kick drum head combination, you'll hardly need any muffling at all. You need just enough to stop the overtones from happening. If you make your head sound like a wood block acoustically, it's just going to sound like an amplified wood block out front. For the rest of the drums, the same rules apply.

Also, if you're in small clubs, you should consider using smaller cymbals. You don't need a 22-inch crash to project in a club. Let the mics do the work. How many times have you seen a bad-sounding band, because all you heard was the guitar on 11 and cymbals blaring over everything? If you're fortunate enough to be playing the 'Enormadome,' big cymbals can be really cool."

14. ALLOW ROOM FOR MICROPHONES

I'm sure I will get some feedback on this one, but someone needs to say it: *Leave some room for mics!* Not everyone does this, and occasionally I will go to put mics up on a drum kit and see six toms with cowbells, blocks, two hi-hats, and eight cymbals sitting right on top of them. And if there were any space left for a mic, I have no doubt there would be something else there. First off, I'm sure it looks really cool and you're a great drummer and you need all those extra sounds to be who you are, but how is anyone ever going to hear it if there's no room for a mic? And if your cymbals are sitting right on top of your toms, how can you get the cymbals out of the tom mics? There is a compromise here, but the reality of it is, "less is more." The less you have to set up, the more you get to play. With the 15-minute set changes in most clubs, you actually wind up with about 7 to 10 minutes to spend on setup. That also has to include setting up the mics. If you really want to sound good, you will give both yourself and your engineer some "space" and "time" to work with. Try to keep your cymbals a foot above your drums, and space them evenly across your kit. It makes the stereo overhead mics sound more even, as opposed to three cymbals on one side of your kit and one cymbal on the other side.

COURTESY OF NICK MENZA

Nick Menza—Drums
Megadeth/Marty Friedman
Deltanaut
www.menza.com

"I like mahogany shells because they have a darker tone to them for rock stuff. They don't project as well as maple, but I get more low end from mahogany. I like the Remo coated heads the best—Emperors, which are two-ply and have more of a slap attack on them as opposed to the clear ones, which have a more rounded tone. *There's a point of diminishing returns when you hit something so hard you just choke the sound.* I see guys do this with cymbals a lot; you have to know how to pull your stick back to get the optimum tone. There's a whole whip thing you have to do to get the tone out of it.

I tune my low toms first, because they're the hardest to get right, and then I'll tune the rest in intervals above them. If you get the lowest tom to sound great, the rest are easy. If I'm playing really fast songs, then I'll use two kicks, but for other stuff I just use a double pedal on a single kick, because it doesn't really slow me down. You don't get the bounce off the head from a double pedal on a single kick that you would from a double kick, because one beater is conflicting with the other on the fast stuff. I don't use the chains on my pedal, it's just too clunky for me. I like the leather straps or nylon, which sound much smoother and more flowing."

Typically, you will only get two to three tom mics to work with at most small to medium shows. If you bring four or five toms, what do you think will happen? Compromise, of course! Either the engineer has to run grab more mics/stands/cables, set up more channels at the console, maybe even gates and compressors for the extra toms, *or* he uses one mic on two toms. This works in a pinch, but is not exactly what you want to mix out front. While it certainly is better than nothing, chances are really good that he's not gonna set up more mics/stands/cables/channels in the middle of a show without costing you some time. If you lay out your drums with this in mind, set up your toms in pairs so that you can use one mic on both and be happy with what you get. The right and wrong way to do this is explained in chapter 4. I'm sure that someone will have something to say about my philosophy of miking space, but I would hardly sacrifice the majority of drummers for the few exceptions to this rule. The additional time required setting up all the extra drums and cymbals will be impossible to avoid, even if they could be miked properly—not to mention that each additional channel will add more bleed to the mix. Bring what you really need for the show. When you become a rock star, you can have whatever you want, and your own engineer to deal with it.

Glen Sobel—Drums
Elliott Yamin/Sixx A.M.
Beautiful Creatures/Impelliteri
P.I.T. Instructor
www.myspace.com/drummerglen

COURTESY OF GLEN SOBEL

   "Regarding tone, the most important thing to me is technique—the sound that a drummer gets from the drums using their own hands and feet. You can put five different drummers on one drum set, and the result will be that it sounds like five different drum sets. *Everybody has their own sound on their instrument.* The snare drum needs to be hit with consistent rim shots. The bass drum needs to be played without "burying" the beater into the head. The cymbals need to be hit right, etc. Playing solid and having good technique does not always mean hitting hard. Sometimes when a certain drum is struck too hard it can "choke" the sound of the drum. Lighter hits can sometimes get more tones and breath from the drum, so it fits better with the music. Stick size should be relevant to the gig, as well as many other variables, like dampening (duct tape, "moon gel," a packing blanket for the bass drum, Richie Ring muffles for the snare, etc.)."

15. PLAY WITH DYNAMICS
While we're actually talking about drums here, this applies to all instruments. It's easy to get caught up in the adrenaline of showtime and the fight to be heard onstage, but the harder you play your instrument, the less room for dynamics you'll have. Now, before you make a snap judgment here, at least take a look at my reasons.

   The kick and snare are the "meat and potatoes" of your drum sound; few would argue with this. However, the snare is in the most natural position to play, and it's easy to get carried away with your strokes on it. A lot of young players play their snare harder than any other drum, not to mention that it has more cut to it as well. When they play a roll across the toms, it's not as loud for three reasons: 1) They are harder to reach; 2) Toms don't cut like a snare; and 3) Toms are played faster than the single strokes of most snare hits. All three of these factors combine to make most tom rolls sound weak when compared to a hard snare lick. Gates and compressors can even some things out to a point, but nothing beats the sound of a naturally dynamic groove.

   Playing with dynamics gives you room to dig into the accents and keeps the softer sounds from being so buried in the blend. Fast tom rolls don't come through as loud as your single-note snare hits, so if you're playing your snare just slightly louder than your tom rolls, then you're probably pretty close to being "balanced," with plenty of room for dynamics. Just keep in mind that the more drums you have and the wider the range of tones, the more dynamic range you may need to keep them balanced. You want to leave some room for not only dynamics within the song, but also dynamics within the licks. When you want something to "cut," you simply lean into it. But let me give you the engineering perspective on just how important this is.

   If you are playing hard and digging in, the engineer will set his gain, compressor, and levels lower than if you were playing a bit softer, so there's really nowhere to go with your dynamics but down; after all, you can't play much louder. This means any fluctuations in level will most likely be dropouts. By playing near the middle of your dynamic range, the engineer will need to have more gain and level on your channels; this translates into more usable level when you need something to stand out in your dynamics. And this puts *you* back in control of your levels. You can get your drums to be louder when you need to and still have room to play softer when required. If you're in a situation where you have to play as hard as you can just to be heard at all, then there's a serious problem with your stage levels.

And I would be remiss not to mention the cymbals as well. Quite a few drummers buy cymbals that don't break easily, so durability takes precedent over tone in some instances. If you are breaking cymbals on a regular basis, there's a problem, and it's not the cymbal! The thicker, tougher cymbals don't respond as well to lighter hits, so you almost have to play them harder. Many players think that because there may not be a set of overhead mics for a drum kit that they should play them as hard as they can. Wrong. There are three to four mics on your kit that will pick them up quite well. Your cymbals should played at about the same volume level as your rack toms, unless you want to bury the toms. Lighter cymbals will give you a better range of response. Listen to your drum kit while you're playing it and see if your cymbals are louder than the actual drum hits. Making good choices in your equipment will allow you to play dynamically and sound balanced onstage.

Atma Anur—Drums
Richie Kotzen/Tony MacAlpine
Jarek Smietana/Cacophony
www.myspace.com/atmaanur

"The basic rule concerning gear is, get the best stuff you can and keep it in good order. Try to put things in cases as you move them; this stops unnecessary wear and tear. Keep things clean and lubricated, this will prolong the sound and the life of your stuff in general. Lubricating your lugs also makes tuning drums much easier. Cymbals can be a bit different, however; clean cymbals look nice, but many times cymbals sound better with age, especially for jazz and fusion.

After 30 years of teaching, I have found that the most prevalent problem is simply setting up in a way that makes it so that you can't just reach everything on your kit without some crazy amount of effort. *Don't let your setup get in your way; be able to play the whole kit!* My students eventually move things in closer. I like having my cymbals much higher than my drums, and I like to sit fairly low. Both of these things give me leverage in my playing, and I use my balance more to play well.

The best advice I can think of is to play at a moderate volume and play with musical dynamics. Most songs will tell the musicians how to play (the songs) correctly. All you have to do is listen. Just play the music and use dynamics."

ACOUSTIC STRINGED INSTRUMENTS

As we have done with everything else so far, set your instrument up, tune it up, and play it in a quiet room where you can listen to it carefully. Listen for buzzes or rattles, look for cracks and warps, and check for proper action and intonation. While most acoustic guitars have a fixed bridge, a good guitar tech can make a "compensated bridge" to get your guitar very close to being well intonated. No matter how great the tone is, if it's not in tune, it will sound bad. You need to be happy with the sound of your instrument acoustically, and this will always be true for any instrument. Once you put a mic on it, it just gets louder, not better.

16. USE A PICKUP ON ACOUSTIC INSTRUMENTS

One of the most important and helpful things you can do for your live sound is use a pickup on acoustic instruments. Microphones can be very touchy on acoustic instruments, especially when a monitor wedge is interacting with them. If you use a pickup whose levels are independent of instrument movement, you will get a more consistent and controllable sound. The pickup will always move with the instrument! You can still use a mic for a different tone, but you don't need it in your monitors to create potential feedback problems. It really doesn't matter if it's active or passive as long as there's something you can plug in to the console. As always, keep a close eye on any battery-powered pickup/preamp combinations. A pickup will be absolutely essential to be able to use a personal monitor.

Most acoustic guitars come with built-in pickups, and if you happen to prefer a guitar that doesn't have one, an aftermarket pickup can slide right in the hole. A built-in pickup certainly is more convenient and will give you more control over volume and tone parameters than a drop-in pickup would, but if it's the guitar that matters, then by all means use it. There are other ways to control your onstage sound by using your personal monitor.

For an acoustic guitar with built-in pickups, there's a rubber sound hole plug that can help eliminate the feedback problems of a poorly EQ'd and set up monitor system, which you will encounter if you play enough shows. Since you never know exactly when this will happen, you may want to have one handy, and they're relatively inexpensive. For acoustic guitars without pickups, this is not an option. The plug simply makes the sound of the guitar unusable. They work by trapping the tone in; if there's nothing inside the guitar to pick up the sound, then the whole purpose has been defeated. Same applies to guitars with built-in mics; the plug keeps the sound of the strings trapped outside of the guitar.

17. USE A MUTE SWITCH TO PREVENT PROBLEMS

You will want a "mute" for the output of the instrument so that you can tune up. Most floor tuners have this mute feature, but you can't use the volume control of the pickup; it is feeding the tuner. Also, you will want to mute the instrument when it is not being played, so it's not feeding back in the PA/monitor system as well as for muting the line when you plug in or unplug your instrument. If you do not have this feature, you can use a simple A/B box. It's cheap, but it'll get the job done, and still allow you to tune silently. This will work for mandolins, ukuleles, banjos, and electric guitars.

If you make instrument changes during the show, having a mute will keep the PA system from making a huge popping noise when you unplug and plug in. Engineers hate that! The proper way to do this is described in Chapter 4: Input Sources, with a diagram and an explanation.

18. USE A STAGE AMP FOR A PERSONAL MONITOR

I recommend using stage amps for anything that isn't loud enough to be heard on its own during the show. Club monitor systems are always hit or miss, and so are the engineers that run them. If this is not a primary instrument or you have a large band, you may not even get a monitor at all.

Having a stage amp will take all the guesswork out of your stage monitor levels. It will also keep the instrument from having to compete with your voice in the monitor wedges. This will put control back in your hands, where it belongs; the engineer has enough to keep up with. It will also allow other musicians to hear your instrument, even when they don't have a monitor right in front of them. I seriously recommend stage amps for all acoustic instruments with the exception of acoustic piano.

Another reason for having a dedicated stage amp for acoustic instruments is that the amp usually has an EQ and an XLR output built in. This will give you some control of your sound in case it starts feeding back or you need something extra. The XLR output serves as a backup when a DI fails or is not available.

Take the time to really work on your tone with your personal monitor, as this is your best bet for getting a great sound onstage. It will always be much more consistent than a monitor wedge, which will vary from place to place, engineer to engineer, and night to night. You never have to ask anyone for more acoustic in your monitor again!

COURTESY OF MICHAEL MESKER

Alex DePue—Violin
Steve Vai/Chris Cagle
DePue de Hoyos
www.myspace.com/alexdepue

"Number one, first and foremost, is practice! If you can really play your violin well, you can take any block of wood with strings on it and make it sound good!

I use an L.R. Baggs acoustic transducer for my violin. This transducer has a remote preamp/direct box with a multiband EQ that gives me some control over my tone onstage. The microphone-based systems run the risk of feedback and background noise. I use my tuner or a volume pedal to mute my violin for tuning or changing my instrument, but typically the volume pedal is strictly fully on or fully off. With Vai, one of the most fun effects I got to use was the Digitech whammy pedal. It was a new experience for me, and I always enjoyed the spots in the show where I was able to use it."

REED AND BRASS INSTRUMENTS

Mindi Abair—Sax
Concord Recording Artist
Duran Duran/Backstreet Boys
Lee Ritenour/Mandy Moore
Adam Sandler/Keb' Mo
www.mindiabair.com

COURTESY OF REISEG & TAYLOR PHOTOGRAPHY

"Tone is one of the most important aspects of playing. You can play faster than anyone else, but no one cares, because you don't have tone. Achieving a great tone is very personal. A great start is to check out the artists who have the tone you like. Try to pick apart what are they doing. Is it a special physicality that is creating the sound, or is it their mouthpiece/reed combination? It's probably a combination of a lot of things. Here's where you might want to start getting scientific.

►How are you blowing through the horn? Are you putting a lot of air through it using a lot of air pressure? Or are you using less pressure and a slower air movement through the horn? Both will achieve very different timbres.

►Check out and play through a lot of different mouthpieces and reed combinations at your local music store. With a little Internet surfing you can check out a few of the mouthpieces and/or reeds that your favorite players use. They may or may not work for you, but will help you home in on what you like.

►A horn is a huge part of your sound. You can have a tone in mind, but not be able to achieve it due to your instrument holding you back. Make sure your instrument will inspire you and allow you to create. Some horns are more contemporary-sounding and some have a darker, warmer sound. You should find one that allows you to shine with what you're planning on playing. You should become one with your instrument, and you should know your equipment. Know when your reed is too shot to get anything from, and know when it is going to roar. Once you have a horn/mouthpiece/reed setup that is comfortable for you to play and allows you to create the sound you're hearing in your head, start practicing and make it you. There already is a John Coltrane, a David Sanborn, and a Cannonball Adderley. Be the best 'you' that you can be; that's what it's all about."

COURTESY OF DAVID PALMER

Earle Dumler—Woodwinds
Frank Zappa/Barbra Streisand
The Beach Boys/The Carpenters
Three-Time Grammy Award–Winner

"Handling my own equipment as much as possible is the best situation. It's not like a guitar; they're much more delicate, and putting them together slightly wrong would damage them. When I'm playing, I run a swab through them at least once during every tune to keep the water out of the wooden instruments. The big sax has a spit key, but on the others it doesn't make that much difference. The wooden instruments can get water in the tone holes, and you have to be careful outside because the moisture and heat will affect them. At the Hollywood Bowl, we have heat lamps on the music stands that we can turn on to keep the instruments warm and dry. I never took my best instrument out, but I did carry two of each instrument. You have to stay on top of them, because they do go in and out of adjustment under the best conditions, so anything you can do to make sure the conditions are as warm as possible will help.

Springs can break, and replacing a spring requires special tools and taking the keys off, so it doesn't hurt to have some rubber bands around if you don't have a spare instrument. On one trip, I left the neck of a bass sax at a gig, and I had to play all the bass sax parts on baritone and transpose, so it's a good idea to be able to play your parts on a different instrument."

19. USE A CLIP-ON MIC WHEN YOU CAN

REED INSTRUMENTS

Saxes and clarinets are fairly loud acoustically, and don't really need a stage amp to be heard by the player, but the other musicians onstage and the audience will want to hear them. A clip-on mic or contact mic is a great accessory; it puts the mic in the right spot and allows stage movement without changing the tones and levels. The one exception I would consider is if a player were playing three or four similar instruments, then one boom stand–mounted mic would be fine. However, if three or four players were each playing different instruments, you'd want a mike on each instrument. The primary reason being that with three or four players, all could play their instruments simultaneously and the engineer could balance them properly. In the case of a single player with multiple instruments, he or she could only play one at a time and could work the mic to get the right signal from the monitors.

As always, go through each instrument and clean it thoroughly, taking care of any squeaks or scratchiness. Keep your keys and levers well-oiled and adjust them to play in tune properly; perform routine maintenance when needed.

Moisture and temperature can adversely affect the sound of these instruments, and your ability to play them. In most indoor situations, this really isn't much of an issue; however, outdoor gigs can be frustrating as the evening rolls along and things change. Try to bring a spare instrument for these types of shows and keep it set up and ready to go. It's important to have a few spare reeds of different types when you go out to play. The newer synthetic reeds have gotten better, and while they might not sound quite as good as a cane reed, they certainly sound more consistent and are able to work in extreme conditions that a cane reed may have problems with.

Another alternative is the plastic-coated reeds that still have much of the natural tone most people are looking for; these don't have the moisture problems of conventional reeds. This is great if you change instruments a lot and can't keep the reeds moist; they're ready to go. They also last considerably longer. I'd recommend finding a brand you like and keeping a couple around for emergencies.

BRASS INSTRUMENTS

Much of what was written above applies here as well. Clip-on mics are a good choice here too. As a matter of fact, *if you want to put on a show while you are playing, you will want to have a clip-on mic!* They come in many varieties: wireless and wired, condenser and dynamic, battery and phantom-powered, cheap and expensive. You may have to try a few to see which model best suits you best. As stated above, if one player is switching between several different instruments, set up one mic on a boom stand and use that for all of them. This makes it much easier for your sound engineer to keep up, and a lot less can go wrong during the show. You can't leave several open channels of mics next to the monitor unless you have some way to mute the mics when they're not in use. Using instrument cues will be discussed in chapter 6.

Tollak Ollestad—Harmonica
Don Henley/Michael McDonald
Kenny Loggins/Jewel/Seal
www.tollak.com

COURTESY OF KEYVON BEHPOUR

"When most people start off with harmonica, they typically go for a pretty simple approach. Few people start off with an old tube amp and a bullet mic to get that classic blues sound, which is cool and I like, but for me personally I don't hear the individual personality. One of my favorite players, Magic Dick (J. Geils Band), used a few different techniques, but there was always a real acoustic sound to his tone that shone through and carried his character. *I think it's more important that your personality comes through in your performance than your chops*; if your tone is recognizable, it's easier to stand out from the crowd. You have to find your 'voice.'

I've been playing Hohner harmonicas for years. I play both the blues harmonicas and a Hohner chromatic CX12 jazz, which are quite different beasts. The chromatic has two different registers and a button that switches between the white keys and black keys. I'll pull them apart and clean them occasionally, but generally speaking they're pretty reliable. Sometimes, I'll just toss a bad one and pick up a new one.

Onstage, I prefer to be on the side with the bass player or keyboardist, rather than the guitarist. If you're moving around onstage, you have to be careful that you don't wander into a hotspot and have your mic feedback. If I'm just playing harmonica, then I like my wedge to be right in front of me, but when I play keys too, my wedge is off to the side, and I have to be a little more careful with feedback considerations.

For keys, I keep it simple and run one or two keyboards, but never more than that. I'll run that right off the PA system. I used to have a whole system, but I've gone back to basic setups. It seems like keys need less help than they did years ago. For me, I'm more focused on the music than getting bogged down in the equipment. Back in the '80s, it seemed like everyone had a big rack of gear, but now it's gone to a cleaner setup. I'm looking at some powered monitors, but they're very simple, very light, and they sound really good."

KEYBOARDS

ELECTRONIC KEYBOARDS

These will be the most common type in the keyboard category. There are also many different types of samplers, beatboxes, tone generators, and the like, but essentially they all produce a line-level signal for amplifiers and PA systems. They produce no acoustic sound on their own, so no mics are needed.

When a keyboardist has only one keyboard or set of outputs, life is quite simple. However, when you start using three to four keyboards and having to control six to eight outputs, life can get messy real quick! It's at this point that most keyboardists use a submixer to balance levels and give themselves some control over their stage sound. In most cases, the mixer will provide a stereo pair of outputs for the PA. The keyboardist himself is mixing the keyboards in most instances, and some people are capable of doing this very well.

20. CAREFULLY CHECK ALL CABLES

If you are at the point where there's a lot going on in your rig—cables everywhere, channel settings to keep up with, MIDI controllers, volume pedals, and the like—it's very likely that you will have a problem. Rackmounting this gear and prewiring it with proper labels on both ends can keep things somewhat cleaner, but there will come a day when something will go out and you will have to make an adjustment or replacement in the middle of a show. Have a few backup items, because eventually something will need to be replaced. If it is absolutely essential to your show, make sure you have a spare. Some ways to get ahead of problems like shorted or noisy cables is to go through your rig at rehearsal and wiggle the cables around the ends, where they usually have the most problems. If you see a cable that is nicked or kinked, it may be the one to watch, or simply replace. It depends on your budget.

21. CARRY BACKUP POWER SUPPLIES

AC power supplies and adapter cables are essential to the operation of these devices, and you will probably need extension cords and a power strip or two to get all of these units fired up. Have a backup in case something gets lost or left behind. This is especially important for power strips, and have a long extension cord for when your AC power is far away. Care and the occasional inspection will help spot problems before they become disasters.

22. KEEP SPARE SOUND CARDS AND DISCS

Digital data is another item you may have to keep up with during your shows. It's always nice when your keyboard comes with all the right sounds in it, but that's not always the case. CDs/DVDs/memory cards are how sounds are loaded. It's a great idea to have a few backups in case something fails. They should be kept with the extra cables and AC power cords. You will want to keep rewritable data away from transformers and speakers; magnets can destroy rewritable magnetic media like tapes, cartridges, and floppies.

23. KEEP YOUR GEAR IN WORKING CONDITION

The mechanical aspects of your keyboard rig can be a problem as well. Bent keyboard stands and broken keys and knobs can make your show a bit more difficult. These are not the easiest problems to fix, but they should be taken care of as soon as possible. A small spare keyboard stand is something you may want to consider getting.

Loose or shorting output jacks can be a problem when a unit has been used extensively. These can sometimes be a real pain to fix, with all the microelectronics that go into some of these modern contraptions! If it's a broken solder joint, it's a bit simpler. If it's a defective jack, then an identical replacement is required, and so is some disassembly. Generally, they are PC-mounted jacks and require a steady hand and a good eye to correctly solder into place.

By far, the most frequent problem with electronic keys are broken buttons and other surface-mounted controls. It's frustrating because they want to work . . . about half the time, but they always seem to act up when you least want them to—onstage. This probably isn't something you really want to do yourself, but fixing it is much cheaper than buying anther unit. When it gets bad enough to be a problem, take the keyboard in for repair. There's no room onstage for crappy gear.

Erik Norlander—Keyboards
Asia featuring John Payne
Lana Lane
Big Noize w/Joe Lynn Turner
www.eriknorlander.com

COURTESY OF KEVIN MERCHANT

"The first thing is to find the right keyboards. For some guys, that maybe digital, for others, it may be analog. There's a reason Stevie Ray Vaughan played a particular Strat. It's the same thing with keys—you have to find the right instrument for you. The second step is to really understand how each instrument works. You can't just go down to the music shop and press preset buttons and expect to sound like a star. You have to learn how it works, how to program it and edit it down to the lowest level. What if you couldn't change the strings on your guitar, or didn't understand the pickup selector? Keys can get awfully complicated, and you want them to sound good; you just have to get inside it and get over it. A lot of players hit a wall there. While there's a lot more information out there in regard to other instruments, keyboards are a bit more difficult with the various models and the way they operate; you just have to roll up your sleeves and go after it. The depth of the parameters is much greater, but if you're gonna play it, you'd better learn how to make it sound great.

I work really hard at balancing all my patches, because nothing blows a keyboard sound more than having patches jump out of the mix; then the sound guy makes an adjustment and your level changes when you go back to your other patches! Try to get the levels as close as possible with programming, but also keep your master levels on each keyboard at about 75 to 80 percent, so you can make an adjustment on the fly when you need to. Stage environments can emphasize or mask certain frequencies, and require adjustments to even the most carefully programmed levels. I don't use volume pedals due to the fact that I'm standing and often have one foot on a sustain pedal. Trying to operate a volume pedal as well isn't a practical option, especially with any accuracy."

ANALOG KEYBOARDS

Hammond B-3s, Wurlitzers, and Fender Rhodes (when used with an amp) are all very classic-sounding devices. Each has its own set of problems and advantages, but is almost irreplaceable as far as tone is concerned. Make sure that everything is working properly and is sounding good. If you are not sure or suspect a problem, take the keyboard to someone who knows. Trying to run it in bad condition could damage it or even ruin it.

For those of you who prefer a vintage tone with modern reliability, using a vintage-sounding tube guitar amp with a digital keyboard can really bring out some old-school tone. Having a channel selector will allow you to drive some of your sounds for an edgy tone. Simply switch back to the clean sound when you want pure keyboard sounds. In many cases, it was an old tube amp that was a big part of the vintage tone, and they really do make a difference! This will be covered in much more detail in Chapter 4: Input Sources.

ACOUSTIC PIANOS

Since very few of you (if any) will actually carry around an acoustic piano, there's little point in getting carried away here; however, some of you may wind up using a house piano in some of the more swank venues. Since these instruments are miked and have to pick up a wide tone area, it would be a great idea to keep them away from loud instruments onstage. Pianos are made to be as resonant as possible and will pick up vibrations from amps and drums very easily. Since some of these "intimate stages" are rather small, this may be difficult to do, but create as much space as you can and keep your volumes reasonable onstage. There are pianos with built-in mics that do a pretty good job of keeping this problem to a minimum, but give it as much chance to work as you can. Using a wedge monitor with a piano can be tricky, but don't place it right on top of a piano under any circumstances.

COURTESY OF NEIL ZLOZOWER

Ed Roth—Keys
Coolio/Rob Halford
Christine W/ Glen Hughes
Bombastic Meatbats
http://onlinekeyboardsessions.com

"First, I try to pick instruments that really sing. Whenever possible, use a real instrument, not a sample. Real instruments, especially vintage instruments, really sing. Next, warm up your tone with an Echoplex or Space Echo. The tape warms up the tone and the Echoplex has a nice preamp that does great things to your tone. Whatever you do, try to use pedals before you use the multi-effects in the keyboard. *Stompboxes give a nice, needed edge and dirt to samples.*

For Clav, Rhodes, or Wurlitzer, try to run through a tube guitar rig, Fender Twin, Music Man, boutique stuff, or even a tube version Peavey Classic 50. Stick with Fender-inspired amps; generally open-back cabinets seem to sound better. If you want solid state, try an old Lab Series.

If you are looking for a B-3 tone with either a drawbar organ or samples, try to use a real Leslie. If that isn't available, try a Motion Sound mini Leslie. If you don't crank it too much and use a stompbox for distortion, they really sound good. Dynacord made a Leslie simulator that was incredible, but it's real hard to find."

VOCALISTS

Vocalists are just as important as anyone else on the stage. Everyone should know how to get the best possible sound, and in the case of vocalists, *the entire monitor system is their stage amp!!* When you look at it this way, you begin to realize the relationships in the system as a whole. It's very important to be a charismatic front person, but you still need to get your charms and talents delivered to the audience through the PA system, and you have to be ready to make adjustments. It takes great mic technique and a solid understanding of monitors. First, let's look at what you should *not* be doing. These are things that require you to pay attention during your show.

24. NEVER CUP THE BALL OF THE MIC
25. NEVER DROP THE MIC
26. NEVER EXPOSE THE MIC DIRECTLY TO THE MAINS OR MONITORS

CUPPING THE MIC

One of the most common mistakes I see singers do is "cup" the ball of the mic. Regardless of what you see on MTV or wherever, I can promise you that your mic will sound like crap! It will sound like you're singing in a tin can, if it's not howling like a banshee in the monitors. Having worked with the legendary Tom Jones on a particular night, I have seen the correct way to hold a microphone—just like a wine glass. And not just Tom, but most of the really successful lead singers I have worked with had an easy style of handling the mic. It wasn't an angry, clutched style like the mic was a weapon; it was almost a part of them. There is something very natural about the way a mic should be handled. I can't tell you exactly how to hold the mic for your show, but I can tell you what isn't going to work. Here are some of the most offensive techniques:

> ►Cupping the ball of the mic. (Sounds bad/feeds back)
> ►Dropping the mic onstage. (Can blow mains/mons)
> ►Lowering the mic into the monitors. (Feeds back)
> ►Bending over into the monitors with the mic. (Feeds back)
> ►Standing directly in front of the mains. (Feeds back)

While there may be some other bad techniques, these seem to be the most frequently committed crimes against the "system." If you make any of these mistakes onstage and it causes a problem, the engineer may immediately turn you down. You really aren't giving him or her much of a choice, it's either blow a speaker or turn your gain down. And often the engineer's reflex will be to pull you down in the mains first, then adjust your gain level. Don't get upset, because if you blow a monitor, you will get even *less* level. Not to mention you could really screw up the show for everyone else. And if you wind up taking out a driver in the mains, it'll be even worse. That affects everyone's tone! Don't disrespect the PA system.

27. BALANCE YOUR STAGE LEVELS WITH THE MONITORS

As the primary vocalist in the band, you have an important role to play: Stage Cop. That's right, you are the *volume police. When standing in your zone, nobody should be louder than your monitor; that's YOUR amp.* Since most vocalists are center stage, you also have the best listening position for managing stage levels. You should be able to hear everyone almost equally, with maybe the drums being a bit louder than the guitars and bass. No guitarist ever thinks he's too loud, and if the engineer is telling him to turn down, then the engineer must be the problem; but if it's the singer telling him to turn down as well, he may be willing to listen. You will have to earn band members' trust by being fair about it, but once you do, everyone will feel more comfortable about your observations. There are many ways to adjust instrument levels besides sheer volume. The principles of Location, Focus, and Balance will be revisited many times in this book.

28. USE YOUR OWN MIC

As the primary vocalist, you will probably want to own and use your own microphone. *A club mic is probably the most unsanitary device that isn't regulated by the health department,* but don't look for that to happen in the near future. A quality wireless mic is always a great choice. If you decide to use a wired mic, choose the same model that is in the clubs you frequently play. Don't try to be creative and get something that is expensive; chances are very good that it will not match up in the monitor system and will feed back like there's no tomorrow! Studio mics don't do well at all onstage, so don't let a salesperson push one on you. The secret is to use the same mic the club is using, because the monitors are EQ'd for that type of mic. No two mics sound exactly the same (unless they are brand-new), but they should be fairly close; close enough to be able to get good stage levels without having to completely re-EQ the monitors.

Jaime St. James—Vocals
Black & Blue/Warrant
Freight Train Jane
www.jaimestjames.com

"I can only speak as a vocalist, because we're a different breed of cat compared to guys who play instruments. *Rule #1: Get tons of sleep.* While the rest of the boys are at soundcheck, I'm in bed. 'The voice works best with tons of rest' . . . that's right—we get to be the lazy ones! *Rule #2: Get in-ear monitors.* Guitarists want to crank it up, and it won't matter as far as stage volume goes if you have your voice in your ears. Let your soundman deal with the house. In-ear monitors are expensive but worth it. *Rule #3: Don't drink alcohol before the show.* There's plenty of time after the gig, but if you're on tour, then you have to limit the party. *Rule #4: Put only your voice in your wedges and make sure you are cranked in the sidefills.* Stage monitors are limited. *Rule #5: Warm up your voice before the show.* I warm up my voice about an hour before the show by singing scales into a towel, so no matter where I am, I feel alone. Just jam a towel on your face and do it: on the bus, in the dressing room—or wake up the old people in your hotel room!"

29. KEEP WIRELESS SYSTEMS IN THE LINE OF SIGHT

Wireless mics are a real convenience, but they do require some consideration. As mentioned before in this chapter, always use fresh batteries. Have one for *every show*, period. Make sure that your wireless receiver is in the "line of sight" with the microphone. Don't hide it under the table, and try to keep it away from magnetic interference like large speakers, power amps, etc. Be sure you have adapters that will convert your receiver's output to both Hi-Z and Lo-Z signals. More details about wireless systems can be found in Chapter 4: Input Sources.

30. LEARN WHAT SOUNDS GOOD ON YOUR VOICE

As a vocalist, you may or may not have a preference for what effects you like on your vocals. Do you know what's available? Do you have something very specific that you need on your voice? And even if you don't want any effects, did you mention that to the sound person? If this is something that you've never considered, then it may be time to sit down and really listen to what can be done with your voice. If you have made a recent recording and you want your voice to sound like the recording (or as close as you can), then you need to find out what was done to your voice and take notes. For those of you who are looking for that something extra in your live sound, Chapter 8: Technical Aspects shows you how to calculate delay times for the musical timings of any song. If you are about to record a demo, then you can find out what effects sound good when you mix down. If you really don't care, then make sure that you don't complain!

dUg Pinnick—Vocals/Bass
King's X/Living Colour
The Mob/Poundhound
www.kingsxrocks.com

COURTESY OF DUG PINNICK

"I sing right on the mic, and actually put my mouth right on it. It seems like that's the only way I can connect to everything, and even without a bass in my hands I'll find myself doing this. Always warm up before you go onstage; never party and try to sing, no matter how much fun it is. It'll really tear up your vocal cords. I'm probably the worst steward of my voice ever. I haven't done much for it over the years, and it shows. However, the last couple of years I've been doing the Brett Manning vocal exercise for warm ups before I go onstage, and it's really helped me get my voice working again. It opens my voice up and I don't have to strain to hit notes. I'm still not up to where I want to be, but at least I'm not embarrassed anymore, lol!

I recommend taking some vocal lessons to learn how to breathe so you don't yell. A lot of people yell and lose their voice. I used to scream at the top of my lungs, because that's what I thought I was supposed to do, and I found that it really wore my voice out. Some of the greatest singers around can't hit quite the same notes they used to, but someone like Nancy Wilson still sounds as great she did when she was 20! It all depends on how you take care of your voice. Yelling is a good thing because it has a lot of passion, but you have to learn how to yell correctly without killing yourself. I used to walk offstage and not be able to talk to anybody after screaming for three hours back in the '80s and '90s. I didn't realize I was ruining my voice. I see other singers like Robin Zander, who can walk off the stage and have no problem; he gets up there and gives it all he has because he knows how to sing correctly."

You do need to have some idea of what you want your voice to sound like, so take the time to figure it out. If you prefer *no* effects, then make sure you specify that to the sound person, but don't expect engineers to know what you want unless you find some way to get that information to them. Many smaller gigs will have limitations on what can be done; others may not have the same gear you're accustomed to, so you may have to talk to the engineer to see what they have to work with before you go crazy with requests. The simpler, the better! Details on how to organize the many aspects involved in a live show are covered in Chapter 5: Getting Organized.

31. KEEP YOUR LYRICS HANDY
It is always a good idea to keep your lyric sheets for *all* your songs and go over the ones you're singing that night. Having all of them will be handy in case you have to change

your set or add a few songs. While you may be pretty good at remembering the words, sometimes it's the arrangements that are forgotten; seeing the lyric sheets will keep those in your memory as well. Besides, someone may want to sit in on a song; having the lyrics will make that possible.

COURTESY OF STEEL PANTHER WEBSITE

Ralph Saenz—Vocals
aka Michael Starr/Steel Panther
www.steelpantherrocks.com

"Since I've been performing three to five times a week for over 13 years, I've been through hell and back with my voice; however, it's given me the opportunity to learn what really works for me onstage. In the past, I would never warm up, because I would be playing the same venues in town on a weekly basis, but as of late I have been doing tons of traveling and not getting the sleep I'm accustomed to. The best thing for my voice is sleep; sleep is my savior, and it can be hard to come by on the road! I usually wait two hours after I get up to sing or use my voice in a loud manner to reduce the chances of my vocal cords swelling. Drink lots and lots of water—at least a gallon a day. And try not to eat right before you go to sleep if you have acid reflux or heartburn; it'll burn your vocal cords and make you sound hoarse.

Good microphone technique is important for any vocalist; I hold the mic up so I have to raise my chin to reach it with my mouth. This opens my neck line, which in turn opens my throat, allowing me to project my voice.

Being nervous before a show is a healthy emotion; however, when it's too great it can be a liability. Relaxing and taking deep breaths before and during the show helps me maintain the proper technique that works for me. When I do get nervous, I'm honest about it and share that with the band; I know they've got my back. We all work together and support each other.

I don't believe in trying to save my voice for the next night; it's just never worked for me. If for some reason it's sore, then I'll rework some vocal lines to give myself a break, but I try to leave it all on the stage . . . every night!"

AMPLIFIERS

32. LISTEN TO YOUR AMP WITHOUT EFFECTS

GUITAR AMPS

It really doesn't matter whether it's a tube or a solid-state amp; you want to plug your instrument in with a high-quality cable and listen carefully before you ever plug in an effect or processor. Do this with just your freshly checked-out instrument (you did this earlier, right?), your amp, and your ears. In the beginning, you will want to set your sounds at a reasonable listening level, since you may be there awhile. Take some time to play your amp without effects to see exactly what the amp sounds like when your effects aren't engaged. Find out how it behaves at certain volumes and settings before you start plugging in your units; otherwise you'll have no way of knowing. Once you hook them up, you may notice some differences even when they aren't switched in.

33. USE FRESH TUBES

If you have already taken care of your instrument, then you are primarily listening to the sound of it in the amp, but that doesn't mean that you won't find any noises that weren't present during an acoustic test. Get the best sound you can, then start to turn it up a little at a time. Listen for blown or rattling speakers, loose/vibrating screws and hardware, and harsh, unpleasant tones in general. Make some adjustments and see what happens, especially at higher volumes. Nothing super loud, just right around the level where you feel comfortable playing. You might actually want to do this in a larger room at some point to be sure that you have enough headroom to work with on larger stages. If you are using a tube amp, I highly recommend you keep fresh output tubes in it. The majority of the high voltage goes through these tubes, and they can be very temperamental when they get old. An excessive eerie "blue glow" from a tube means it is damaged and should be replaced. Glowing bright-red tubes usually indicate a shorted tube or an "over bias" in the adjustment. It takes an experienced eye to tell the difference in most cases, so if there's any doubt, have it checked out!

34. BUY AND USE A VOLT-OHM METER

Tube amps must also be properly loaded with the correct impedance; otherwise they can easily be damaged. That damage isn't cheap. Fuses and breakers are placed in the output section to protect the amp, but that won't protect you from everything. An inexpensive volt-ohm meter will save you a lot of worry and trouble when using strange speaker cabinets or connecting different speaker loads. Even when an impedance is marked on a cabinet, you need to be sure. *You can run a load that's higher than your amp setting, but never run a load that is lower than your amp setting.* While running a higher rating than your amp setting will work, it may not sound like you're used to, and can screw up your carefully dialed-in settings. Volt-ohm meters can be used to check cables, fuses, and power supplies. It's a $20 investment, but it is guaranteed to save you much more than that if you actually use it. Chapter 8: Technical Aspects contains information about the proper use of volt-ohm meters.

35. CHECK FOR MICROPHONICS IN YOUR RIG

The term *microphonic* means that something in the signal chain is picking up other sounds, including the resulting sound itself. This can really affect your tone, especially at higher volumes, and you may notice squealing and excessive noise in your setup. One way to test for microphonics is to rap on different components in the signal chain as if you were knocking on a door. While you can expect to hear something from your guitar and its pickups, you are primarily concerned with items that are supposed to be silent, like footpedals, connectors, amplifiers, and even cables. Crackle, noise, or anything that is noticeable in a component could be the first sign of a problem. Yes, it still works, but how well and for how long? Since it's a good idea to have spares of the various cables lengths that you use, swap out any suspected offender with your backup and see if that helps. If there's no change, keep looking until you have narrowed it down to the source.

In some cases preamp tubes will be the villain, and output tubes can have the same problem, but they're usually more noisy than microphonic. Remove or replace the suspect and see if this solves the problem. You should always have a matched set of output tubes at all times, since they are the first to go. Keep looking until your gear is solid and quiet before hooking up your effects; it makes troubleshooting much easier.

COURTESY OF BRYAN BASSETT

Bryan Bassett—Guitar
Wild Cherry/Foghat
Molly Hatchet
www.myspace.com/bryanpbassett

"For me, it begins with a quality tube amp. Because we use rental backline amps for our shows, I request Marshall 900s, which seem to be the most consistent amp available for my sound. I don't use distortion pedals, so the amp needs to have good tubes and be properly biased to get that singing quality I'm looking for. I run into some that are dead-sounding and don't have any sustain, and that's a very critical factor for me. I'll use a wah and a T.C. [Electronic] G-Major very sparingly for a little chorus and echo here and there on solos, but really the amp tone is everything!

Wooden stages are my favorite: they sound the best because of the reflections off the floor. On a concrete stage, I've actually placed a sheet of plywood on the stage in front of my amp to eliminate the harsh concrete reflections. I prefer playing from stage left. This way I can use minimal monitors and I can position myself between the drums, my amp, and the wedges and sidefills to get a good stage balance.

I like all my time-based effects to run in an effects loop, but it really comes down to the way you run your amp; I run mine with a bit of preamp crunch. Most time-based effects sound better in the effects loop between the preamp and amp rather than on the front end of the amp if you use the preamp in your amp for distortion.

If you're running loud and clean and are using distortion pedals, then it'd be fine to run your effects on the front end, because the preamp won't distort your delay sounds. I use a small Tech 21 MIDI Mouse to change my effects back at the amp; it's only a three-button unit that gives me control over the three to four programs I use, and it's hard to get lost with that! My priorities are "lean and mean" for most shows: I'm just going for a good straight-ahead guitar sound with minor embellishment."

36. TRY YOUR EFFECTS ONE AT A TIME TO FIND PROBLEMS

Most people use the floorboard-type footpedal effects units: they are cheap, easy to hook up, and take up very little space compared to rackmount units. However, they can be battery-hungry little noise makers! Most floorboards now come with power supplies built in, but that can also transfer hum into all of your units, or create a ground loop—not all footpedals will play nice together. You should check them out by adding them and removing them one at a time from the signal chain to see what difference they are making, even when they aren't being used. If there seems to be a problem with one unit, try hooking it up by itself and see if it is in fact the real source of the problem. Sometimes it's a combination of two pedals that creates a problem. That's when running a separate power supply for that unit may help solve the issue. It may need to be on a separate transformer, or it may need to be on a completely different AC outlet. These are just two ways you can fix ground problems. They may or may not always fix your problem, but you might want to try them before you spend money on a new gadget. In some cases, you may have to run one unit on battery power to stop it from humming or creating hum in other units. If a unit is causing a serious problem, it is not worth using.

37. USE ONLY THE EFFECTS YOU REALLY NEED

There is no denying the fact that the less effects you use, the cleaner your tone will be and the fewer problems you will have; however, they do offer some nice tones when used properly. Just be aware of the fact that since many footpedals are wired right into the front end of your rig before the preamp, any problems that happen will be amplified by this factor. For every cable you add to the floorboard, you have introduced four opportunities (each end of the cable and each input/output jack that they are plugged into) for something to go wrong, not to mention the unit itself. Only put up what you really need to have, as you will lose gain for every device you add. This is called "insertion loss."

Sean McNabb—Bass
Montrose/Dokken/Quiet Riot
House of Lords
www.myspace.com/bassriff2

"With tone, everybody's different; everybody's hands are different, and nobody's got the same tone. What a lot of people don't understand is that midrange is a very important part of getting a bass sound that will be able to cut through everything so you can hear your notes. Midrange is a very fine line: It can really make you sound awful, or it can really make those notes jump out. It just kind of opens up the frequencies to where your instrument doesn't sound like it's in a box— you get a low mid that opens the whole thing up, and you're like, 'Wow, the notes really sing now!' instead of being all low endy and muddy. So it's a fine line between adjusting the mids so that you can cut through the guitar. Most people—and I see this with younger players all the time—will punch in that extra-low button on the amp, which immediately kills the midrange. And there's nothing worse than having a guitar with so much low end on it that it's killing all your bass frequencies. To me, you got to have a tone that you can distinguish under that guitar, and your notes will cut."

COURTESY OF MICHAEL HERBACH

For every physical connection in your signal path, you will lose approximately 1 dB of signal strength, which can add up quickly. If you can find a unit that does several effects, this is preferable to having several individual effect units.

Rackmounted effects are usually much higher quality than your typical foot stompers, and some are studio-quality units capable of a wide range of effects. Most of the time these effects will be patched into an effects loop built in to the amp between the preamp and the power amp stage. This is where they generally sound the best. By being close to the amp, shorter cables can be used and less noise will be introduced into the system.

With all these advantages, why would anyone use the cheap, noisy stompbox units? It's simply *easier* to use footpedals. People go buy a couple, then they get a couple more, then they get a pedalboard and power supplies. By the time they purchase two or three pedals, most people feel obligated to use them. They didn't have to commit to it all at once, they didn't have to figure it out all at once, and they surely didn't have to pay for it all at once. Rackmount effects require a bit more expertise and a lot more time to program and set up, especially if they are MIDI-controlled units. If you haven't worked with MIDI, it can be quite daunting to a beginner. Even experts can be baffled by the myriad features available with MIDI implementation. You will have to spend some time with the manual to figure it out, as each device is different, even though the MIDI protocol is universal. It's the actual programming of these devices that varies, not so much their abilities. When there is a malfunction with a unit, it's almost always a programming error, and since there are very few visual inspection points, these problems seem to be more difficult to diagnose. It will most likely be worth it when you have it mastered, but it may not happen on the first try. The possibilities of MIDI-controlled devices far exceed anything a footpedal could ever offer, except one thing: convenience! It's very hard to deny the accessibility of plug-and-play devices.

38. DON'T WEAR EARPLUGS—TURN DOWN

There can be no doubt that loud sounds have an effect on your hearing, especially if you are playing a lot, but I'm not convinced that wearing earplugs solves the problem for anyone. In fact, they may actually create more problems than they solve. My opinion on this is that if you're playing loud enough to need them, you may be *too* loud. Why would you ask other people to listen to something that is too loud for you? There are several issues that are created when a musician wears earplugs onstage.

▶**It's Too Loud.** That's what the master volume control is for; reach over and give it a little counterclockwise twist. If it's another musician's instrument that's too loud, then there may be a problem with the way your band is set up. Try relocating their amp closer to them and farther from you. If space is limited, then refocus their cabinet toward them and away from you. If it's the drums that are killing you, then it could be acceptable to wear *one* (1) earplug on the side that is really loud. This will sometimes happen on small stages where there is no room to retreat, but anything that can be turned down should be turned down.

▶**Earplugs Change the Frequencies You Hear.** Most earplugs will typically filter out highs and mids much better than lows. This can cause you to turn up the highs and mids to compensate for this effect. Now you really have a problem! Not only are you too loud, but your tone is brittle and honky sounding. This is very difficult to mix around, especially in a small club.

▶**Earplugs Affect Your Pitches.** While the actual physics of this phenomenon are complicated, the effect is simple; wearing both earplugs can flatten your pitch very slightly. It's enough to make your vocals or your playing seem "off key." You will find yourself groping around for the pitch, but nothing ever really sounds right. Your ears are designed to operate with equal pressure on both sides of your eardrum. You should be able to understand this if you've ever had to "pop" your ears. Have you ever seen a singer put a finger to one ear? By wearing *one* (1) earplug, you can hear yourself with that ear, and the stage with the open ear. This is exactly what they are doing. Use one earplug only if you can't fix the problem on a small stage. The bottom line is that earplugs aren't the right way to solve a level problem. They cause too many problems. Use location, focus, and balance to get your stage sounds right.

▶**Earplugs Affect Your Ability to Hear the Monitors**. Stage monitors will almost never get loud enough to hear with earplugs in, and even when you can slightly hear them, you won't be able to jack up the highs and mids enough to make them sound right without risking feedback. This alone should be enough reason to not use them.

So if you want to hear something onstage besides yourself, take your earplugs out and turn down to a reasonable level; reasonable means that everyone can hear themselves. In chapter 2 we will look at alternatives to setting up onstage that may help solve the volume wars and prevent you from making things difficult to work around. As a guitarist or bassist, you actually have more control of your sound than any other musician; therefore you should not be the main cause of any stage level problem.

EFFECTS

This is something that all players should understand, not just guitarists. Vocalists, keyboardists, bassists, and drummers will all benefit from reading this part of the book. And while we have looked at some of the basics of effect pedals and rackmount units, let's get a better look at what they do and how to make the best use of them. By examining effects in general, you will gain insight into both onstage footpedals and the rackmount units behind the board. A lack of knowledge regarding their use has caused many a player to just say no to effects; however, they can be very handy tools for taking control of your sound—the sound inside your head.

39. PLACE YOUR EFFECTS IN THE CORRECT ORDER

Effect units can be divided into four primary categories: Dynamics, Tone, Pitch, and Time. To get the most natural sound from these units, they should be run in this particular order as well. Years of studio engineering has shown this to be true for the vast majority of sounds regardless of the instrument. Keep in mind that this is for those of you who want a *natural sound*; those of you who are looking for something out of the ordinary should really pay attention to this so you can see what rules to break. Why does this matter? Each category of signal processor has a particular function, and if placed in a different order it can interact or defeat the purpose of the effect. So let's look at the sequence of these units and why they should be run in this order.

DYNAMICS PROCESSORS

Gates, compressors, and expanders are often the leading processors. These devices are meant to correct signal levels and eliminate noise. While many people put their noise gates after some of the gain and tone processors to cut down on hiss, compressors should be the first in the chain if a noise gate isn't being used in this stage; otherwise the gate should be first. Why? Both compressors and gates are very input-sensitive devices, and even a slight amount of signal variation can engage them. Anything that was placed in front of a gate or compressor would affect its operation. Practically speaking, you wouldn't be able to switch effects in and out in front of one without having a problem with one of the dynamic settings.

TONE PROCESSORS

This category includes EQs, distortion, and level boosters. The vast majority of tone processors will affect the gain and signal level of your sound, which is why you want them after a compressor or noise gate, especially if you're switching them in and out of the signal chain. Otherwise, if you turn up the EQ, the compressor would turn down the entire signal, and the gate would open before you wanted it to. The exception to placing a gate after a tone processor is when it is set up in a "loop," which we'll look at very shortly.

PITCH PROCESSORS

Harmonizers, octavers, digital whammy, chorus, flange, and vibrato will change the *tune* of your sound. You want to get your sound right before you add these effects, so dynamics and tone processors should come before other effects. Adding distortion to a harmonized signal can sound rather nasty, which is why you want to harmonize your distorted signal. Each unit will not adversely affect another when correctly sequenced.

TIME PROCESSORS

Delay, slapback, and reverb will all change the length of time in your signal. These are the most popular effects processors, and most of them occur acoustically. These are the units you want last in your signal chain. If you engaged your reverb before your compressor, you'd turn it down—not just the effect, but the entire signal. If you engaged your preamp after your reverb, you would distort your reverb, and that doesn't sound natural. If you were to chorus your reverb signal, it'd sound washy and pitchy, because that's what a chorus does. Harmonized reverb sounds like poop! This also applies to delays and slapbacks. But if you're looking to create a unique sound, these are the rules you must smash. But keep in mind that once you start running things out of sequence, every setting becomes highly interactive and very specific; they may only work for one or two sounds. Fig. 1.1 shows a diagram of effects types and sequencing.

Fig 1.1.
Effects
sequencing

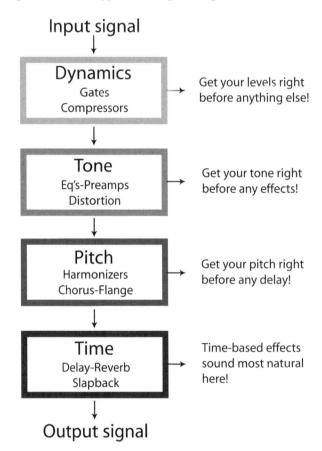

Input signal

Dynamics
Gates
Compressors

Get your levels right
before anything else!

Tone
Eq's-Preamps
Distortion

Get your tone right
before any effects!

Pitch
Harmonizers
Chorus-Flange

Get your pitch right
before any delay!

Time
Delay-Reverb
Slapback

Time-based effects
sound most natural
here!

Output signal

COURTESY OF JIM CORSO

Doug Doppler—Guitar

Favored Nations Artist
Guitar Hero Studio Musician
http://dougdoppler.com

"I think that one of the biggest mistakes some players make (including myself) is to forget to adjust the amount of time-based effects they are using to the room they are playing in. The amount of delay that makes a small room sound cool can bury you in a larger venue like the Ventura Theater."

40. USE LOOP SWITCHING TO CREATE UNUSUAL EFFECTS

There are times when you want to create a sound that is so unique and individual that it goes against some or all of the rules previously discussed. This would be a great place for a loop-switching device. Called "loop selecters," "switchers," and by a few other monikers, these devices allow you to set up a group of effects and switch them all in at one time. They can have multiple ins and outs, or they can be simple one loop in/out devices. There are even some complicated units that place each effect in a separate loop and allow you to set up many different combinations in whatever sequence you like.

One aspect of most loop switchers you should be aware of: they switch everything in the loop either in or out. And unless you have the more sophisticated variety, anything in the individual loops will remain isolated when disengaged. In other words, you won't be able to use one of the effects without using *all* of them, exception noted. You may, however, turn something on or off when the loop is engaged.

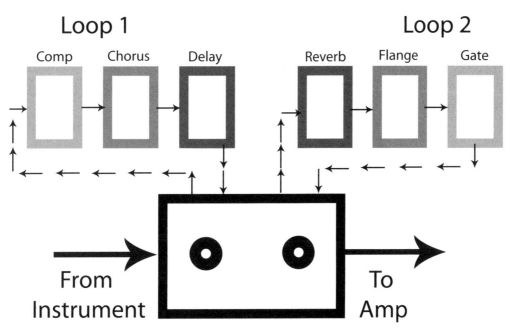

Fig. 1.2.
Effects loops

As you can see from the diagram, there are two separate loops that don't interact with each other. Each one has a specific sound, but some loop switchers allow you to engage both loops, with Loop 1 running to Loop 2 in sequence. The above setup is designed to be separate and may not sound that great when both loops are combined together, but a different combination might sound good. In this instance, there is a conventional sound in one loop and a nonconventional sound in the other. Here's where your creativity can be wide open; you are free to roam about the effects plane. Just be careful what you ask for—you may not like it! It's easy to get carried away by some of the interesting sounds these units can make, but always keep in mind that it's about the notes you're playing. *Interesting sounds make interesting notes* more *interesting!*

All of the aspects we have just looked at apply to rackmounted effects as well. While these units are certainly more complex and usually more expensive, they often have far more capability and flexibility. Often a single multiprocessor can emulate an entire pedalboard and offer a hundred programming combinations. Also, a rackmounted device can offer real-time adjustments of the specific parameters in its arsenal. Most manufacturers have gotten hip to what's really usable by most players, so you typically will have a choice among the most obvious adjustments. In many cases, effects are laid out in a particular order that prevents many common sequencing problems, but also prevents more unusual combinations you may want to try in your quest for tone. As you can see, there are no easy answers or a single product that will do it all, regardless of what people tell you.

AMPLIFIER EFFECTS LOOPS

No discussion about signal chains, effects sequences, and loops would be complete without covering the gain structure aspect before or after the preamp of the amplifier, i.e., the effects loop. While most of the previous information is useful to practically any musician, amplifier effects loops are used mainly by guitarists and keyboard players.

Not to be confused with the previous examples of external effects loops, most quality guitar and bass amplifiers and keyboard mixers have a built-in "effects loop" (called INSERT). Some are switchable, some are not. The difference between this effects loop and the others is that amplifier effects loops are located between the gain stage/EQ of the amp and the output stage. Because the effects loop comes *after* most of the amp's gain, it is less likely to create any noise, and it also has a better signal level for driving long cables. In cases where the effects are placed before the amp, any noise is amplified along with the signal. And due to the often sizable length of cable and unavoidable inherent signal loss created by the effects themselves, more gain equals more noise. Fig. 1.3 shows an amplifier's effects loop in the signal chain.

Fig. 1.3.
Amplifier
effects loop

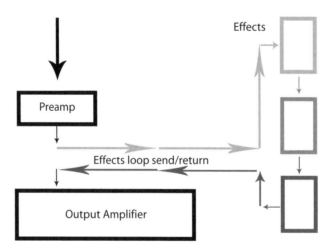

After reading this, one would assume that this would be the best placement for *all* effects, but that is not always the case. When you have multiple channels and different gains, effect units can either distort (under extreme gain settings) and/or create a loss of internal gain level to the output stage, causing you to have to add even more input gain. While there are line drivers than can bring your return level up, each unit will sound different depending on its placement in the signal path and whether it's before the amp or between the preamp and the power amp stage. The bottom line is that you'll have to try both to see what works for your amp and your ears, which are the most important judge.

We have already covered the fact that the more you put in your signal chain, the greater chances for noise, loss of level, and reduced reliability, so use discretion when deciding on the effects you use. Having seen more than 12 effects pedals on a single guitar input, I can say that it will work, but expect some noise! For this reason, we should look at both places where your effects can be located.

▶**Front End.** If your effects are plugged in between your guitar and your amplifier's input, you will have placed them in the "front end" of the signal chain. Since this is *before* most signal amplification, any noise produced by your effects will be amplified.

►**Gain Staged.** If your effects are placed between the amp's preamp and the power amp, you will have placed them in the "gain stage" of the signal chain. Since it is *after* most preamplification, the noise produced by your effects will be amplified less. As mentioned before, this is generally the best place for effects, with the exception of compressors, especially if there is gain switching in the amp. Some of you have amps that *don't* have effects loops; the front end is your only option. For those of you who do have effects loops, don't feel that everything has to go through the loop. Some of you have separate preamps and power amps, which is essentially the same as having an effects loop: simply patch any effects between the preamp and the power amp if that's what you want.

I suggest that compressors and tuners be placed in the front end. Noise gates should be used in the effects loop after any gain devices; otherwise noise will be present from them. Pitch- and time-based devices should come after any gating or they'll be chopped off.

These are simply guidelines; always use your ears to make the final decision. You don't have to place all your effects in one position; try some in the front end and others in the loop, but still maintain the recommended sequence for each effect type. Fig. 1.4 shows these two placements.

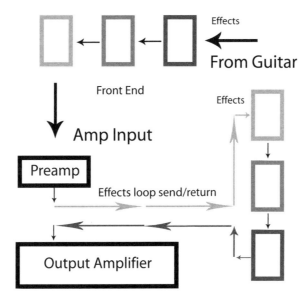

Fig. 1.4. Loops placement

While it's important to know where to place effects, it's also very important to know how to use them . . . and abuse them! Most people have a general idea of what each effect sounds like, but if you are aware of how an effect is being created, you may get a better idea of how to set it for a desired application.

GATES

A noise gate doesn't really change your sound at all. It simply opens up when your signal has reached a desired strength (Threshold), opens at a specific rate (Attack), stays open for a designated time after the signal has gone below the threshold (Hold), and closes at a particular rate (Release). These extra functions allow you to tailor the response of your gate to not chop off your notes or sound jerky when opening and closing. The primary effect of a gate is to quiet noise, whether it's hiss buildup from an effects chain or background noise picked up from a microphone. When you are actually playing, the gate will open and allow your notes to be heard (and the noise too). When you aren't playing, the gate closes and shuts out any unwanted noise.

COMPRESSORS

Compressors and gates are actually the same electronics used in different ways. As opposed to completely opening and closing, compressors ride your signal level. When your signal reaches a certain strength (Threshold) it begins to turn the signal down at a specific rate (Attack) and by a certain amount (Ratio), and turns it back up once you have gone below the threshold (Release). It would seem like this would be the perfect effect; however, it comes at a price: *noise*. Extreme ratios and very low thresholds will essentially turn down every note you play, yet turn up the noise when you aren't playing. Compressors can also remove all the life and dynamics from your playing as well. These effects aren't meant to replace your ability to control your instrument, but they help if you're in the range. A rule of thumb to consider when using them is, for every 1 dB of compression in your signal chain, you will add 1 dB of noise. Light compression and lower ratios should be your first choice for a natural sound.

EQs

When properly used, these are incredibly handy devices that can change not only your tone, but your level as well. There seem to be two schools of thought regarding their use: one group of users simply cut out frequencies for the proverbial "smiley face" EQ setting, and another group of users just push everything up (though not quite equally), then leave it on pretty much the whole time. Often the amp needs adjusting to make either of these approaches work. I question both philosophies. Wouldn't it be easier to set your amp to the right rhythm tone in the first place, then use the EQ for a lead tone or gain boost? It could also be used to balance the tone of a second guitar; i.e., one sound for the Strat and an EQ for the Les Paul. You shouldn't need an EQ to make your amp sound right if you choose the right amp.

If you're sitting in on other people's gear, an EQ is almost essential. Instead of tearing up their settings to get your sound, simply use your EQ to compensate for their settings. I seriously recommend this for any bass player or guitarist, especially for an acoustic instrument.

GAIN AND DISTORTION PEDALS

These are probably the most misused devices of all the effects. While they can make a marginal amp sound better, they can also make a great amp reek! There is no substitute for having a great amp and getting great sounds from it. If you can get a great sound from your amp without these units, effects can make them sound even better when used reasonably. And like any processor, they can make you sound really bad when pushed to their limits. They should enhance your tone, not become your tone! Very few of them have adequate tone control over the drive they create, making them a liability at higher settings. Using them to go from a clean sound to a saturated lead tone is risky at best; if you need a two-channel amp, then get one! Don't try to use a footpedal as a substitute; use it to enhance a great amp sound.

HARMONIZERS AND OCTAVE PEDALS

While nothing beats a well-played harmony, it's impossible if there's not another like instrument in your band. Many high-end harmonizers claim to be able to follow the intervals correctly in key, but a song rarely stays in one key, and pitch shifters aren't really capable of playing through changes or following movements correctly. They do provide some harmony effects, and used occasionally they can sound very interesting. If you balance them correctly, even the off notes don't sound so bad when they are blended behind the dominant pitch. The only pitch intervals that sound right on most of these units are an octave above and below, or the unison, which essentially is a doubler. As long as you are aware of the capabilities and inadequacies of harmonizers, you won't be misled to believe the many outrageous claims made by their manufacturers. Cool effect, but rarely true harmony.

FLANGERS/CHORUSES/PHASERS

These units are all similar in that they mix a processed signal with the original unprocessed signal to produce a particular sweeping or swirling effect. Flangers and choruses both change the speed of a delayed signal to produce a swishy or sloshy sound, depending on their settings. Phasers shift the phase of a signal by using a filter to sweep the frequency range. They all sound different when you hear them one after the other, but they are remarkably similar. Extreme settings on a flanger or chorus will produce a warbling effect known as vibrato. While phasers have Speed and Depth controls, flangers and choruses can also have Sweep in their settings.

An ordinary delay unit can be used to produce a flange or chorus effect if it has a modulation control, which automatically varies the speed of the delay. Sweep is the equivalent of delay time, Speed is the equivalent of modulation, and Depth is the equivalent of the feedback or repeat control of a delay unit. With no modulation and longer delay times of 40-60 ms, this is called a doubler, because it sounds like two people playing the same thing ever so slightly out of time.

DELAY

Delay is an effect in which you can hear the individual repeats of a signal. Often called "echo," this is one of the most popular effects in the history of audio. There are many types of delay units, from old tube Echoplexes to pristine-sounding digital delays, but they all perform a similar function: to repeat a given length of your input signal at least once, often more. With each succession or repeat, the volume decreases; at least for normal delay usage. Most delay units have a control for length, another for feedback (the number of repeats), and a mix control that allows you to balance the delayed signal with the original signal. Delay is best used before any reverb, as this is what occurs in the real world and sounds most natural to us.

REVERB

Often confused with delay, a reverb unit produces a large number of "reflections" by means of a digital algorithm. No discrete "echoes" can be heard; instead it sounds like you're playing in a cave. The evolution of the reverb effect went from using a microphone and speaker in a tiled room to a long box with a "plate" in it or a small box with "springs" to the now famous digital reverbs with complex space modeling, backward reverbs, and "gated reverbs" that build and end abruptly.

The operation of these units will vary considerably, but there are three main parameters on most digital reverbs: Room, Density, and Decay. Smaller rooms produce shorter, tighter reverbs, Plates produce medium-length reverbs, and Halls produce longer reverbs. Each program uses a different algorithm to produce a particular tone for each reverb. Density controls the amount of reflections produced by each program. Decay determines how long the total reverb time is from the initial sound until the final reflection has decayed. While there are often a few more parameters, each unit has a different set of features, sometimes even for different programs.

Reverbs should always be last in the chain, as they usually sound most natural after everything else. The tails they create would sound quite unusual before other units like harmonizers, choruses, and delays, but if you're out to discover that "unique tone," this may be the one rule you'd want to break, and my leading choice for a strange effect.

LINE DRIVERS

A line driver really isn't an "effect"; it simply amplifies a signal that has been weakened by multiple effects units in series to a level that will drive a long cord to an amp without a significant loss of gain. This unit will rarely be switched in or out of the signal path; it is usually left in the whole time. It doesn't provide "distortion" as we know it—its main purpose is to *cleanly* amplify a signal without changing the quality, just the level.

These units are best used *very last* in your signal chain, even after any reverb. If you only have a few effects, you may not need one at all. If you have six or seven units, you may need one. It really depends on how much gain your amp has. If you have plenty of gain left over after all is said and done, you don't need one. If your gain is cranked all the way up and you could use some more level, then you definitely need one.

An entire library could be devoted to just effects, but that's just not practical for the purposes of this book. There are quite a few other effects—some of them one-of-a-kind specialty units that nothing else can replicate, but in the end, they will typically fall into one of the four categories we have discussed here. As long as they are sequenced correctly, you should be able to make what you have work with few problems. Just keep in mind that people come to hear *music*, not *effects*.

IN CONCLUSION

As stated at the beginning of this chapter, really listen to your instrument. "Become one with your tone," or as Ira Black says, "Own your tone!" Take the time to learn how to adjust it and make it sound the best you can. Listen to your instrument in complete silence without an amp to hear what it is really doing. Visualize what is happening when you play your instrument and you will start to see things that would have never come to you otherwise.

Think about all the aspects of your tone on its way to the PA—your cords, effects, amp, speakers, the mic. Everything counts! Don't be afraid to admit when you get in over your head and need some help, but don't just let someone fix it; fix the problem with them and you will have earned the money you paid them to teach you. Try many different combinations with your setup. Most discoveries were accidents waiting to happen, but in a good way. Practicing at home and rehearsals are the places to do this, not during showtime! Never forget that it all begins with your tone—it has to be at its best! This is the first and most important step in taking control of your stage sound.

Here is a checklist of points that were made during the chapter. It is a good idea to look these over before every rehearsal and get into the habit of doing this for shows as well.

1. Always Use Fresh Strings
2. Listen in a Quiet Room
3. Eliminate Buzzes and Noises
4. Intonate Your Instrument
5. Check All Batteries and Keep Spares
6. Use a Quality Guitar Strap and Fastener
7. Secure Your Instrument Cable
8. Adjust Your Action Properly
9. Adjust Your Pickups Properly
10. Keep Strong Magnets Away from Pickups
11. Eliminate Squeaks and Rattles
12. Use Fresh Drum Heads
13. Tune Drum Heads Evenly
14. Allow Room for Microphones
15. Play with Dynamics
16. Use a Pickup on Acoustic Instruments
17. Use a Mute Switch to Prevent Problems
18. Use a Stage Amp for a Personal Monitor
19. Use a Clip-on Mic When You Can
20. Carefully Check All Cables
21. Carry Backup Power Supplies
22. Keep Spare Sound Cards and Discs
23. Keep Your Gear in Working Condition
24. Never Cup the Ball of the Mic
25. Never Drop the Mic

26. Never Expose the Mic Directly to the Mains or Monitors
27. Balance Your Stage Levels with the Monitors
28. Use Your Own Mic
29. Keep Wireless Systems in the Line of Sight
30. Learn What Sounds Good on Your Voice
31. Keep Your Lyrics Handy
32. Listen to Your Amp Without Effects
33. Use Fresh Tubes
34. Buy and Use a Volt-Ohm Meter
35. Check for Microphonics in Your Rig
36. Try Your Effects One at a Time to Find Problems
37. Use Only the Effects You Really Need
38. Don't Wear Earplugs—Turn Down
39. Place Your Effects in the Correct Order
40. Use Loop Switching to Create Unusual Effects

Paul Doty
Pro FOH Sound Engineer and Lighting Designer
CEO, West Coast Sound & Light
www.wcsl.org

COURTESY OF PAUL DOTY

"I see all kinds of mistakes being made onstage:

Guitarists. 1) A big mistake guitarists make is using crappy amps. I just did a pro gig, and the guitarist showed up with a 5-inch practice amp that sounded like a 100,000-watt practice amp when amplified. C'mon: *Use pro gear.* 2) Don't play so loud that the engineer can't bring you up in the mix. You will achieve the best tone when amplified through the PA. Cranking it up on stage so it sounds good to you means it sounds good *only* to you.

Bassists. 1) The quality of your instrument and your playing style is paramount. 2) Don't EQ mud frequencies between 100–300 Hz at the head. Remember, low-frequency wavelengths can be 60 feet long. You're not hearing those fully develop onstage. Work with the FOH engineer to achieve your best tone.

Drummers. 1) The biggest mistake is heads that drone or ring. Gates should be used to keep everything else out of the drum channel, not the drum itself! That being said, a good, tight drum can sound even tighter with a proper gate. 2) Obviously, know how to tune your drums. 3) Failing to cover a set on an outdoor stage. Sun + drum heads = doo-doo.

Vocalists. 1) Easy—mic technique. Don't cup, don't pull far away, be consistent, and sing out. You know . . . *mic technique!*

Keyboardists. 1) Use pro gear. The *less* your engineer has to do here, the better you're going to sound. 2) Feed your FOH consistent levels in your patches.

Percussionists. 1) Technique and consistency is your best friend, right up there with quality instruments. Once again, the *less* your FOH engineer has to do EQ-wise, the better you will sound. Remember also, if you are entirely acoustic, put as little of yourself as you can in your monitors so the FOH is not amplifying the stage sound as well as your primary signal. Loud monitors will cause phasing problems and poor tone.

Harmonica. Tone here is somewhat subjective. Just don't be overbearing in the monitors.

Horns/Woodwinds/Violins. Play on your mics. If you buy your own wireless system, get a good one. If you buy a $400 toy, it will sound like a 100,000-watt toy!"

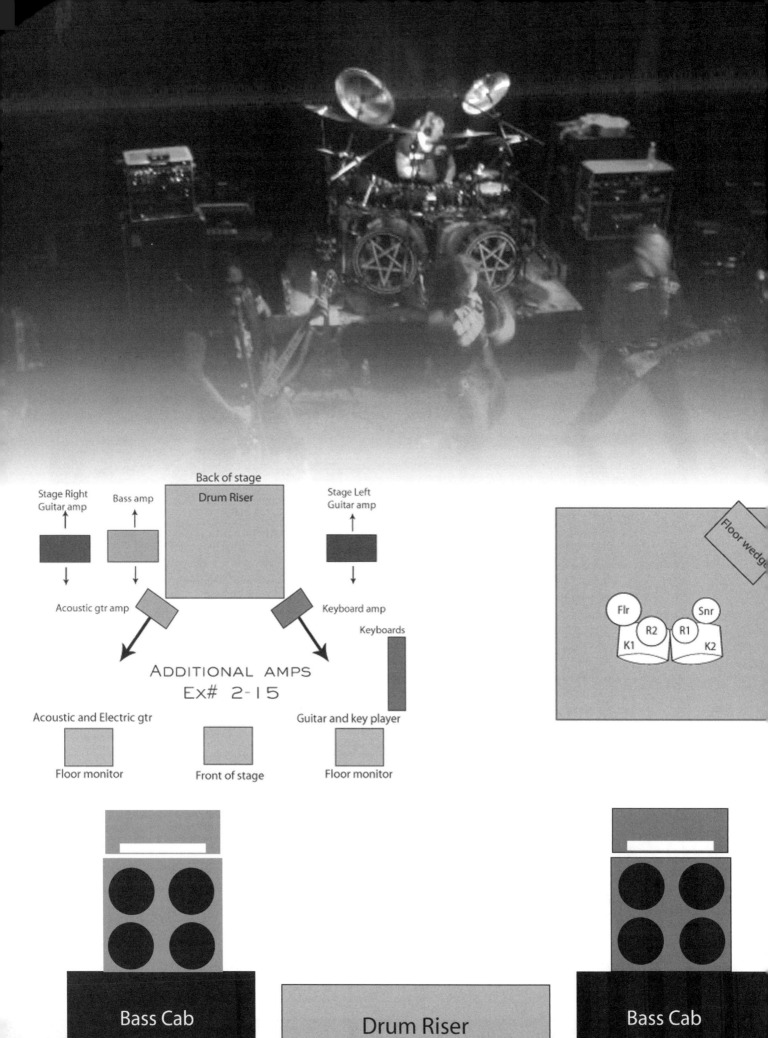

Back of stage

Stage Right
Guitar amp

Bass amp

Drum Riser

Stage Left
Guitar amp

Acoustic gtr amp

Keyboard amp

Keyboards

ADDITIONAL AMPS
Ex# 2-15

Acoustic and Electric gtr

Guitar and key player

Floor monitor

Front of stage

Floor monitor

Floor wedge

Flr

Snr

R2

R1

K1

K2

Bass Cab

Drum Riser

Bass Cab

Setting Up: Using Conventional and Radical Setups to Solve Problems

SETTING UP

In chapter 1, we looked at individual instruments and how to get each one to sound its best. The trick now is to get all of your instruments to sound good together as a band. Since there are so many instrument combinations to consider, we'll have to look at a few different approaches to setting them up. In this chapter you'll learn different ways to make your equipment more effective without actually having to use more equipment. For those who prefer more equipment, there are a few techniques for that as well. In fact, you should often examine both the simple and the advanced methods for handling most situations you encounter so you can figure out what's best for you. You'll also find several different ways to adjust your setups, but feel free to combine these approaches to get what you need. This chapter contains both unconventional setups and some unusual approaches to conventional ones, but the real point here is to "think outside the box."

The logic here is simple, but the applications aren't: You need to be able to hear yourself properly and you need to be heard properly. You have already worked on your individual sound and made it as good as it can be, now you have to blend your great tone with the rest of the band's great tones. The first thing to consider is that if you can't hear yourself properly, you can't play properly. The second thing to consider is that if you can't be heard properly onstage, it will be difficult for everyone else to play in time with you. There are a lot of cues to the feel and dynamics that come from your playing; without these, something will always be amiss in your show. The solution will come from a proper balance onstage, where everyone can hear both themselves and each other as they need to. The key to this solution is using Location, Focus, and Balance to make adjustments that will allow you to hear yourself better without simply using sheer volume. Having your equipment set up in the right location is absolutely essential! It must also be focused in the right direction to make the best use of the level. These two aspects are often the root of the problem for most bands. It is these two first principles that determine the proper balance. These three elements are combined to form a zone. You will see how these three principles work together as you go through this chapter.

THE 5.1 SURROUND SOUND THEORY

No matter where you are, you are always listening in 5.1 surround sound. No, the world hasn't changed over to surround sound just because it's popular—it's been a part of your perception since before you were born. When you hear a sound in a room, you can almost instinctively look in the direction of its source; *your mind is finely tuned to Location, Focus, and Balance.* You can easily tell which direction a sound is coming from as well as its proximity and intensity; if you don't believe me, just close your eyes and listen in a noisy room.

Unfortunately, this 5.1 concept has been overlooked by many, and the common misconception is to attempt to solve problems onstage with a one-dimensional approach: volume up/volume down. It's either too loud or not loud enough. I personally feel that this is just one of the three dimensions of sound, but let's take a look at why I believe this to be true. I'll use the differences between recordings as an example. It's really quite simple.

MONOPHONIC SOUND

In the beginning of recorded sound there was only one format: mono. There was only one *location* and one *focus* for all the different *balances* a mono mix would have. Results? One dimension. Mixes had to be carefully balanced to distinguish a number of different sounds, but it just never sounded real. This is what you get from a stage monitor.

STEREOPHONIC SOUND

Over 50 years ago, someone was brilliant enough to link a pair of mono mixes together to bring us stereo. And while it was much better than mono, it still lacked that something extra that made it *real.* Having a stereo pair of speakers gives you an additional dimension with the sound's left-to-right placement within the mix. Results? Two dimensions. Even with all the left-to-right placement, it still lacked *depth.* This is what you get from headphones.

SURROUND SOUND

This is where recordings took on a whole new dimension. The extra speakers placed behind the listener added the depth of a real acoustic area, which was the missing dimension in the equation. And while surround sound is the standard for film, it still has yet to catch on within the musical community. Maybe this is the reason why most musicians think in "stereo" rather than 3-D surround sound, but I would like to see this book change that mentality. The ability to feel and hear the depth of sound onstage is what makes it so unique . . . and confusing for many! These three examples should illustrate the differences in your perception of sound, regardless of where you are listening from. The rules don't change just because you set up and play!

OK, so now what? It's right here where you can break free from the ordinary and grasp the concept that will allow you to make the right choices for setting up your equipment onstage: the 5.1 Surround-Sound Theory! You need to think of your stage as a big mixing console, but instead of having to twiddle a bunch of knobs, you will physically place your gear where it works best for you. Just set up your gear as you would like to hear it. Think of the amps and drums behind you as the surround speakers and the stage monitors and sidefills as the front speakers. And let me introduce you to a new set of tools:

▶**Location.** This would be the equivalent of the "gain" control on a channel strip. What this means to you is, the closer you place your amp or monitor to you, the better you will hear it, period. You can turn your amp down, but if you place it correctly, you can still hear it just as well.

▶**Focus.** This would be the equivalent of the "pan" control on a channel strip. What it means to you is, the more you turn your amp toward you, the better you

46

will hear it, period. Now you can turn your amp down even more, but still hear it just as well if you point it in the right direction.

▶**Balance.** This would be the equivalent of the "fader" control on a channel strip; your volume control. What this means to you is, the better your location and focus, the less volume you'll need. Truthfully, the volume control should be the last thing you adjust to get the level you need. If the first two principles are properly adjusted, you will need less volume level to get the exact same perception of your sound.

Unfortunately, many bands use the same old setup, with their amps pointed out into the audience, not necessarily at each band member. A lot of wasted volume goes out into the audience because of inefficient placement and projection. You can barely hear yourself onstage, but the front row of the audience is in pain! Since most amp's speakers are below your waist, you're not getting the real volume—the audience is! Take a good look at the setups in this chapter and find out how each of them can change your perception of the sound onstage.

Jon Butcher—Vocals/Guitar, Multimedia Producer
Jon Butcher Axis
Barefoot Servants
Johanna Wild
www.jonbutcher.com

COURTESY OF JON BUTCHER

"While I perform from center stage, I prefer my amp to be stage right, and I'd probably be thrown off if it were the other way around. I'm just used to hearing my guitar in my right ear. And I'm not a fan of hearing everything from one spot, either; I think you need to use the dynamic range of spatial placement—the panorama. It's a pretty standard stage setup. I rarely get very much guitar in my monitors and depend on an ambient level onstage from my amp, but on a larger stage I'll need some in the sidefills; I prefer the sound of my amp onstage.

I think staying healthy is one of the most important things I do for my voice. I'm very lucky to have figured out a long time ago how to sing and play at the same time. It's a skill that people work on for a lot of years, and I'm fortunate that it came quite naturally. When I'm playing, I can hear my guitar in my head, so I want to hear more of my voice in the monitors; I can play my songs in my sleep. Preparation is the key.

For me, my approach to playing is so organic that there are no affectations; I don't have any smoke bombs in my guitar or fireworks shooting out my butt, just the simple approach of a player!"

These are simple little tricks you can use to make things sound just a little better onstage, but there are many more options that aren't quite as simple. While they aren't too complicated, they do require more than a few words to be understood. This chapter will examine several setup techniques that aren't conventional, as well as some that are. I ask you to be open-minded and encourage you to try some of them before you jump to any conclusions. Each setup will sound quite different, even those that seem to be similar, so experience the differences yourself. Don't just be like everyone else, unless you want the same results. Going through the various setups in this book will reveal the true nature of the 5.1 Surround-Sound Theory. It might even cause you to think outside the box! Your stage setup is the second most important aspect of your stage sound; we've already covered the first—your tone!

STAGE LOCATIONS

The stage has been around for centuries, and there are some very specific terms for its locations that are used by the pros. All of these location references are from the stage's perspective. "Stage right" means that if you are onstage facing the audience, you would be to the right of the stage. From the audience's perspective, you would actually be toward the left of the stage. It is here where much confusion often happens; when discussing stage locations offstage, many people forget to reverse their thinking, and their mind automatically wants to think literally. If you aren't very familiar with these terms, you may get confused and in turn confuse those around you. So let's get this straight before we move on to setting up.

Fig. 2.1 shows the stage and its stage location names from the audience's perspective. I have chosen this perspective since it is used in most of the illustrations that will follow in this book. What you are looking at is an overhead view, with the front of the stage at the bottom of the illustration, and the back of the stage at the top. The large gray rectangle represents the drum riser, and the small gray rectangles represent stage monitors. This is the basic layout you will see onstage most of the time. There is usually a stage monitor on the drum riser itself, but for simplicity's sake we will leave that off for now. It will appear when we are actually discussing the drum wedge. It would be a good idea to get used to seeing the stage this way, as you will see it in most of the illustrations and stage plots you encounter. This is the most common representation of a stage layout, and is used by most national acts.

As you can see, there are three different lateral locations (left, center, right) and three different longitudinal locations (up, center, down) that can be combined to describe any relative location onstage. You can use any combination of these terms to get your point across, but always remember that when you are onstage, right is right. When you are in the audience, left is right. These terms are far less confusing when you are backstage: left is left and right is right.

Back of Stage		Back of Stage
Downstage		Downstage
	Drum Riser	
Stage Right	Center Stage	Stage Left
Upstage	Upstage	Upstage
	Monitor	Monitor	Monitor

Front of Stage
From Audience Perspective

Fig. 2.1.
Stage
locations

These terms are universal and are used on every professional stage in the world—for music, theater, and television. Take the time to get used to these terms and try to use them as much as you can. I would advise this for anyone who wants to make the stage their home. Every time you see a stage, go through these locations in your mind until they become second nature. The pros who work on them every day have an advantage over those who don't, and they have no idea that you actually mean "the other left." By then, it's usually too late.

STAGE TERMINOLOGY

Upstage means toward the front of the stage, closest to the audience.

Downstage means toward the back of the stage, away from the audience.

Stage Right means to the right of the stage when facing the audience and to the audience's left.

Stage Left means to the left of the stage when facing the audience, and to the audience's right.

Center Stage means exactly what its name suggests—the very center of the stage.

Downstage Right means the back of the stage to the audience's left.

Downstage Left means the back of the stage to the audience's right.

Upstage Center means the front of the stage in the very center.

Upstage Right means the front of the stage to the audience's left.

Upstage Left means the front of the stage to the audience's right.

Stage Right Center means to the right of center stage when facing the audience, and to the audience's left.

Stage Left Center means to the left of center stage when facing the audience, and to the audience's right.

Louis Metoyer—Guitar
4 Non-Blondes/Stanley Clarke
Terence Trent D'Arby
New Edition
www.myspace.com/louismetoyer

"I prefer to set up on stage right so I can watch for any visual cues from my fellow musicians and see my position on the guitar neck. It's also very important to understand the stage terminology that the pros use, like FOH, FOB (monitors), stage right/left, upstage/downstage, etc.

If you are a guest in another band, don't try to play louder than the band you are performing with. If it's a gig they are familiar with, you should listen to the tonal and dynamic suggestions they give you. They probably know more about the sound qualities of the room.

Dynamics are the secret weapon of any band, so use them wisely. Bring down your verse volume in order to pull your listener in. This automatically makes your choruses sound stronger when you bring up the volume on those sections. Playing dynamically always leaves you somewhere to go with the energy."

COURTESY OF MCNULTY

INTRODUCTION TO STAGE ZONES

It was important to take a look at stage locations before introducing you to stage zones. While this may seem to be the most commonsense issue discussed in this book, I often see examples of it not being so, so let's set the record straight and define the term. You will see lots of references to zones in here.

A *stage zone* is an area dominated by a particular instrument and its performer. It is important for this area to have a good level of this instrument so that the performer can hear himself properly. If it is an electric instrument, this is generally not a problem.

If it's a drum set, once again this should not be a problem. Other instruments like acoustic guitar, violin, and others with lower stage levels may require a personal monitor to help create a zone. In chapter 1, we looked at the importance of having personal monitors; now it's time to show you just how important they are to controlling your stage sound. You absolutely need to have a zone for each player. Even when you don't use a personal amplifier, you will need a stage monitor, which will create a zone for you that you have little control over. Wouldn't you rather have that control at your fingertips? Use a personal stage amp when you can.

Stage zones can be rather large, in the case of three-piece bands where the guitarist and bass player dominate an entire side of the stage, or smaller, where there are five, six, or even seven players onstage. The more players onstage, the smaller the zones need to be, which means lower stage levels for each zone, especially when the stage itself is small. The trick is to set your volume loud enough to hear yourself without overpowering the next performer's zone. That means being within a reasonable distance of your source. Most stage problems are a direct result of zone violations: Someone is too loud! When everyone is balanced, the stage seems to blend nicely and the monitors work.

"Out of bounds" is a familiar sports term that can be used to describe leaving the area in which you can hear yourself; i.e., your zone. Don't expect to walk completely across the stage and hear your amp really well in someone else's zone; you would have to be too loud, simple as that. While stage monitors can help get your levels to that location, don't try to do that from your stage zone. If you are in your zone, you should never have a problem hearing yourself.

COURTESY OF MICHAEL HERBACH

Sean McNabb—Bass
Montrose/Dokken/Quiet Riot
House of Lords
www.myspace.com/bassriff2

"I prefer playing on the hi-hat side, just because I feel like I'm right in it. When I'm on that hi-hat side, I can always go back there and listen. On some stages, you can't hear that well, but you can always walk right back to that hi-hat and know exactly where you're at. From my experience, I think most drummers like the bass cabinet a little bit behind them so they can hear what's going on, but everybody's different. I prefer it to be at least even with the drums or a few feet back from the drums. I would prefer it to be as close to the drums as possible, but a lot of times you go into these festival situations and you play wherever it is, because the set changes are so quick, they call it a "throw and go." You get out there, make sure you got a tone, get some kick, snare, and hat in your monitors, some vocals, maybe a little guitar, and let her rip. Something I read on Duck Dunn: he says you've got to EQ a little bit bright onstage to cut through; you can always back it off if it's too bright. It helps you cut through everything. There's a fine line between being clacky—where you're hearing the fret noise—and having a warm sound, so you got to be right on the edge so you still have the warmth. If you can get right on that edge, then you can cut through anything, and they'll warm you up in the PA if you need it."

Now we have arrived at the main point: *Use the setup options in this chapter to create a zone for each player.* There are many different ways to do this, and they can be tweaked to suit just about any situation that your band comes across, but you will have to try some of them. The equipment you choose and the way you set it up is how you take control of your stage sound. This is something even a sound engineer can't mess up! *If you can't hear yourself onstage, it's because you are not doing something right.*

Location, Focus, and Balance are the key principles to creating zones. A zone is where you and your equipment are located, and how you focus your equipment will always determine your balance (levels). These principles will show up in almost every aspect of your sound onstage: amps, monitors, and input sources! It's more important to hear yourself onstage than it is to have the audience hear you from the stage, so don't concern yourself with trying to mix—that's the engineer's job. Your job is to sound great onstage!

James Kottak—Drums
The Scorpions/The Cult
Montrose/Kingdom Come
Warrant/Kottak
www.jameskottak.com

COURTESY OF JAMES KOTTAK

"From a visual standpoint, the audience came to see a show, so I put some of my cymbals out of the way or a little higher. They want to see you doing your thing, and this is something I do because it looks a little cooler. I keep everything symmetrical and flat so the people in front can see me. It really bothers me when I see a kit and there's a cymbal right in front of [the drummer's] face; I want to see the drummer! We use cameras for the video wall, and it makes no sense to have a bunch of drums and cymbals in front of it. People want to see you.

One of the most important things to our backline is placement; from where I'm sitting, I can just see the front of the guitar cabinets . . . I can barely see the logo. If I'm one foot farther out, it kills the drum sound because it bleeds into the drum mics; if I'm back too far, then you don't get any of it. Even though I'm using in-ear monitors, I can still feel it. Everyone likes something different, but this is what works for me. With The Scorpions, we have the luxury of bringing all our own gear. We have three complete sets of gear, so we can send our show out in three different directions and just fly in to each show. When we're over here in the States, we do a typical tour with one backline and go show to show. At soundcheck, I just try to get a simple compact mix. "The Zoo" is one of the songs we typically use for soundcheck, but sometimes we'll check a song we need a little work on; we rotate the show a lot."

Stage monitors will be part of the final equation, but the less you depend on them for things that you can control, the more consistent your show will be. Since every venue will have its own quirks and every night will be different in some way, you want to be able to control your zone! Creating your zones onstage and properly controlling them will eliminate many unnecessary monitor requests. This in turn will allow you to make the best use of them for things you don't have control over, which is why they are there. Monitors also have their zones, and setting up a good stage zone for yourself will include this monitor zone as well, but it all begins with having your equipment in the right place. The more effective your stage zones are, the more useful the monitors will become!

So go through these setups and learn how to adjust them. Simply looking at the illustrations will not reveal all the subtleties that are involved; you must read the text to get an idea of how they work. The bottom line is that you'll have to set up your gear and see how it sounds before you'll know if it's the right setup for you. Each one has a different feel to it, even when they look very similar on the page. Each example will usually have two different versions or adjustments, but it is more of an exercise in creativity than a hard and fast rule. Sometimes, two or even three of these techniques can be combined to form something that is uncommonly effective for unusual situations, but don't overcomplicate matters; try to keep things simple. Try setups individually before you start blending techniques. Sometimes the differences won't be revealed until you try back-to-back examples, but keep track of something when it puts you in the ballpark. Keep improving it until it's right. Only you can be the judge of what is truly working, but you'll never know unless you give it an honest try. So keep an open mind as you go through these examples and don't be the person who is looking for the problems; be the person who is looking for solutions. You will find many in this book.

SMALL-FORMAT SETUPS

1. PUT THE RIGHT SOUND IN THE RIGHT PLACE

When a band isn't set up properly and one person can't hear herself, she will turn her volume up until she can. Now someone else can't hear themselves, so they turn up as well. At some point, the singer can no longer hear the floor monitor! Sound familiar? This is one of the most common mistakes I see onstage, and one of the most avoidable. As human beings, we can be creatures of habit even when there's no real justification for it. It is right here where creating stage zones becomes an obvious solution to most stage level problems. If you are a lead singer/rhythm guitarist and you are center stage, don't put your amp on the far side of the stage! Locate the amp directly behind you just in front of the drum riser, if you can. If you set up on the far side, then your volume level has to be much louder than the amp that is actually closer to you; now that player can't hear themselves, and it's off to the races. Let the volume wars begin! You have violated his zone. Don't be fooled by the old misconception that the bass has to be next to the drummer; the drummer can't hear the timing of the bass notes from behind the amp anyway. Crossing zones never works. You'd be much better off putting some of his bass in the monitors; it's a much more effective use of volume. Once again, this example should illustrate the importance of putting the right sound in the right place.

2. FIND THE RIGHT SPOT FOR YOUR BACKLINE

STAGING

Let's take a look at what the "right spot" could actually be. Fig. 2.2 shows a standard four-piece rock band setup. Note that the gtr/bs amps are pushed back even with the drummer. This is the best choice for smaller stages. There will be some bleed from the cabinets into the drum mics, but usually not enough to cause a problem unless you are really loud. Oftentimes the drummer will be able to hear enough of the amps to not require much of them in the monitors.

Back of stage

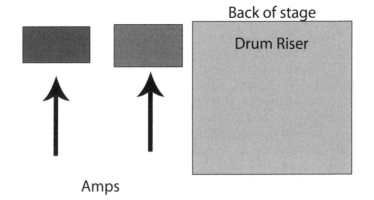

Drum Riser

Amps   Amp

Fig. 2.2.
Downstaging
amps

Floor monitor   Front of stage   Floor monitor

Burleigh Drummond—Drums
Ambrosia/Tin Drum
Mighty Mo Rodgers
www.ambrosiaweb.com

"Everybody's gonna set up their drums differently because it's a physical instrument; however, your body has to be comfortable with the layout. It's all got to be in your flight path. Typically, when I play on a huge stage and the guys have our gear spread from end to end, I immediately tell them to 'bring it in,' even the monitors. *The farther the band is away from each other, the looser it gets.* I try to bring them in so that they're not so dependent on the monitors and they're hearing me. As the show goes on, each player will want more of something, and pretty soon the balances will change, and even though the monitors are there for a purpose, you're all supposed to be connected no matter how far away you are. Physical proximity can make a dramatic difference. I prefer not to have my monitor full of instruments, because I'd rather hear them live. I'll always probably need a little bass and some vocals and a little kick and snare so I don't have to play so hard and can keep my natural dynamics. It's all about the vocal, because if the vocal is happening, then everything's happening!"

In Fig. 2.3, you will see a similar setup, but with the guitar and bass cabinets pushed up even with the front of the drum riser. This is the best choice for larger stages because you have more space to work with. While you'll get less bleed in the drum mics, your drummer will probably need more of these instruments in his monitors than in the setup in Fig. 2.1. The players will get more of their amp's sound without having to raise their volume, and in some cases, they may actually turn them down. Imagine that!

The secondary effect of this up/down stage technique is that your drummer will hear more backline volume, as the frontline players hear less stage volume when the amps are pushed back. The players up front will hear more level, as your drummer will hear less level when the amps are pushed forward. It doesn't have to be "fully forward" or "fully back"; you can move your amp to just the right spot that will allow the player to hear his amp, and allow the drummer to get some of that sound as well. This is just another form of Location. Find the right spot for your backline that works with your volume and the right volume for that spot. You have to work them both. And everyone doesn't have to play on the same even line, either; it may be wise to push the loudest player forward some so he doesn't dominate the backline and can bring his levels down a bit. Two birds with one stone!

For other instruments like acoustic guitar, violin, and keys, this is where it becomes really important to have a personal stage amp as a monitor; otherwise you won't be able to do this with your setups. Having them gives you options; not having them leaves you depending on a different engineer every night, so you're gonna get some really good nights, some average nights, and the occasional disaster. Wouldn't you want to have a great night every night? Allow yourself the opportunity!

Fig. 2.3.
Upstaging
amps

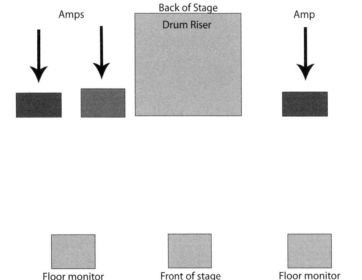

There will be times when staging may not be an option or has a reduced area of adjustment. Some clubs "layer" the backlines from front to back with the band order; if you are in an early band, you may get pushed up toward the front as the later bands occupy the back. In other cases, the headliner may not strike their drum kit, leaving you with a compromised stage. This may put your drum kit further upstage than you'd like and with little room to use any staging techniques for your backline. It may also put an excessive amount of drums in the frontline and make things really difficult to hear. Since the gear is pulled from the stage as the show moves along, you will get more room to work with if you are scheduled for a later time slot, but a nonstriking headliner may create other onstage disadvantages that make things difficult to work with. See the extra chapter "Unusual Stages" at www.rockinyourstagesound.com.

3. USE DOUBLING TO GET MORE STAGE LEVEL

Doubling. Using the same four-piece setup we just looked at, let's add a cabinet from each player to both sides of the stage. Fig. 2.4 shows an example. This gives you all instruments on both sides of the stage. Now, it's very critical that your volumes are properly balanced with each other so no one is much louder than anyone else; however, this greatly reduces the need for anything in the stage monitors but the vocals. Each player has more possibilities for setting up their own 5.1 surround sound by placing the cabinets in any configuration on each side of the stage. Luckily for the bass player, he will be able to hear himself no matter where his amps are placed; low frequencies are omnidirectional and can be heard everywhere.

Doubling has an advantage because it creates a "wall of sound" onstage and feels like more of a "mix." The presence is felt everywhere and it sounds powerful. The problem with doubling is actually created by its "advantage": louder stage levels. By staging your amps toward the back of the stage, you'll be able to reduce some of this effect, but this setup is better suited for larger stages. While it's conceivable to combine both staging and doubling in larger venues, the "up-staging" technique will have problems with smaller stages, and "doubling" them makes this problem twice as noticeable. For narrow stages, doubling may not be an option.

One thing to consider before you overcommit to this setup is the fact that it will take some additional time to get everything in place and dialed in. You really need a wide stage and more than the 15-minute set change that you will find in most clubs, so keep this in mind before you lug all your gear out to a show. If your band is getting a soundcheck and your gear can stay onstage, then you're good to go. However, when "doubling" your cabinets, check your volumes carefully; your offstage volumes will be fairly high. If you have a lot of vocals to balance out front, it's even more important to keep your stage levels reasonable.

Frankie Banali—Drums
Quiet Riot/Wasp
Billy Idol/Hughes-Thrall
www.myspace.com/frankiebanali

"I've always preferred to be center stage in order to have a decent opportunity to hear the instruments to the left and right of me acoustically. There is no substitution for hearing your fellow musicians while the sound is being generated from their equipment. I really enjoy not being set up on a drum riser because I like feeling the sound vibrating off the floor of the stage and it sounds so organic, which really appeals to me. While this is almost a necessity of drum setups in most clubs, it's hardly practical in an arena scenario.

I have always tried to have my drum set positioned so that my ears are even with the side of the bass and guitar cabinets, rather than being in front of them. This affords me the luxury of hearing the instruments acoustically, while at the same time not being bombarded by them. I grew up playing in equipment-conscious bands. It was not unusual for me to play with like-minded musicians where a typical setup has two Marshall 100-watt stacks each, right and left, and four Ampeg SVTs somewhere within firing range!"

COURTESY OF FRANKIE BANALI

Fig. 2.4.
Doubling
amps

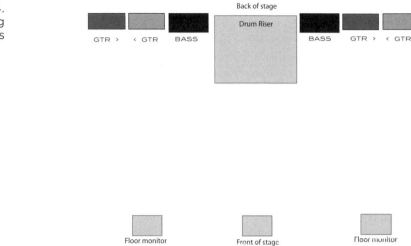

Back of stage

Drum Riser

GTR >   < GTR   BASS   BASS   GTR >   < GTR

Floor monitor   Front of stage   Floor monitor

COURTESY OF BRUCE BOUILLET

Dave Foreman—Guitar/Bass
Snoop Dogg/Christina Aguilera
Jay Z/Rihanna/Boyz II Men

"I can work with either side of the stage as long as I have a good balance. Part of that has a lot to do with the distance of the amp; this determines how I can set my tone. I generally like my amp even with the batter of the kick drum. If I go too far back, then I have to run my amp louder and that can bleed into the drums. *I can set my tone better when everyone is playing*; it's hard to do without this. *I'll find a place where it fits in with the frequencies well.* I usually start with everything toward the middle of the adjustment ranges, including my guitar; this way I always have somewhere to go with EQ and volume. This also helps with the monitors in case something gets missed; I can pick it up from there.

A lot depends on where I'm playing; I'll choose the right amp according to the size of the venue. In a small club, I don't really need monitors to hear myself, but in larger ambient venues there's a lot more coming back at you, and I may need more from the wedges to keep it tight. Sometimes I'll set up my amp on the side of the stage; other times I've had my amps right behind me, tilted up to hear them better. I prefer the open-back tone of combo amps because I don't have to ride the bottom end as much. Whatever I need to do to hear myself onstage, I'll make the best use of my locations!"

When you use doubling there will be times when balancing each side of the stage is difficult. What is working on one side is actually not working on the other side. Stage left's guitarist may have a level that is perfect for him, but is too loud for stage right's guitarist, who is comfortable with her level. There is a very easy way to deal with this problem: simply change the Focus of the opposing guitarist's cabinet.

Note that the cabinets from the player on the other side of the stage are placed to the outside. This will allow you to turn them outward if the other player is too loud. Fig. 2.5 shows this method of controlling the problem. Another idea would be to put a speaker attenuator on that cabinet alone, and then you could turn the volume down on your side without affecting the player's volume on the other side. Attenuators are discussed in Chapter 8: Technical Aspects.

When using this doubling technique (I want mine in doubly!) try to downstage your backline to get a better blend of all three cabinets per side. Upstaging may put them too close and overemphasize a particular one. When you find a spot you like, measure it to see what works.

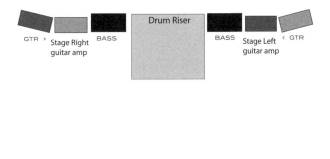

Fig. 2.5. Doubling amps adjustments

4. USE CROSSFIRING TO USE LESS OFFSTAGE LEVEL

Crossfiring. This method involves placing the guitar amps on the edges of the stage pointed inward. Fig. 2.6 shows an example. Crossfiring works well on smaller stages with smaller PA systems. It allows you to put more of your levels "onstage" without them being directed toward the audience as much. In the previous demonstrations, the amps were facing the audience, and will produce a fair amount of offstage level. Most engineers will run your instrument levels lower in the PA when you have a generous amount coming from the stage. Crossfiring will give you the same onstage levels with less offstage level. Most engineers will run your instrument levels higher in the PA when you have a moderate amount coming from the stage. A moderate offstage level will give your soundperson more control out front, which will be very helpful if you have lots of vocals or acoustic instruments onstage.

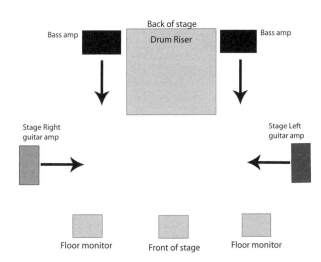

Fig. 2.6. Crossfiring amps

Rob Marcello—Guitar
Danger Danger/House of Lords
Marcello/Vestry
Twenty-4 Seven
www.myspace.com/dangerdangerrob

"When you're rehearsing with your band, you're like your own soundman in a way; you find a sweet spot in the room where the speaker moves air and everything sounds nice, you get a little ambience. It's the same onstage. When I'm at home, I want the dryness, but onstage I like that vibe, I want the *bigness*. In a perfect world, I'd have an amp with the most beautiful clean sound and the perfect crunch, but I like an amp with clear distortion and a lot of note definition to it.

I like to be stage right—it's always been my spot; for some reason I can hear everything better from there. I like to push my amps as far back as I can get them and still hear it [well]. There's a fine line when they're too far back; you get too much ambience, but right before that point is where you get a great blend of the room and your tone. We set up close to the drummer's line of hearing. The straight cabs give me more low end than slant cabs, and I usually only use the bottom cabs.

In smaller places, I'll turn the cabinet around or set it on the side like my own sidefill, then look for the sweet spot. I try to keep my stage volume reasonable and give my soundman something to work with."

5. USE CORNERING TO GET MORE STAGE COVERAGE

Cornering. This technique uses two cabinets per amp, and each guitar amp has one cabinet in the "crossfired" position and the other cabinet in the "staged" position. Fig. 2.7 shows an example of this. The bass amp is usually staged on each side of the drums. By properly staging the backline, you should find a good balance with the crossfired cabinets. This method will give you a good stage level, and allow you to run less volume because you have better coverage. The audience will get some too, so be reasonable with your volume.

With both crossfiring and cornering, you may want to push the cabinets as far back as possible when they're on the sides of the stage. This will allow you to hear them as you're used to—from a slight distance; however, when you're on a tight stage and this isn't

Fig. 2.7.
Cornering
amps

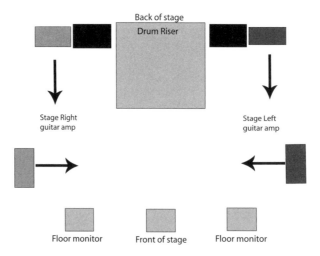

practical, find a way to elevate them. Milk crates, chairs, or even concrete blocks will help, but the higher up you can get them, the better.

David Garfield—Keys
George Benson/Boz Scaggs
Natalie Cole/Smokey Robinson
Karizma/Los Lobotomies
www.creatchy.com

"Every stage has its limitations as to how you can set up, so you have to be flexible with your setup. I'd prefer to be on the side of the stage with the bass player (stage left) for harmonic reasons, but I wouldn't want to be right in front of his cabinet. When stages are tight, we angle his cabinet so I'm not getting killed!

I have a couple different setups. I used to have my own stereo amps, like a guitarist would, for my electronic keys, but now I use them primarily for my stage monitors on smaller gigs. I don't play my keyboards through guitar amps because I can't get any clarity with them. I've been using Barbetta keyboard amps, which are biamped and sound amazing. Most small clubs don't have adequate stage monitors, or enough of them for both vocals and keys, but when they do, I'm more than happy to use them. Ideally, I'd want a stereo pair of wedges onstage on bigger show as my monitor sound, but I'm okay with a mono wedge if I know it's stereo in the PA. *As I learned the intricacies of PA systems in smaller venues, I realized that I didn't have to reach the whole club with my stage sound.* When I'm in that situation, I just use the PA for my house volume and my amps as stage monitors."

COURTESY OF DAVID HAPLEY

6. USE A HOTSHOT FOR TIGHT SPOTS

Hotshot. This technique is a bit more involved. It requires converting a medium-size floor wedge into a guitar or bass cabinet. Take an old floor wedge, put in a full-range speaker rated for the amp's wattage and ohmage, and bypass the crossover by wiring the speaker directly to the input jacks. Ten-inch and 12-inch floor monitors work best for guitars, and 15-inch floor monitors work best for bass. I can't recall ever seeing a floor wedge with 18-inch speakers in it, but if you can find one it would probably be too big for a small stage. You can use any cheap used floor wedge with the right size speaker, but you are going to have to put in some work. Bypassing the crossover is important; if not, your amp will probably blow either the crossover or the tweeter, leaving you with a honky, muddy, unusable sound. You don't have crossovers in your Marshall cabinet, so you don't need one in your hotshot. It is fine to leave the horn/tweeter assembly in the cabinet as it keeps the cabinet closed and correctly ported, it just doesn't need to be hooked up. This is detailed in Chapter 9: Technical Aspects.

Fig. 2.8 shows examples of hotshot placements. You could crossfire the hotshot from the side, you could place it next to a vocal wedge pointed back at you, or you could use it for level on the other side of the stage. The two examples on the bottom are when the hotshot is being used for yourself, and the example on the top is when the hotshot is being used for other players.

Hotshots also come in real handy for keyboards and acoustic guitars. They can be set in places that would not be acceptable for a combo amp or a full-size cabinet. The same principles that make a wedge monitor useful for a PA also apply to its use as an instrument cabinet; better location and focus means less balance (level) is needed. A hotshot allows you to make the best use of this technique when other cabinets aren't practical. Since we are discussing small-format setups, we'll come back to these ideas when needed.

Fig. 2.8.
Using a
hotshot

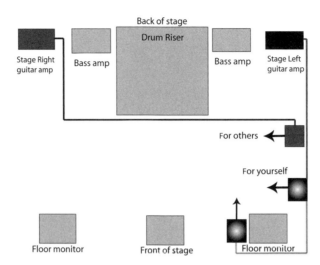

This is just another example of "thinking outside the box." The most important thing to remember about hotshotting is that *it can put your sound exactly where it is needed in more places than a normal cabinet.*

7. USE STACKING AS AN ALTERNATIVE

Stacking. This is an uncommon trick where you put a bass cabinet on each side of the stage with a guitar cabinet placed on top of it. Fig. 2.9 shows an example of this. The bass cabinet is laid down on its side and becomes a great-looking "riser" for a guitar rig. There is usually less of a volume battle when the cabinets are stacked. The bass cabinet is also lower and therefore less present, but when the guitar cabinet is elevated, it becomes much more present onstage. Essentially, the differences are subtle between "stacking" and "doubling" bass cabinets, but you should be aware of both techniques. You may prefer one over the other. This works great on tight stages.

Fig. 2.9A.
Stacking
amps #1

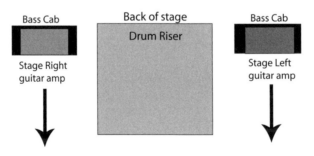

The stacking technique works very well when you *angle* (to be discussed next) your cabinets; the elevated cabinets have more coverage. It may seem louder, but it isn't; it's just the effect of Focus. Stacking sure does look cool when done with the right gear. Fig. 2.9A shows the front perspective of this setup.

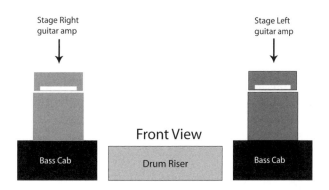

Fig. 2.9B.
Stacking
amps #2

Front View

8. USE ANGLING FOR WIDER COVERAGE

Angling. Angling is just another example of thinking outside the box. I have to give credit where it is due: I picked this up from Greg Leon of the Greg Leon Invasion, and thought it was rather clever-looking with two stacks angled back to back, but I also immediately spotted the advantage. This trick requires the use of an angled 4×12 guitar cabinet set on its side. The "bottom" speakers are then pointed to the front and the "top" speakers are now angling toward the center stage. By placing them in the right spot, you can cover more of your stage area with the same cabinet. And while better coverage is just one benefit, it also keeps everything from loading up in a particular direction as well. The speakers can be angled inward or outward, depending on where the sound is needed. They can also be "corner angled" for even more stage coverage. Fig. 2.10 shows both versions of this setup. When "angling" your cabinets, it's a good idea to elevate them slightly with a milk crate or something when they are in close range. This allows you to hear them better and keeps your levels lower. This is highly recommended for spreading your tone out over a larger area.

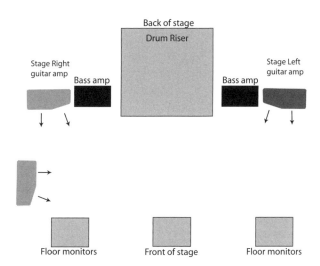

Fig. 2.10.
Angling
cabs

9. USE SIDELINING AS AN ALTERNATIVE

Sidelining. This is essentially an extended version of crossfiring, but the cabinet is upstaged to make best use of its projection. On smaller stages or where you are close to the cabinets, you may want to use a pair of slant cabs. This will give you upward projection and allow you to hear yourself better. On larger stages where you are off the cabs more, you could use any combination of vertical slant cabs or horizontal slant cabs. Figs. 2.11A and B show examples of this. Fig. 2.11A is more for crowded stages, but Fig. 2.11B is more of a semicircle that many acoustic bands prefer and is exactly the same as crossfiring. It's given simply for comparison.

This is one of the more unusual setups and was originally a concept for crowded stages with other bands' gear taking up the majority of the backline. You may run into some situations where you just don't have any room to set up like you normally would; this may help. As with many of these alternate setups, it is given to show you how to think outside the box for solutions. I had not seen this setup used very often, so I was about to pull it from the book until I saw a legendary metal band use this very same technique! In their case, the stage was so full of centerstage props that a conventional setup wasn't possible. It's something to think about when your band starts adding props to the show.

COURTESY OF ALEX SOLCA

Mike Hansen—Drums
Tribe After Tribe/George Lynch
Souls of We/Leif Garrett
The Pointer Sisters/Paula Abdul
www.myspace.com/cymbalcrasher1

"I use my kick drum as the target point for my backline. It's not an issue of the drum riser. The front of my kick drum is where the back of the cabinets should line up for the backline. Essentially, I'm behind everything. You can't just get up there and put your stuff in a different place every night; you need to find a spot that works for you. It doesn't matter where you prefer it, *pay close attention to what's working, and this will help improve your consistency from night to night.* I don't want them any closer than a couple feet to the sides of me, but no further than four feet away from the sides.

Some of the bass cabinets are really directional, and I don't get much tone from where I'm at, so I'll need some of this in my wedges as well. I really don't need much rhythm guitar in my monitors or backup vocals, but I do need some lead vocals.

I like a lot of my drums in the monitor, but if there's too much feedback caused by the toms, then I'll have the engineer take them out. I don't want gates or overcompression on my kit, which would sacrifice my tone. I'm a very dynamic player, and I don't want the gates chopping my drums off. *It's also a great idea to keep a bit of kick and snare in the whole band's monitors to keep everything tight and cohesive.*

I prefer conventional monitors to in-ears, but I can work with either one. If I had to choose, it'd be a wedge. I want to hear the ambiance of the cabinets onstage, then add what I'm not getting. With George Lynch, it depends on whether his cabinets are facing forward or backward, which is what we do for small stages and small PA systems. If they're facing the audience, I'll get more in my wedge. If they're facing me, then I just get a little. None of this is really about volume—it's more about balance!"

At this point, we have looked at several variations of conventional and unconventional approaches to setting up your gear for a small-format band. As mentioned before, these techniques can be mixed and combined to accommodate just about any situation that arises. What works in a large venue may not work in a small one, even when you have the space to work with. Sure, it's nice to have a few options for setting up, but the real point here is to think outside the box! If the stage is very wide but shallow, try setting up where there is the most room—on the side. This can also apply when other bands' equipment has taken up the downstage backline; set your equipment on the sides if you need to. If the stage is very narrow but deep, then the obvious choice is to use the back rather than the sides. It doesn't have to be all the way to the back; use staging to get comfortable levels.

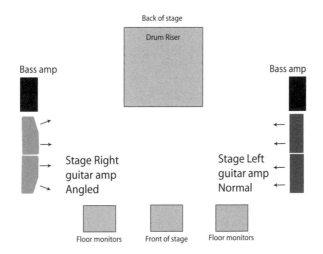

Fig. 2.11A.
Sidelining
cabinets A

Back of stage

Drum Riser

Bass amp

Bass amp

Stage Right
guitar amp
Angled

Stage Left
guitar amp
Normal

Floor monitors   Front of stage   Floor monitors

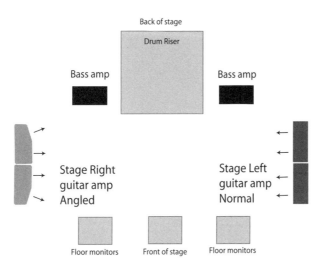

Fig. 2.11B.
Sidelining
cabinets B

Back of stage

Drum Riser

Bass amp

Bass amp

Stage Right
guitar amp
Angled

Stage Left
guitar amp
Normal

Floor monitors   Front of stage   Floor monitors

Try some of these setups in rehearsals before you commit to any one in particular. Don't let a short cable decide which setup you will use; that's just too easy to fix! When you find something that really makes a difference; take note of it, but don't let it stop you from trying other things too. This way, when you have made your decision, you will know exactly what is working best. You now have options.

MEDIUM-FORMAT SETUPS

Using the above techniques for a four-piece setup, we will look at what happens when we add another instrument. What if the lead singer plays guitar? Now we can take a look at some of these medium-size setups with a variety of instruments in different positions. While it really doesn't matter if your frontperson is playing acoustic guitar, keyboards, or a full guitar rig, the trick will be to get his or her sound to the player without disrupting anyone else's zone. This will be true even if he or she isn't a primary player and only plays on a few songs.

10. USE A COMBO OR HOTSHOT FOR ACOUSTIC INSTRUMENTS

Acoustic instruments played by a frontperson located center stage should have a "personal monitor." Either a small amp designed for the instrument, or a hotshot cabinet will work very well. In case you haven't noticed, there is a "void pocket" often created by the drum riser that pushes the backline to the outer sides of the stage. If it is a couple feet tall, it also blocks sound from being directed to the singer's area. This allows the singer to hear more of her monitors and less of the surrounding stage volume; however, this spot will always get more drums than anywhere else.

Fig. 2.12 shows a small acoustic amp placed behind the singer, directly in front of the drum riser. This void pocket is also a great place for the singer's personal monitor. In chapter 1, we discussed how important it is to have control of your own levels onstage. Having the amp at your back isn't always the best location to hear it from, so if you are having problems getting this method to work, then get it up off the ground a couple feet or angle it upward slightly. If this doesn't cut it, you may want to place a hotshot directly next to the singer to get the level you need. While it seems like the simplest solution would be to add some of the direct signal to the wedges for additional level, this could create a loss of presence if the direct signal is out of phase with the acoustic signal onstage. Even slight differences in phase could cause it to sound funny. Moving the microphone will bring this back into coherency. You now have several options to work with—choose what's right for you!

Fig. 2.12.
Fronting
amps

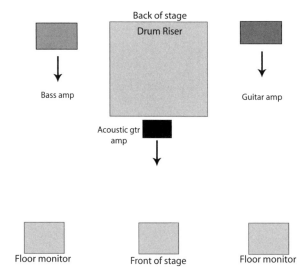

Fig. 2.13 shows a hotshot setup next to a vocal wedge. If you have a choice, place the hotshot on the *neck side* of an acoustic guitar. It will be less likely to feed back than if it is placed on the body side of the guitar. The reality is that some people hear better in one ear than the other, so you may have to place the monitor on the side that hears best. Since an amp is required to power a hotshot, you can actually use both at the same time by simply plugging it in as an extension cabinet. Your frontperson will get his instrument on both sides from different directions, and this greatly reduces the need for levels by increasing the coverage. It really doesn't matter what type of instrument it is; this setup works well for anything. The trick is always to get the right sound in the right place. Location! Location! Location!

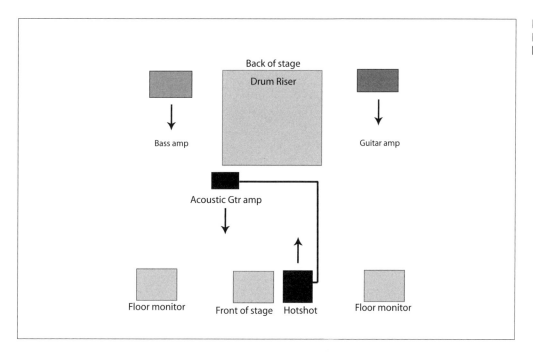

Fig. 2.13.
Fronting
hotshot

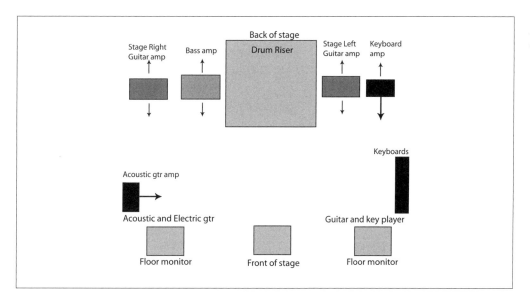

Fig. 2.14.
Additional
amps

Fig. 2.14 shows a setup for the additional amps that a multi-instrumentalist located up front would want. As you can see, a zone has been created for each player, and both musicians have personal monitors set up in their zones. While most people would simply run these instruments into direct boxes and through their monitor wedges, this won't give you the control you need to have. Unfamiliar venues, no soundchecks, and inadequate monitor systems make personal monitor amps the choice of consistency; without them you are at the mercy of chance.

Each multi-instrumentalist is using a different technique; the stage right player has his combo amp in the "crossfired" position, and the stage left player has his combo "staged" on the backline, as he has more room on his side of the stage. This works well for small, narrow stages, but on wider stages, everyone could be set up on the backline. You can still make a stage balance adjustment by staging the backline cabs forward as you need to.

11. USE A FULL-SIZED AMP FOR SOLOISTS

Sometimes a frontperson will have a very strong presence onstage, and in addition to primary vocals, may be a primary instrumentalist. Electric instruments played by a frontperson require a second look before deciding on the right approach. If he/she is using a small- to medium-size combo amp, then you could use the same technique as you would for acoustic. However, if your frontperson is using a large combo or full-size rig, then they should set up with the backline, staged to the inside, where the bass is typically set up. You don't want this amp to be on the outside of the backline or there'll be a volume war between the two players. *Make sure that there is a zone for every player, and always keep your amps as close as possible to you.*

A hotshot in addition to that would be helpful, or it can be used as the cabinet itself. If your frontperson is also playing leads, then a full-size rig should be onstage. Nothing replaces the tone of a full-size rig, especially on a larger stage. It projects well, and the extra stage level is helpful for someone playing leads, especially when there's a lot of interaction with other players. Trying to get this much level with stage monitors is asking a lot. If your frontperson is a keyboardist who is trading licks with a guitarist, this setup should also be your first choice. This is exactly the same as if the frontperson were a lead vocalist and primary guitarist; why should keys be any different? Fig. 2.15 shows an example.

Fig. 2.15.
Soloist
frontman

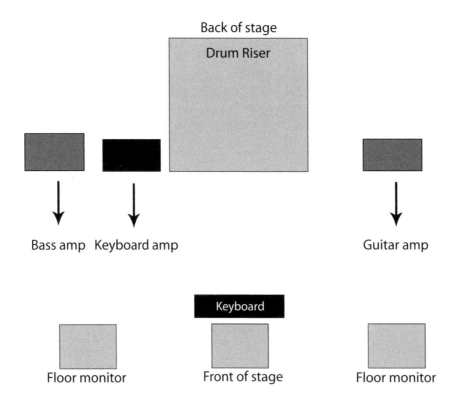

Ed Roth—Keys
Coolio/Rob Halford
Christine with Glen Hughes
Bombastic Meatbats
http://onlinekeyboardsessions.com

"Try to set up on the opposite side of the stage as the guitar. The two of you are in the same frequency, and both of you will have problems hearing if you are too close together. Always set up so you can make eye contact with everyone in the band. If you don't listen and pay attention to what everyone else is playing, you are not a musician.

Make it clear to the monitor engineer what you want, and ask him to check your mix in his cue wedge. If it's brutal after that, better get a couple of adult beverages! Always try to remember that it usually sounds 100 percent better out front than onstage, so just try to stay in the vibe and don't think; just play!

Nothing blows more than bad sound on stage. *Everything I play depends on what I hear.* Try to use a keyboard amp as well as the monitors so you can hear yourself no matter what. Know that everyone is going to turn up even more as the set goes on and their ears get burned out. With that in mind, leave yourself a little room so you can turn up if you need to."

COURTESY OF NEIL ZLOZOWER

12. KNOW EXACTLY HOW LONG IT TAKES TO SET UP

Large keyboard rigs that include several different types of keys like Fender Rhodes, Hammond B-3s, and Leslie cabinets need *lots of room*. Oftentimes, these setups are so large that they will take up an entire corner of the stage. Cornering will allow them to run in both directions and still leave room elsewhere on stage.

Fig. 2.16 shows this type of setup in a five-piece band. In this illustration, there are two players on each side of the stage, as well as a frontperson. When a large key rig is located upstage like this, it can sonically take over the zone and create a problem for the other player located on that side. Upstaging that player's amp will bring back some of the presence needed for him without having to jack the levels up to a ridiculous setting, but it will take careful balancing of both players' levels to keep a battle from ensuing on this side of the stage. *Try to keep everything within the volume level of the stage monitors if you want them to be of any use at all!*

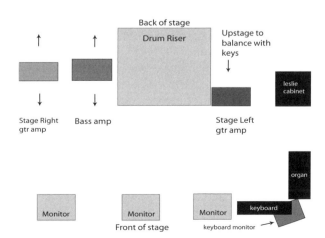

Fig. 2.16. Large keyboard rigs

I really love the sound of these rigs, but if you aren't headlining with a full soundcheck and a limited strike, you may be asking for trouble. It's been done, but rarely in the 15-minute set change that most bands get. You have to make sure that the stage is large enough and that there is enough time to set up and line check. The place to figure this out is at rehearsals. Try pulling up to your rehearsal room, start a stopwatch, load in and set up, wire it up and get mics in front of it. Then test your sounds, check them in the mixer, assign monitors and levels: *now* you can hit the stopwatch again. After you time yourself, then pull out a tape measure and write down just how much space your rig needs. Oh, and don't forget that you will need a stage monitor wedge included in that space as well. This is helpful if you want to hear the rest of the band or your vocals. Just make sure that you know exactly how much time it takes to set up, how much space you need to set up, and don't bite off more than you can chew. At some point, this will become essential to know if you plan on touring. Most national acts keep track not only of how much space each member needs, but also exactly how much space the whole band needs, among other vital information.

COURTESY OF SCOTT HONSBERGER

Scott Honsberger—Keyboards
Spencer Davis Group
Bo Donaldson & the Heywoods
www.myspace.com/multikeyboardist

"Hello, I am a soundman's best (worst) friend (nightmare)! I am a large-scale MIDI nuisance, a poster child for cable manufacturers, and the torturous test track for any and all audio equipment. I am a spoiled, petulant child and I have *all* the toys; however, I don't want anyone to have to deal with my uh, um . . . self-indulgence!

I will climb onto a stage and set up my rig in 15 minutes or less. I smile and say I only need one AC outlet, two input channels, and one monitor mix (I have a stereo pair of balanced outputs, but can go mono if the situation calls for it).

How do I do it? Drum roll, please . . . *prewire is the correct answer!* The more thought you put in before you get to the arena, the more likely your rig will *not* annoy the overworked, underpaid soul sitting on the console for 16 excruciating hours a day!"

No wonder electronic keyboards have become so popular over the past couple of decades, but even they have many of the same problems. Bad cables, forgotten adapters, and stands, and incorrect wiring can all affect your setup time. The more you can prewire, the better! It's also a good idea to mark both ends of every audio cable and your AC power cords. Once they get tied up together, it's darn near impossible to tell which is which unless you separate them, which not a practical idea in a live performance. Using different colored cables is the very best way, but even this can be hard to coordinate. Also, use the right length cable in the right spot. Custom lengths are recommended for really sophisticated rigs, but this won't be necessary for the spares. Marking both ends also keeps the same cables in the same location of the signal path. If a particular unit keeps having the same intermittent problems, you have a good idea of where to look first.

This comes in very handy when troubleshooting problems in the middle of a show. If you used the same problem cable in a different place every time you played, it'd be much harder to find, and would make it seem as if everything were having a different problem every time, so spare yourself some insanity. The setup suggestions in this section are designed to give you a variety of perspectives in regard to your stage setup, so don't feel obligated to conform to the norm. And while they may not solve every situation, they will solve most. These are the basic components of the more complex stage setups that you may be faced with, and it's important to have a firm grasp of these concepts in their basic forms. Take the time to get familiar with these individual concepts so that you can seize opportunities when they arise, as they surely will. You will recognize them in various forms in the next section on large-format bands.

LARGE-FORMAT BANDS

You may be asking yourself, "What the h#%! does a symphony have to do with my band?" But there was a very good reason for choosing this image in regard to large-format bands: *If they can do it, so can you.*

For centuries, long before mics and amps, PA systems and monitors, these orchestras and symphonies have been able to accomplish what many modern bands haven't: *balance.* It's one of the principles I've been trying to drive home in this book. Location, Focus, and Balance are what makes an orchestra sound as incredible as it does. And while there are many great recordings that get close, nothing can compare to the impact of actually being there. This is the "gold standard" of live performance, and there's a lot to be learned from orchestras, especially in regard to dynamics. But take a look at the way they're set up; does this resemble crossfiring? Very few orchestras set up exactly the same way. So before we jump right into large-format bands, let's take a closer look at orchestras and find some common elements you can use for your band.

Location. While there are endless possibilities for setting up a 96-piece symphony orchestra, there seems to be a common practice among all of them called *dynamic placement.* This means that particular instruments are located in certain places to achieve a desired effect. In all actuality, the softer instruments are usually placed toward the front, where you can hear them better, and the louder instruments are often placed toward the back so that they don't overpower the quieter sounds. Isn't this what you do with vocals and drums? What would happen if this were reversed? However, there's more to this than meets the eye; risers are used to help backline instruments project.

Zones. Another common practice among these giants is the use of zones. All of the violins are grouped together to form a single zone. You wouldn't scatter them throughout the orchestra in a random fashion, would you? When grouped together, they form a single area where the violinists can hear themselves better than if they were placed otherwise. While there are quite a few reasons for this that have nothing to do with your band, it does illustrate the importance of having zones in your setup.

Focus. Not only are instruments grouped and placed in specific locations, but also face in particular directions. Interesting . . . *that's* what this chapter has been about! Of course, there's a considerable difference between an acoustic instrument and one with an amp or monitor; an amp gives you the choice of exactly where your tone is projected as well as the opportunity to hear yourself better. This is the primary reason I have been emphasizing the use of personal amplifiers; without them you have no choice but to depend on the house monitor system. Depending on monitor systems to solve all your problems is like asking a waiter for more vocals on your plate. He may get around to it, sooner or later . . .

Balance. Originally, symphonies didn't require microphones to perform, but they still had a sound engineer—called the *conductor. That's right, conductors were the very first sound engineers in history.* One of the conductor's many responsibilities is to control the dynamics of certain instruments and the levels of the orchestra as a whole. This sounds like a soundperson to me. Since you don't have a conductor, you have a sound engineer, it would be wise to follow his or her stage level cues.

Many times during a difficult soundcheck, I will bring down the PA system to hear the balances from the stage, and almost every time there will be one member that is substantially louder than everyone else. Not only does this create a problem for the rest of the band, but it's a problem for the engineers that have to mix *above* this level. It's an easy problem to fix: *balance*!

In a large-format band, you need to have a zone for each player, but there's only so much space onstage. Your zones will have to be smaller, and your stage volumes will have to be lower than they would for a trio; everyone's a little closer together. More often that not, you may be short on stage monitors with a large-format band. This means you need to find a balance that is good for everyone: not too soft, not too loud; present, but not overbearing. This includes drummers, too. Just because you don't have a volume control doesn't mean that you don't have to "turn it down" a bit. If the verses are as loud as the choruses, you may have a problem. Dynamics are very important with a large-format band.

COURTESY OF TIM FRANQUIST

Tim Franquist—FOH/Monitors
Cheap Trick/Robert Palmer/Night Ranger
Grand Funk Railroad/Ray Charles
James Brown/Jerry Lee Lewis
www.myspace.com/sonicnomad

"When it comes to the stage, don't overcomplicate your setup—the simpler it is, the better. Your band needs to focus on a controlled stage volume, and then they can enjoy the monitors. You can't just turn up and then try to fix it with excessive monitor levels. *It's been my experience that the best-sounding bands get a great sound onstage before the PA is ever turned on.* 'Less is more,' and louder doesn't mean better. Get a great sound at the source and the rest is easier. Start with great drum sounds and go from there.

At soundchecks, play like you do in your show. Make sure your volumes are at the same level and have the same intensity as well. Having stage plots, input lists, and cue sheets for mix and monitor assignments are great, but make sure they're up to date. *Whatever you do, don't expect engineers to read your mind; let us know exactly what you need.*"

Now that we've had our orchestral history lesson and made some comparisons, it's time to look at what all this means to a large-format band. Most bands of this type have the basics: drums, bass, guitar, keys, and vocals. This is the core of the band, and under normal circumstances would not be much of a problem. We have already looked at what it takes to get these elements working together, but a large band will often have another two or three players to contend with, and this is where the problem lies—creating effective zones for them. Since everything will revolve around the core of the band, you should examine these instruments first and decide who belongs on the frontline. Typically, it should be the players that sing the most, because this is where the monitors are, and they will need them.

Now before anyone gets their panties in a bunch over being stuck on the backline, let's get something straight. You're putting on a show, right? You *do* plan on moving around the stage, right? Good. Because standing on the frontline and making funny faces while you play isn't really putting on a show. There are a couple ways to get you back into the spotlight without having to bask in it.

►Guitarists and other mobile players can simply step up to the frontline when it's their turn to shine. It takes a bit of coordination between the players in that area, but once the idea of shifting positions onstage sinks in, it becomes second nature.

►Stationary players like keyboardists and percussionists can have stage lighting focused on them. By dropping the frontline lighting and spotlighting them onstage, they can get their five minutes of fame without having to be up front the whole night. It also helps when the frontline players move out of the way for the audience to see them do their thing. Choreography and good lighting are essential to any professional live performance. We'll look at that in Chapter 5: Getting Organized.

If your core players don't sing, they could become the backline, and a conventional setup should be fine. This leaves the frontline open for some noncore players, and this should take care of bands that have seven or eight players. Fig. 2.17A shows an example of this type of setup. Each player has their own zone in a different shade. You could have two lead singers, two background vocalists and two sax/horn players for a total of 10 players onstage with room to move around. This is a *two-layer setup*. Larger bands will want to become friends with this concept.

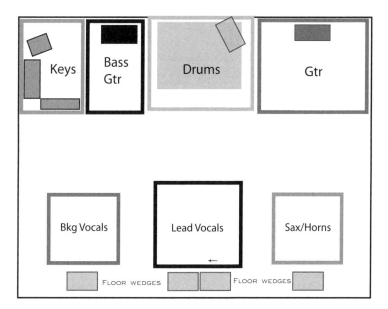

Fig. 2.17A. Large format #1

This setup uses some of the orchestral techniques we discussed earlier:

►Dynamic placement puts the louder sounds toward the back and the quieter sounds toward the front. It also groups like sounds together.

►Zones have been created for all players, and like instruments are grouped together.

But there are also other variations to consider, such as what if your guitarist is a primary vocalist? This setup can be adjusted to handle that by swapping zones with the sax/horn players.

Fig. 2.17B shows a variation of this. Not only did the guitarist swap locations with the sax/horn players, but his amp was relocated as well. This keeps his amp close enough to him to not have to turn it up or cross the sax/horn player's zone. Your band may or may not have the exact same type of players, but the idea of this layout will work for most instruments regardless of type. The real point here is the proper use of zones in your stage setups. Every player that needs an amp has one close by, and every singer that needs a mic has a monitor close by as well. While this chapter is mainly concerned with your setup, monitor zones will be discussed in the next chapter.

Fig. 2.17B.
Large
format #2

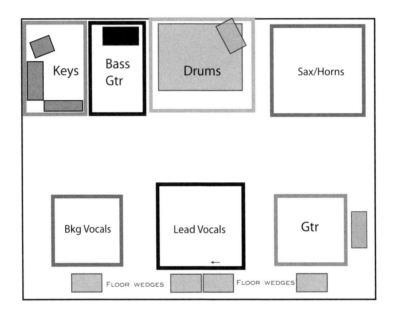

Large-format bands can be complex, and the resources they have to work with can be rather limited. When equipment resources are lacking, you must make the best use of physical resources through dynamic placement, zones, and location, focus, and balance. Usually an approach can be found by combining these principles. If your band has even more players than shown on the previous pages, then you might want consider these next setups before picking out a location for them: they all interact together. In reality, *these principles apply to all sounds placed onstage.* You can use the previous examples as a starting point.

Choosing Stage Locations

Looks are important—after all, you are putting on a show—but so is your ability to get up there and sound good. Finding a balance of both is essential to both looking and sounding great. You're going to have to be flexible and adjust your setup for different venues and the various member changes that happen with larger bands. I can't tell you what "looks good" to you; that's a decision you'll have to make on your own, but I can tell you what to look for when choosing stage locations for various members.

There are three general concepts you may want to consider for any member's location onstage: *what, where,* and *how.* What is it? Where is it? How are you going to make it work in the PA system? These are the questions I ask myself any time someone sets up on my stage. But don't just ask yourself these three questions; use the following criteria to arrive at some useful answers.

13. consider the dynamics of the sound

1. Dynamics. This is the What in the equation. Is this a loud (dominant) sound? If so, consider the backline as a first choice. Make sure it doesn't violate a quiet sound's zone.

Is it a quiet sound? If so, consider a spot up front. Make sure it isn't close to a loud sound. Is it similar to one of the other instruments onstage? Consider grouping it with like instruments. Horns and reeds belong together and voices belong together, especially when they are blending together. For acoustic guitars, violins, and other instruments *that use a personal monitor*, you will have more options to work with. Once you have fully considered the dynamics of each sound, then you can select a proper location for them. Some bands may need a two-layer setup, and others may need a three-layer setup.

14. CONSIDER THE LOCATION OF THE SOUND

2. Location. This is the Where part. Where will this instrument be located in relation to the other dominant sounds? Microphone bleed increases with every mic that is placed on the stage. Try to find a spot where there is some "sonic space." You want to make sure that this member is not blocking the sound from anyone else's monitor or cabinet. Each player needs a zone, or at least share one. Does this player use an amp? That not only requires more physical space for the amp, but it makes their zone larger. These aspects should be considered when picking the right spot for an instrument.

Earle Dumler—Woodwinds
Frank Zappa/Barbra Streisand
The Beach Boys/The Carpenters
Three-Time Grammy Award–Winner

"I don't want to be too close to the drums, and not so much the drums themselves, but the *cymbals*. The cymbals absolutely absorb the sound of the wind instrument; they just suck it right up. If a drummer is riding a cymbal behind a wind solo, you'll hardly hear any of the woodwind's notes; that 'white sound' just sucks up the tone of a woodwind instrument. I also wouldn't want to be close to the bass unless it's someone I know who understands the instrument.

Sax and brass instruments are less tricky because they've got a lot more volume and the sound is very dominant. If you had a trumpet, trombone, and sax, I'd want them together. These instruments often play a lot of background riffs, so if they are together, you can get more vibe. If you're going to do something with one of the gentler wind instruments, what you do around that is pretty important. The subtleties of those instruments are very difficult to capture, and there are some things you just can't do live."

15. FIND THE BEST WAY TO MIC THE SOUND

3. Input. The is the How part of the equation. How are you going to mic it? No matter what instrument you place onstage, you will need some way to get it into the console for mixing and monitor returns, and this makes your choice of location very important. If it requires a mic, then be sure you have some separation from other dominant sounds. You want to select the right mic and the miking technique that will get the best sound. If it has a pickup or direct out, there will be less to worry about, and this is the best way to get a signal into the monitors. We will look at your options in Chapter 4: Input Sources.

16. FIND THE BEST WAY TO MONITOR THE SOUND

4. Output. Last but not least, the player has to have some way of hearing themselves onstage. An electric instrument has the ability to use an amp, and it should not be a problem to hear. A dynamic acoustic instrument like sax or horns should also not be a problem for its performer to hear onstage, but vocals, flute, and delicate percussion may often require a stage monitor for its performer. If you decide that this instrument needs a monitor, then it may need to be relocated if monitors are limited.

Putting all this into action may be simpler than you think. Fig. 2.18A shows a three-layer setup that could handle up to *12 performers* onstage.

Fig. 2.18A.
Large format
#3

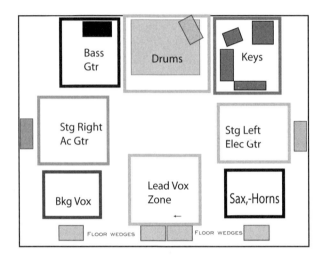

That's right, I said *12*! Drums, bass, acoustic guitar, electric guitar, and keys = five, plus three sax/horn players, three background singers, and one lead vocalist. And more importantly, everyone has a zone!

Why this setup works: When you look at a large band as a "small orchestra" and employ some of the principles that allow it to function properly, it becomes easier, but never simple.

▶ Similar instruments and vocals are grouped together.
▶ Instruments and vocals are dynamically placed onstage correctly.
▶ Effective zones are created for each group.
▶ Amps and personal monitors are located and focused correctly.
▶ The stage monitors are maximized.

These illustrations are three-layer setups: there's a frontline, backline, and a middle layer. Let's take a look at even more players onstage. Fig. 2.18B shows 15 performers. This should cover the majority of fairly large bands, but it's possible for an additional zone to be created center stage. If your band has even more performers than this, I would suggest posting specific information on the www.rockinyourstagesound.com website and include exact stage and equipment dimensions for best results. Don't forget to list the stage monitor resources as well.

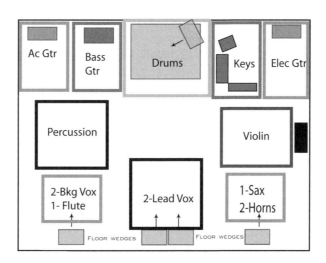

Fig. 2.18B.
Large
format #4

USING PERSONAL MONITORS

17. USE A PERSONAL MONITOR FOR BEST RESULTS

Just as guitarist needs an amp and a singer needs a monitor, any other instrument that can have a pickup mounted on it should have a monitor of some kind. One of the main purposes of this book is to put control back in your hands! If you don't have control of your ability to hear yourself, you will always be at the mercy of someone else. Here are some of the reasons why you want this control.

> ►**You can control your stage level.** You don't have to ask for more, you just reach over and get what you need. Even more important, you get control over the EQ, which is something you don't get on most small and mid-size PA systems. Your tone is just as important as your levels.

> ►**The engineer is usually busy with your mix.** There's a lot to a FOH mix, and it's not like the engineer is just standing around waiting for a monitor cue, unless you are working on a Type III or IV system (this will be discussed in the Chapter 3: Monitor Systems).

> ►**The more you put in the vocal wedges, the less you can hear the vocals.** It's only a mono mix, and things get jumbled up real fast when you load the wedges. This amp can be focused precisely without sacrificing the vocal monitor. Having a personal amp onstage will give you staging options as well.

> ►**A personal monitor will allow acoustic instruments to compete with the more dominant sounds onstage**, instead of Bambi vs. Goliath! It allows other musicians to hear these instruments much better than simply through a wedge.

You want to remember that some of the sound being heard out front is coming from the stage in smaller shows, so if a loud guitar is onstage and a soft acoustic with no stage monitor is playing, chances are good that the other players won't hear that acoustic very well. Using just the monitor system for acoustic sounds requires it to be assigned to all the monitors onstage, and that means more time and details. It also clutters up their monitor mixes. Give the acoustic instruments a chance to be heard by using a personal monitor.

Anything that can have a pickup should! While most people would readily agree that a mic sounds better, using a microphone exclusively on a sound is very limiting. Using a mic means having to remain precisely in the same position for the sound to be consistent. Move away slightly, and the tone goes away. Move into the mic slightly and it may feed back. Nobody ever goes on stage and is perfectly still when performing, so right away the mic becomes a bit of a problem, even with a compressor on it. Slight movements onstage can really be a devil in the monitors.

This is why it's a good idea to use a pickup or a transducer: It always stays near the sound. You can move around and the level never changes. Another reason for using a pickup is that it is often closer to the sound. This means less background noise and less chance of feeding back. These two points alone make the use of a pickup your first choice for monitors, even if that is the only reason for using a pickup. You need to get your sound into your personal monitors and/or stage monitors, and pickup/transducers are the best way. These devices don't have much, if any, control over their sound, so you will want to use a personal monitor when using them.

18. ALMOST ANYTHING CAN WORK AS A MONITOR

There are several different kinds of "purpose made" monitors, like acoustic guitar amps, keyboard monitors, and even small PAs, but they are all essentially similar: preamp and EQ, power amp, and speaker, even when they are all one unit. You can use one of these purpose-made units with nice features like XLR outputs for the PA system and pre/post EQ switching, but even a practice amp works just fine. If you have a lot of money and want the convenience, buy one of these dedicated units. However, if you are looking for something different and don't mind experimenting, try using a tube guitar amp.

TUBE AMPS

For an acoustic guitar they might not be the best, but for keyboards they are awesome. They seem to warm up all that digital sound and take the edge off the harsh tones, which is precisely why we love them on guitars. Set them for clean tones and your digital sounds will come out as you want them to in most cases. If the amp has a couple channels and a footswitch, you can get creative with some of your unusual sounds. If it has an effects loop, you are in for even more fun. Since a digital keyboard isn't subject to feedback like an acoustic guitar would be, you can create some crazy stuff with a decent keyboard and a guitar rig with effects. You will want to put a mic on all this craziness; otherwise it will just get lost onstage. Using a direct box off the dry keys *and* a miked guitar rig with effects could be just what you're looking for. No doubt someone has already done it, but it hasn't become an everyday item yet.

DIGITAL MODELING AMPS

Today's technology has gotten very advanced, with sounds and options that you could never get on a standard guitar amp. The programmability of these units makes them very useful for this purpose. They even have controller inputs for parameters that aren't available on a standard amp. Consistent, portable, and reliable, these units are a great choice to create something new with.

PLAIN OLD AMPS

If all you are looking for is good, clean volume, a solid-state guitar amp will work great. If you have great sounds and don't want to spend much, you can find lots of these lying around pawnshops for a reasonable price. There may be one already available in your band. For those who prefer the convenience of a special-purpose unit that has all the dedicated features you would need for that instrument, they make some very nice keyboard amps with multiple inputs for several sets of keys, EQs, and levels. They come in all sizes and price ranges, so take a look at some of them and give them a try.

But for those of you who don't mind experimenting and insist on the very best, a small PA system is a great choice. You can place a set of speakers on both sides of the stage, like you would with the guitars. You can have your keyboards "spread out" in stereo, or have one keyboard sound on one side and another sound on the other. You could even program your keyboard sounds to certain "panorama" positions and have them move around the stage as you change sounds. Even the PA system would reflect these changes, enhanced by the moving stage sound.

This suggestion is meant more for the adventurous type with some technical expertise, but sometimes you just have to roll up your sleeves and get dirty. We will be examining these types of systems in the next chapter, so you should find all you need to know about operating a small system as a stage monitor.

19. KEYBOARD AND GUITAR SOUNDS SHOULD BE BALANCED

Balancing your patches and channel levels is really important. This is true for both keyboards and guitar amps alike. Anything that has multiple sounds and levels should be carefully balanced to dynamic levels. The gain structures involved in PA systems can greatly exaggerate the volume changes between patches, and what may seem just fine onstage can be excruciating in the system. If your patches aren't balanced, the engineer will turn down your channel to make the loudest sound work. *If one is particularly loud, the rest will often be undermixed.* This is the instinctive reaction by almost every sound engineer on the planet. They can't possibly imagine when your changes will happen and how much to compensate, so they will always be chasing your levels around. At some point they will just set it for some compromised balance and leave it. Is this what you really want?

Another consideration is the monitors—these drastic changes will come blaring out of other player's wedges as well! They may not get noticed as quickly by the monitor engineer and become irritating onstage. This is why it is important to grasp the concept of balancing your sounds. Using a compressor on your outputs can smooth things out. Different techniques should be used for different applications.

KEYBOARD PATCHES

Luckily, most keyboard patches have individual levels for each sound, as well as an overall master level. Having individual levels for each sound does not mean that you can set them all to "7" and they will all match. A "bell" patch will need to have a different volume level than a "square wave synth" patch. The majority of keyboardists have gotten used to using a volume pedal to control these differences on the fly. Most of the time this works, but it is extremely difficult to memorize all the changes. This process becomes even more difficult when a player is using several keyboards at once. There is an alternative to this method: by using some mathematical magic in the individual volume assignments of each patch, you can get them to come very close without having to rely so heavily on the volume pedal.

This is a two-step process that requires setting *all* patch levels to 66 percent, whatever that may be for each type of keyboard. Some keyboards have volume levels ranging from 0–127; others range from 0–99. Some of the simpler and older keys have 0–9 or 0–67. There is a very good reason why a level of 66 percent was chosen; it brings all sounds to the upper middle of the adjustment range. Once all patches have been set for a 66 percent volume level, you can then go through every patch and match them correctly. Otherwise it would be difficult to make a simple downward adjustment of the loud sounds because there is no true perspective.

Mitch Perry—Guitar
MSG/Cher/Edgar Winter Group
Asia Featuring John Payne
www.mitchperry.com

COURTESY OF CINDY CRAMER

"I don't really have a particular stage setup; everything changes from stage to stage, so I make my adjustments once I'm there. I just like to be on the side of the stage where all the hot chicks are! I like my cabinet off to the side, angled slightly away and generally to the outside; I don't like getting smacked directly with it. I hate putting my amp on the side of the stage; it just doesn't sound natural to me. Guitar cabinets throw kind of weird; they sometimes put 20 times more guitar on the other side of the stage than yours. I don't even like sidefills on the stage.

I will not listen to my amp through a monitor; after all the trouble we go through picking the right cabinet and dialing it in, why would I let an engineer have total control of my sound onstage? On bigger stages, you'll have an engineer who can get you a sound you can live with. *Monitors are there to fill in the missing blanks.* A lot of people think they're supposed to hear their stereo through the monitors; I want very little. When the band's playing and I don't hear enough of something, I'll ask for it. I don't need a whole lot, just enough to be able to hear it. It's live rock 'n' roll—learn how to deal with it!"

If you tried to turn down the loud sounds to match the softer ones, you might have to go back and adjust every patch whenever you find a softer one that doesn't work, because you would have no way to turn up the softer sound as well as turn down the louder one. Setting them all to 66 percent gives you a reasonable amount of upward adjustment for the softer sounds, while giving you considerable downward adjustment on the louder sounds.

There is no escaping the fact that you will have to balance them all against each other, and the closer you can get them to match each other, the better and more consistent your patches will sound. This is *very* crucial to large multiple-key rigs. It is a big time saver in the end, especially when a new module comes in and you need to dial it in. This should make things adjustable without having to commit to either end of the adjustment.

GUITAR PATCHES AND CHANNEL SWITCHING

There are many different methods of channel switching: some people use dual or multi-channel amps, some use amp-modeling devices, and others use stompboxes to change sounds. Each method should be approached differently, but the results should all be similar: consistency of tone. Some of you may disagree with this, but you may change your mind after you consider the implications involved in a PA system.

Why should your tone be consistent? Most people think that having the ability to radically change their sound means that they should. I agree with this to some degree, but it should be done with a specific range in mind. This is because your rig is dialed in and set for stage levels, then a mic is placed in front of it and dialed in as well. The levels and EQ settings on the PA are *very specific* for that sound. If your level and/or your tone changes drastically, those settings no longer work in the PA.

The PA may be multiplying certain aspects of the sound by a factor of three (or more), and if your level/tone changes by 4 dB in any way, you have created a 12 dB (or more) difference! This is how gain structure works in a PA system. Everything is very specific.

When there is no mic involved, larger differences in gain/tone can work just fine onstage, as a certain amount of distance "tempers" and softens the changes, but between the combination of the gain/tone change onstage *and* the exponential increase due to gain structure in the PA, it can jump out of the mix and become obnoxious. Guess what happens . . . yep! The engineer turns your PA level down instinctively, and it probably won't come back up. Now your loud channel works, but everything sounds "small." If these channel settings were relatively close in EQ and level, then this phenomenon would not happen. It should be apparent that serious level and tone differences will not work, but how much is enough? This is the most difficult part: finding a balance that does work. This will depend on your style of playing and range of tones. Make sure that they are "progressive," meaning that the clean sound is the lowest and the rhythm sound is slightly louder, and lastly that the lead sound is slightly louder still. They should all be fairly close so that you can hear them well onstage, but progressive enough to get the dynamic range you need.

DIGITAL MODELING AMPS

These seem to be the easiest to program of the bunch. Line 6 and other similar amps will have several choices for each program, A/B/C/D or whatever. You will want to find your primary sound first. This is the one that you play the most and are most comfortable with. Try to set the controls as close to medium as possible, as this will allow you to copy this program and vary it according to your range.

By using this main program as a master model, you can copy the program and back off the gain for crunch or clean while keeping the same EQ and level. Slight adjustments are okay, but don't change too much. This closely resembles the way a real amp would work. For the other side of the spectrum, you can copy your basic program and make gain and/or level adjustments to get your drive or lead sound.

Keep the EQs and levels close; only moderate adjustments will work. Save this to a different program bank. You can copy it and add effects for variety. Store your programs in a left-to-right order, beginning with the cleanest first, and step through the channels progressively with the loudest and dirtiest channel last. You should be able to step through your programs with only dynamic changes in volume and small EQ differences. The actual sound can change as a normal amp would, but the levels and EQs should be fairly close; just like a normal amp would. I would like to make the point of not having your clean sound louder than your crunch sound: It's just not natural sounding and will make your crunch sound "small." For those of you who prefer many different sounds and find this a bit confining, you could set up other program banks if available. Just bear in mind that if the levels and tones change drastically, you will probably be disappointed with the end result in the PA. There will be nothing an engineer can do to fix this, except turn your mic down to where the loudest sound works. Even when you have your own sound engineer and he is willing to ride the fader for you, it would only compensate level changes, not EQ differences.

Todd and Troy Garner—Vocals
Lenny Kravitz (background)
The Seventh Hour (lead)
www.myspace.com/theseventhhourmusic

Troy: "With Lenny, Todd and I were set up on stage left, but since we operated as a unit within our own zone, we could have been just about anywhere onstage. We both had a monitor and like pretty much the same mix, which is primarily our vocals. As long as I can hear the bass drums and guitars, not necessarily loud but there, I can hit my pitches."

Todd: "Typically I don't need a whole lot in my wedges because I'm hearing most of the instruments from the stage. I need to feel the beat of the song. My hearing is very key to my performance onstage, so I try to take care of it as well. Most of our soundchecks go pretty smoothly, because we have a good idea of what we need to have onstage and we don't need to compromise the FOH mix to get any more than that."

Troy: "We also had in-ear monitors and loved it, but I always took one of mine out. I still like to feel the impact of the sound onstage. When I could hear myself really well, like with in-ears, I didn't have to force my vocals and I could sing with dynamics. This kept my voice in better shape all the way through the show. No matter what type of monitors you use, you have to know what you want to hear onstage."

Todd: "You also have to be very concise when you ask for adjustments in the monitors and do so in a way that doesn't disrespect the engineers. They can't read your mind, so you have to let them know exactly what you need, and most guys will give you what they can. Make sure this is dealt with before you leave soundcheck. You gotta be humble and very nice, because sometimes this makes the difference when you need a little something extra. Being cool and thanking the guys I work with always seems to make things just a little better!"

CHANNEL-SWITCHING AMPS

This should be a bit easier, but you will often have less options. The separate channels should sound similar, so setting up a consistent tone from channel to channel should be easy. Keep your settings dynamically progressive and smooth.

Most amps have two channels, and that isn't quite enough for most guitarists. The use of a footpedal with a slight gain and level boost will give a lead sound for both clean and crunch settings. It doesn't have to be much, just enough to take the sound of each channel up to a dynamic difference. While it won't give you "four channels," it will give "four ranges" of two channels.

FOOTPEDAL OVERDRIVE

This is one of the more tricky setups to dial in: not only do the tones of these devices vary *dramatically*, but you usually have very little control over their tone. Most guitar rigs should have three sounds: Clean, Crunch, and Drive. They should all sound like different gain stages of the same amp, not three different amps. If you engage a pedal and it sounds like a completely different guitar, this may not be the right pedal. Stay away from dramatic EQ changes; they just don't translate well in the mix. Be careful to keep everything dynamically progressive and smooth and you should have no problems.

IN CONCLUSION

By now the idea should be apparent: *Think outside the box!* The gear that you set up, the way you set up, and how you run it can set you apart from the crowd. Moving a sound just a few feet can make all the difference in your show. I suggest you start at rehearsal with a simple setup and try moving one thing at a time to different places. Push your backline all the way back one set, then push it all the way up front the next. Stark changes made back to back like that will reveal hidden subtleties that wouldn't be noticeable any other way.

Once you have found the right spot for your backline, try using different equipment or running your equipment differently until you are sure you know what will happen when you have to make a change. Once you have a simple setup dialed in and you feel confident about getting it set up correctly every time, then you can add some of the more complicated aspects. When you run into a small problem, look this chapter over and decide if it is a location issue or an equipment issue. There are tools for both in this chapter. Always create zones for each player and use Location, Focus, and Balance when you can to solve problems.

Remember to use a personal monitor whenever possible. This will enable you to take control of your sound. Your levels and EQ will be important to making yourself feel comfortable, and don't forget that they can be set up in several different places and several different ways.

Keep in mind that stage problems begin at rehearsal; if you have bad habits there, they will come back to haunt you onstage. For this reason alone, rehearse with what you perform with!

There are some of you who are making use of some less-than-adequate places to rehearse, but if this is forcing you to set up incorrectly, then it will be a problem later. Anything you save by using a rehearsal space like this will cost much more in the long run. You are not just rehearsing your songs; you are rehearsing your sound as well. Rehearse as you would perform! This is the only way to resolve the minute details that will present themselves at showtime.

So let's take a look at what we have covered in this chapter.

1. Put the Right Sound in the Right Place
2. Find the Right Spot for Your Backline
3. Use Doubling to Get More Stage Level
4. Use Crossfiring to Use Less Offstage Level
5. Use Cornering to Get More Stage Coverage
6. Use a Hotshot for Tight Spots
7. Use Stacking as an Alternative
8. Use Angling for Wider Coverage
9. Use Sidelining as an Alternative
10. Use a Combo or Hotshot for Acoustic Instruments
11. Use a Full-Sized Amp for Soloists
12. Know Exactly How Long It Takes to Set Up
13. Consider the Dynamics of the Sound
14. Consider the Location of the Sound
15. Find the Best Way to Mic the Sound
16. Find the Best Way to Monitor the Sound
17. Use a Personal Monitor for Best Results
18. Almost Anything Can Work as a Monitor
19. Keyboard and Guitar Sounds Should Be Balanced

Understanding Monitor Systems and Their Limitations

MONITOR SYSTEMS

Monitor systems are probably the least understood of all PA components. They get kicked around, stood upon, have drinks spilled on them, are used to hold set lists, and are cursed at when they don't perform. There is no doubt that they are greatly underappreciated by their owners. The cost of a good monitor system can often exceed the cost of the main PA system, so it's understandable why club owners usually cut corners here. There are several different levels of monitor systems, and each level costs exponentially more than the previous one. That will become very apparent as we examine them. In any system, the path to a successful stage sound will be to personalize your sound using the many tools you have been given in these pages. While most of these techniques are simple and easy, some require expertise, but there's something for everyone.

Monitor systems have one of hardest jobs in audio; they have to send an amplified signal back toward the microphone that is providing the signal. This is one of the things that most people fail to realize when they start asking for "more monitors." Right about the time you start hearing your monitor pretty well is also the time the *mic* starts picking up sound from the monitor. It doesn't take much to get feedback at that point. So essentially, you are only going to get so much monitor, and there's a narrow margin between where you can hear it and where it starts to feed back. Excessive stage volume will render monitors useless. You can never play any louder than the monitors; that is, if you want to hear yourself. It's not really a matter of how big the monitor is, it's a matter of how well it's set up and EQ'd.

The Logic: Regardless of what system you are using, there is a philosophy that should run through your monitor approach: *zones*. By using the setup techniques in the previous chapter, personal monitor systems and proper use of a stage monitor, you can get a comfortable sound onstage without having an enormous amount of equipment. Balance your zone carefully with the right level from your instrument and the right level of monitor. The term *right* is entirely subjective, but you should have no problem at all if your expectations are realistic. Monitor systems are very much like stage amps and personal monitors: Location, Focus, and Balance will be essential to making them work, but you have to give them a fair chance.

There are some enormous differences among monitor systems. You will need to know what each system is capable of before you can have a realistic expectation regarding any of them. While you may think that the local club's monitor system should be better than your rehearsal system, you may find that sometimes it isn't. In this chapter, we will look at why this can happen as we examine each type and its capabilities. When you get to the arena level, you will find a monitor system that has all the capabilities needed to make your onstage mix sound awesome, but you still need to know what to ask for.

Regardless of what system you are working with, pay attention to what you are hearing; not just from the monitors, but also from the stage. All of these things work together to form your "5.1 Surround Sound" stage sound, so it's important to know what you need to hear in any venue, large or small. If you know what you need, you will know what to ask for. Engineers will have an idea, but knowing what you want will make all the difference.

MONITOR ZONES

In chapter 2 we took a look at stage zones and what they mean to your ability to hear yourself. Now, it's time to have a look at monitor zones and how they work within the stage zones.

A *monitor zone* is an area that sends PA signals back to the performer. Monitors can vary from the simple two-speaker system that you see in rehearsals to 10 or 12 different mix systems that have a dedicated monitor operator. The number of available mixes and monitor wedges determines how many monitor zones you will have to work with. In some cases, one mix will feed two wedges; this is often the case with paired front wedges. This allows for the mix to be in two places at once, but both monitors still share the same common blend, so it's a bit of a compromise. This is usually the case for lead vocalists who often need more level onstage.

A monitor cannot send anything to the stage that is not in the PA system. This is why chapter 4 will become very important: it will show you how to select the correct input sources for your signal applications.

Creating an effective monitor zone depends on several things:

▶ Having a good stage setup that includes stage zones for each player.
▶ Having a reasonable stage volume that is balanced between musicians.
▶ Placing the monitors in the right location and focusing them.
▶ Keeping your monitor mix as lean as possible.
▶ Having realistic expectations of stage monitor systems.

If your expectations are unrealistic, you will always be disappointed! You may have gotten an awesome stage mix at one of the venues you played, but don't expect that to happen all the time. As a general rule, most engineers put as little as possible in the monitors to reduce the number of interactive combinations, limiting the potential for feedback. You should ask only for what you need. Having monitor cues for each player can help get things started, but it still takes time to dial them in correctly. We will be looking at stage cues in Chapter 5: Getting Organized.

THE ROLLOVER POINT

Vocal monitors are different from many other monitor assignments because they are pointed directly at the source of their signal: the vocal mic. Since the human voice is usually not the loudest sound onstage, they also require substantially more level to compete with guitar and bass amps and any heavy-handed drummers in close proximity. There's a point where the vocalist can begin to hear him- or herself properly, and any additional monitor level will cause him or her to either back off the mic or lay back on projecting their vocals, *but only if the stage levels aren't overpowering the monitors.* This is what you are looking for in your monitor assignments: the Rollover Point. It is where you don't have to strain to hear yourself. It's not just a "setting on the console"; it requires several things to be done correctly first.

> ▶**Proper Mic Technique:** You have to sing *on the mic.* Holding it more than a few inches away won't give you this level, and you really have to project your voice; singing at a low level won't get the job done. When you do sing quietly, get right on the mic.

> ▶**Proper EQ Adjustment:** For any monitor to reach the rollover point, it will have to be properly EQ'd to remove problem frequencies. Using a different type of mic may render a carefully EQ'd monitor useless. Use the same type of mic as the house mic.

> ▶**A Balanced Stage Level:** By "balanced," I mean a level that does not render the stage monitors useless. This can be rather difficult on smaller stages. If you start hearing feedback in your vocals and still can't hear yourself, the instrument levels need to come down to where you can hear yourself in the monitors.

Without these three things, you won't be able to find the rollover point for your vocals—you may find feedback instead! Even when you do find the rollover point, it may not be without some considerations. Raising the level past the point where you can sing comfortably will be asking for trouble.

A monitor system can never be louder than its source. Let me clarify this statement, as it may not make sense without qualification. A monitor signal can never be louder *at the source of its signal* than the signal itself. A prime example is your vocal mic: While the monitor may seem quite loud coming from the wedge, if it is as loud as your voice is to the mic, it will feed back. As a matter of fact, it will affect your tone just before it gets to that level.

The difference lies in the fact that the mic picks up sound better from in front of it than behind it, but the reflections from your face can cause spontaneous bursts of feedback when monitor levels are very high. If you hold your hand up to your ear, you can actually hear the change that happens. This very same thing occurs as soon as a microphone gets close to an object: it picks up reflections. This phenomenon is highly apparent when the ball of the mic is cupped.

It is important to remember that a high level of monitor signal will also affect the tone of a microphone. Too much monitor will make your vocals sound honky or muddy, depending on the prominent EQ settings of the monitor. Essentially, the mic is hearing the monitors as well as your voice, and the interaction is very dynamic and will change with every adjustment you make. This applies to pretty much any microphonic sound source, including internal mics and contact mics that are interacting with stage monitors. Even excessive FOH mix levels can affect your tone if the mic or the cabinets are not placed well, but this is rarely a problem with well-situated main PA systems.

This observation regarding mic/monitor interaction is not strictly limited to the mic that is feeding the monitor; high levels of other elements in a monitor mix can leak back into a vocal mic and cause additional problems. Anything that is significantly louder than your voice at the mic can leak into the vocal mic and create a tone problem for the mix engineer. If a lead singer is asking for a lot of backing tracks or guitar in her monitor, guess what will be in her vocal mic channel? You got it! This is another reason to keep your monitor mixes lean and simple. Try to hear as many sounds as you can from the stage; personal stage amps will help out with this. The mic will pick up anything that is as loud as your voice, so be careful what you ask for in the monitors.

COURTESY OF ALBIE BURKE

Mo Rodgers—Vocals/Keys
Mighty Mo Rodgers
Sonny Terry & Brownie Magee
Brenton Woods
http://mightymorodgers.com

"As a singer, all I can say is, you don't want to blow your voice, because you can't hear yourself. I always want monitors on the stage and on both sides. I know very little about EQs and high and lows, etc., like most singers, but I know what sounds right for me: a slightly bright sound with a little echo. I like a natural sound with little or no artificiality. And again, you really got to hear yourself as a singer. I have the other instruments mixed in the monitors, including my keys. Not loud, just there.

It's also important for the other musicians to be able to hear the singer in their monitors. 'Breaking the Sound Barrier'—this is what I call that sweet spot in the sound where the mix is so right that the sound is transparent. So clear and pure that you feel a natural high from the sound and you and your fans go on a journey of wonder and discovery."

IDENTIFYING MONITOR SYSTEMS

While the term *monitor system* can mean different things to different people, there are some distinctive characteristics that are common to each type of monitor system. Learning to identify the different types of monitor systems can greatly increase your understanding of what to expect from each type. Here is a quick look at what you will see.

Type I Monitor System. This is a very small and simple type of PA system. You may have used it at rehearsals to hear vocals. It usually consists of a small powered mixer, a pair of small or medium-size speaker cabinets that broadcast toward the stage, and a couple of microphones. There is generally no full-time operator for these systems.

Type II Monitor System. This is a typical small club monitor system, with good-size main PA cabinets and several small wedge-type floor monitors. A Type II PA will have microphones for every sound onstage rather than just a couple vocal mics, so everything will be available for assignment in the monitors. This system has only one medium-size mixing console for both FOH and FOB (monitors), and has one full-time operator.

Type III Monitor System. This type of system is what you will find in most arenas. It typically consists of multiple large main PA cabinets and more than four monitor mixes that use both floor wedges and sidefill monitors. This system has two large consoles, one for mixing FOH and another for mixing monitors. There are almost always two operators for these systems.

Type IV Monitor System. This type is identical to a Type III system with the addition of in-ear monitors onstage. It can be in-ear only, or any hybrid combination of both, but is primarily an in-ear system. If there are more conventional monitors than in-ear systems, it should be considered a Type III hybrid.

All of these systems are substantially different from each other, not just in size but also in capability. You will have options on some that won't be available on others, so you need to know the differences to make the best use of each system. In this chapter we'll take a good look at what these differences really mean to you. It's not necessary to be an engineer to get good monitors, but you will have to understand the range of abilities each system has. We'll spend some time with the system you will likely see the most in rehearsals and will probably purchase at some point. It will be the one that many of you actually operate.

TYPE I MONITOR SYSTEMS

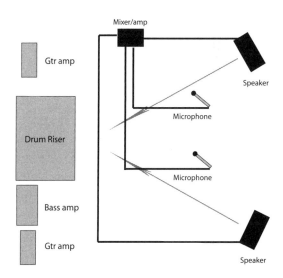

1. A TYPE I MONITOR SYSTEM IS REALLY A PA SYSTEM

Consisting of a small mixer and amp, microphones, stands and cables, and a couple of speakers, this is often confused with a "PA" system. Actually the only real difference between the two is in the way that they are used. If the speakers are pointed at the audience, it's a PA. If they are pointed at the performers, it's a monitor system. Since this chapter is on monitors, we'll examine this type of system in that role. It really doesn't matter if it's an "all in one" system or not; it will have these basic combinations: mics/stands/cables, mixer/EQ, and amp/speakers.

Fig. 3.1 provides an example. This type of system is usually run by the band, and the speaker cabinets will be pointed back at the band. This is generally a "vocal-only" monitor system. You will need to educate yourself on this type of system, as you will often be the operator. The more you know about working one of these, the better your rehearsals will be. And while this is only a single element in a larger monitor system, it is the building block that will help you understand the essentials of how to make the best use of any monitor system. We are going to take a very good look at this system and go through the things you should consider when working on it, and each system type will become progressively more complicated.

Just as Location, Focus, and Balance play a role in your stage zones, they will be equally important in coordinating your monitors in that zone.

Fig. 3.1. Type I monitor system

2. IDENTIFY THE ZONES OF THE SYSTEM

The biggest indicator of a Type I monitor system is that the "main" outputs of the mixer are used to feed the speakers that the band is hearing, and floor wedges are rarely used. Essentially, a Type I system will have two zones: left and right. However many mixes and output systems it has, that is how many zones it will have, regardless of the number of cabinets you put on each channel. You will need to identify the monitor zones when you are working with any system, and this type should be quite familiar to you.

Because the main outputs are being used to feed the monitors, all the features of the console are available for adjustment. The channel EQs work in the monitors, unlike a Type II system, where the monitors are being fed from pre-fade and pre-EQ auxiliaries. Most people take this convenience for granted, and when they work on a mid-size system, they wonder why it isn't there.

What does this mean to you? You have more control over EQ with a Type I system than you do with a Type II system. Adding effects is considerably easier on a Type I system as

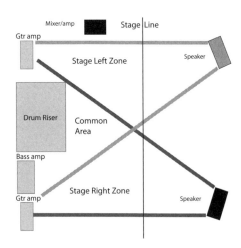

Fig. 3.2. Type I monitor zones

well. While I suggest you don't get too accustomed to having effects in your monitors, and there are some types of effects you don't want at all, it is much easier to add a little reverb.

So now, let's take a look at the *zones* in a Type I monitor system and see how they will work with the stage zones you created in chapter 2. It's really quite simple: you have a stage left, a stage right, and a common area zone. The center of the stage gets a bit of both sides, and toward the outside it becomes more individual. If you have four players on stage, the two outside players primarily get the left or right signals, and the two inside players get both. This helps overcome the fact that they are farther away from the cabinets; having some of both brings up their levels. While there's not much in the way of separate mixes because both speakers cover the entire stage, this works just fine for vocals and CDs. Besides, there's really not much to mix unless something is being miked or has a direct input to the console. For rehearsals, it's usually vocals and a couple of DI's.

Fig. 3.2 shows a simple diagram of a stage and a typical downstaged setup in gray. The monitor system is indicated in black and medium gray, and the left and right coverage patterns are in medium gray and dark gray. This shows a pair of speakers located in the ideal spot for this type of application. Toward center stage, you can see where the coverage from both speakers meet; this is referred to as the "common area." While the speakers could be located farther to the outside, this is generally the best layout.

3. USE LOCATION, FOCUS, AND BALANCE TO GET WHAT YOU NEED

It is not uncommon to see two speaker cabinets on each side. Not only does this give you more volume, but you can easily point a pair in the direction needed for additional coverage, or move them to a better location. Location, Focus, and Balance are always the keys to a successful stage sound. You can extend a zone simply by spreading out the coverage. This will not give you another zone, but it will expand the coverage of that zone, thus making it more effective.

If you own this type of system and would like to make it more powerful, the most cost-effective way to increase its potential is to add a pair of identical cabinets. There are very good reasons for adding identical cabinets. First, they will closely match in frequency response, which will make your EQ adjustments predictable and controllable. If they aren't matched, your graphic and channel EQs will not be able to remove troublesome frequencies properly because of the differences between the two. Second, being of similar impedance and wattage, they will almost double the potential of the output amp. This is true only when you are discussing passive output speakers, however.

Fig. 3.3A. Extending monitor zones A

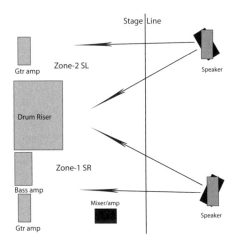

Powered speakers don't have shared output amps and are limited to the power that their internal amp produces. While they are simpler to set up and use, they don't offer the versatility of a component-type system. Being considerably more expensive to purchase and service, powered units offer only a marginal improvement when doubled. However for most people, these systems are quite convenient. (Note that convenience does have its price.)

Fig. 3.3A gives an example of adding another pair of speakers to a Type I monitor system. Notice that the added pair is *located* in close proximity (same place), but *focused* (directed) differently. They are also *balanced* (volume) identically. This is just one illustration of using Location,

Focus, and Balance. You use different techniques to set up monitors than to set up stage equipment.

With a small stereo PA system, you can use the pan control on your mixer to send more of a particular signal to the side that needs it most. In larger systems, this is done by simply increasing the level to the particular auxiliary feeding the signal to that zone. On a Type I system, the main outputs are feeding the monitor cabinets, so all the features of the mixer are available, including EQ.

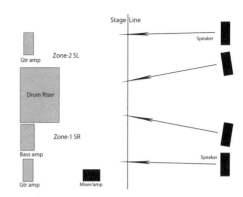

Fig. 3.3B shows another example of adding a pair of speakers to a Type I monitor system. Notice that the additional pair is *located* differently, but *focused* and *balanced* identically. This is another illustration of using Location, Focus, and Balance. Just as an example, if you were to "crossfire" a pair of your monitor speakers, then you would be changing both the location and the focus; therefore you would more than likely have to change their balance (volume levels) as well.

Fig. 3.3B. Extending monitor zones B

Adding a pair of speakers to your system will save you money as opposed to having to upgrade your whole system, or purchasing a very large and expensive single pair. You also don't have to commit financially to a large system initially. Should you need more capability than these speakers provide, I would suggest moving to a larger single pair, larger sets of pairs, or consider a set of floor monitors, which would give you more of what you will be getting onstage anyway. Regardless of what you use, note that monitors can only get so loud before they start to feed back.

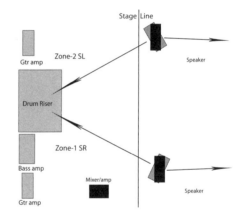

Another little known benefit of having two pairs of monitors is that one set can be turned around and directed toward the audience as a PA system. This can be quite handy for small parties where you just need some basic sound out front. Surprisingly, the same levels needed for your stage monitors are often the same ones needed for your outfront speakers (FOH). Fig. 3.3C shows an example of this.

While this isn't your ideal situation, this solution is certainly better than nothing at all. Having the extra speakers gives you this option. This is just another example of thinking outside the box!

Fig. 3.3C. Extending monitor zones C

We have looked at several different ways to adjust or improve the typical Type I monitor system, but since you will be using this system without the benefit of an engineer in most cases, it would be a good idea to go through some of the proper techniques for using it. While it is not really the intention of this book to teach you to be an audio engineer, you should be able to make the best use of rehearsal systems. By now, you should have a good idea of how to set up a Type I system, so we will start by going through some of the functions of a monitor system.

COURTESY OF BRUCE BOUILLET

Bruce Bouillet—Guitar
Racer X/The Scream/DC 10
Epidemic/Bottom Dwellerz
Grammy-Winning Producer/Engineer
www.myspace.com/brucebouillet

"From a guitar standpoint, you should be able to get your stage to sound just like at practice. Let your singer get most of the monitors, because he needs them more than anyone else. When I do get monitors, it's mainly kick, snare, hat, and bass; I get what I need from my amp. I like to be able to walk around and get more or less of me.

Unless you have your own sound guys, you're playing roulette, and the odds aren't in your favor. In one of my bands, we had loops running through the whole show, but wound up with a new guy on the monitor console one night—he couldn't find the loops and killed the show! After that we brought our own small PA and set [the speakers] up on each side of the drums so it sounded like two drummers. We do it in rehearsals; we do it onstage.

One of the things I like to do is cut a yellow earplug in half and put each half in; it doesn't kill all the sound, but enough to keep my ears from ringing at the end of the night. *If you've got bad monitors, turn them off, which goes back to balancing your stage first.* On bigger stages you need to have them, but if you're in a club setting and they're sounding really bad, just tell the house guy to shut them down. If you're a singer, you're in trouble!"

Fortunately, these systems are quite simple. Manufacturers have been incorporating more functions into a single unit and reducing the number of devices to get lost in. We are going to look at a flow chart for one of these combo units. Essentially, there are six elements to any monitor system, regardless of which type. If you are using in-ear monitors, this is where you will learn the basics of setting them up and dialing them in. Since singers will be getting the most benefit from these systems, it would be wise to step up to the plate and learn how to use your "stage amp."

> ►**Inputs/Microphones:** Direct boxes, CDs, samplers, keyboards, etc.
> ►**Mixers:** Multichannel mixers, line mixers, mic pre's
> ►**Graphic EQs:** 5-band, 10-band, 15-band, 31-band
> ►**Power amps:** Single-channel, stereo, multichannel
> ►**Speakers:** Passive, active, in-ear, floor wedges
> ►**Accessories:** Mic cables, line cables, speaker cables, mic stands

Fig. 3.4 shows an example of how the signal travels through the monitor system.

4. SET UP YOUR SYSTEM PROPERLY
Using the diagrams and suggestions in this chapter, decide on the best way to set up your monitors so they completely cover the stage area. Set up your mixer combo or system where the cables can reach the speakers and you can easily reach the controls from the stage. This is important, as uncontrolled feedback will destroy your monitors; you need to be able to rectify it quickly.

5. SET GAIN CONTROLS TO CENTER WITH THE MASTER DOWN
Before you turn your system on, you should check to see that nothing has been

Fig. 3.4.
Type I flow
chart

inadvertently turned to an absurd setting. Set all EQs to flat. With the master volume and all channel outputs down, plug a mic in, check the level with a normal singing volume and adjust the gain until it slightly peaks, then back it off just until it stops peaking. You won't hear anything while this is happening; you are simply visually checking to see where the proper input gain setting is. If the unit has a PFL (pre-fader level) switch, you could use this instead.

Then, turn the master output up to about 3/4 and *slowly* turn up the channel output to an appropriate level as you are "checking" it. Set it as loud as you can without feedback. If it's too loud, you can always back it off a bit. If the channel's output control is very low, reduce the master until you can get it to 2/3 of the way up: if you need more level later, you can always turn it up. This is the proper technique for setting gain structure on this type of system. You should completely dial in the lead vocalist's mic first before bringing up any other channels, so wait until you have gone through this entire procedure before opening up any other channels.

6. START WITH YOUR EQS SET TO FLAT

Type I monitor systems have channel EQ and sometimes a graphic EQ between the mixer and power amp stages. The difference between the two EQs is that the graphic EQ is used to balance the overall system, and the channel EQ is used to balance the individual channel. The graphic EQ is a precision EQ, and the channel EQ is a general EQ. It would be wrong in theory to use the channel EQ to eliminate feedback, but in reality that sometimes happens. If a particular mic was brighter than the others, you would need to trim some of the highs on that channel as long as the other channels were pretty close to flat. If it was dull sounding, then adding some highs would be appropriate for that channel. If you notice that all the channels are being cut or boosted at a particular frequency range, then you would reset them to flat and use the graphic EQ to make up the overall balance of the output system. You want your channels to be as close to flat as possible, but definitely no "extremes"! Any time you have to use *all* of the adjustment on an EQ, something is wrong! Try to use mics of the same make/model, rather than random choices.

7. ADJUST THE GRAPHIC EQ TO CONTROL THE OUTPUT FIRST

With only your lead vocalist's mic set up in its location, turn the PA up slowly until it starts to feed back and turn it down until it just stops. Go to the graphic EQ and test each band in the suspected frequency range until the offending feedback is found; *turn that frequency down 3 dB*. Repeat this procedure until you have enough PA volume without feedback. Pretty soon you will have a good idea of what frequency is feeding back. This is called "ringing out the system," and works for most monitors as a general rule. While this is more of an art than a science, avoid large cuts in multiple adjacent frequency bands if possible. Treat *feedback like a rat: If it squeaks, KILL IT!*

8. ADJUST THE CHANNEL EQ TO CONTROL THE INPUT

After you have set the lead vocalist's mic to its best sound and volume level, then duplicate the channel setting for the other mics as long as they are the same type of mic. If not, work the channel EQ to get them to sound right without adjusting the graphic EQ; otherwise you will have just undone your job! Keep in mind that the backing vocal mics should be a bit lower in volume to prevent them from becoming an interactive feedback problem. Keep in mind that if there is a Lo-cut/Rolloff filter, use it. There's nothing in the human voice that belongs in that range. Even 3–6 dB of low frequency cut on all vocal channels is appropriate; this keeps you from having to kill too much low end on the graphic EQ.

9. AVOID EQ CONTRADICTIONS

A principle you should also follow when dealing with EQ levels is eliminating "contradictions." An EQ contradiction is where you have boosted or cut a certain frequency range on the channel EQ only to have to do the opposite on the graphic EQ stage. Fig. 3.4A gives an example.

Notice that even the gain settings are contradictory on the incorrect example. This is something that commonly happens on PA and monitor systems. Once you turn something up on one stage, many people often compensate by turning the next stage down, instead of going back to the original source of the problem and reducing the level there. Try to avoid turning something both *above and below unity gain*. Unity gain is explained in chapter 8.

With a Type I system, you are "broadcasting," which is something that requires some expertise on a crowded stage with microphones. This is what you will be using for the majority of your rehearsals. The idea is to be able to hear some vocals, a CD, and maybe an effect.

Fig. 3.4A. Correct and incorrect EQ settings

CORRECT EXAMPLE

Normal gain settings.
Both EQs boosting highs.
Channel EQ used to cut lows.
This allows other sounds to work properly with minimal EQ.
Flat EQs show a balanced system.

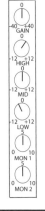

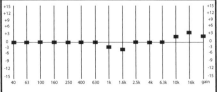

INCORRECT EXAMPLE

Contradictory gain settings.
Contradictory EQs settings.
Channel EQs have to be pushed to balance other sounds.
Peaked EQs show an unbalanced system.

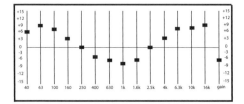

Trevor Thornton—Drums
Asia/Saxon/Nelson
Michael Lee Firkins
www.myspace.com/theseventhhourmusic

"The size of the venue determines the size of the monitors you will be using. A fairly small gig will just have a small wedge, and chances are you will only have your kick drum miked. I also like to have bass and vocals in the monitors. *Having monitors allows you to set up slightly behind the backline.* This way you don't have to put up with overpowering guitarists or bass players; you get what you want to hear. People sometimes ask if it hurts your ears to play with really loud bands, but if you set up behind the amps, it's not nearly as loud.

If it's a small wedge, I liked to raise it up a little to get it as close as I can, and I always put my monitor on my left side because there are no floor toms in the way. If I am using an earpiece for a click, I put it in my right ear. On smaller gigs I never have trouble hearing my snare or cymbals.

If you are able to do a soundcheck, try not to use it for rehearsal; make sure you can actually hear everyone you need to hear. If there are any parts of a song that you use for cues, then try those parts out and make sure you can hear them. If you are used to hearing certain things in a rehearsal room, they may sound very different on a stage and through a monitor."

10. AVOID GAIN CONTRADICTIONS

Just like when a guitar amp has its preamp turned up and its master volume turned down, gain contradictions create distortion. If your channels are all the way up and your master output is down, you will have noise and distortion, or a serious lack of headroom. If you have a modular system, this is important to check. Don't turn down the power amps or graphic EQ and then run the mixer wide open. For PA systems, it's better to do the opposite, but a balance is always best.

At this point, you should have a well-balanced system that has plenty of room for adjustment and a fair amount of headroom. Even a seemingly small system can perform surprisingly well when it's set up properly. Once everything is up and working well, take a quick look at the channel EQs: are all the channels cut/boosted similarly? If so, then you can rebalance them by cutting/boosting those frequencies on the graphic EQ and resetting the channel EQs to flat. As you can see by now, there are many different approaches. Some work better than others.

If for some reason you aren't getting a good sound, then you may need to go back and repeat the above steps until you are comfortable with "ringing out" your system. This is an important procedure to learn, since you will be doing it quite often.

11. USE THE SAME EQUIPMENT AT REHEARSAL
THAT YOU PLAN TO USE AT THE SHOW

While it's tempting to just plug into your rehearsal system, don't try to use it as an excuse for a lack of stage equipment. Your instruments should have personal monitors. We have already covered why it is important to have them. Don't try to cheat here at practice—you only cheat yourself. You should rehearse with what you plan to use at the show and the way you plan to use it at the show. This is the only way to develop consistency in your shows.

Not only should you rehearse with the correct equipment, but you should get used to bringing all you need, setting it up, moving it around, and testing it out. This is how you find shortcuts and gauge how long the setup process takes. If you're going to have a problem, then it's better to find this out at rehearsal. If you are going to find a solution, it's better to do this before the show. The only way to do that is to rehearse with the same gear you will be using at the show. Don't get accustomed to using something that isn't going to be there or will change every place you go—eliminate the variables as much as you can.

TYPE II MONITOR SYSTEMS

This type of system will generally be run by a single engineer. And while this seems to be a much better system than your rehearsal PA, it has some limitations you should be aware of. The indicator of a Type II system is that the monitors are being fed by auxiliary sends from a *single* console that runs both "mains" and "mons." The mixing console is usually located in a listening position offstage. Other characteristics often include the use of a "mic snake," wedge monitors, and multiple output speakers. A system of this magnitude is considerably more expensive than a Type I, but is a good compromise from the enormous cost of a Type III. While this type of system isn't a full-fledged PRO rig, it's a decent rig for the money. You will see this type of system in most small to medium-size clubs, but rarely in arenas or at the concert level.

Fig. 3.5 shows a Type II PA and monitor system. In this diagram, the monitors are in black, the PA system is in dark gray, and the stage setup is in light gray. While we are primarily concerned with the monitor aspects of this system, it illustrates the increasing complexity from a Type I to a Type II system.

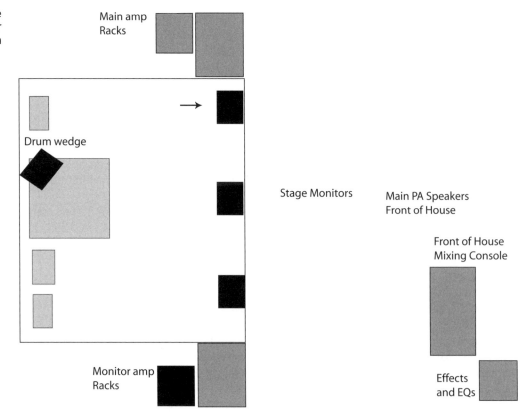

Fig. 3.5. Type II monitor system

Main amp Racks

Drum wedge

Stage Monitors

Main PA Speakers Front of House

Front of House Mixing Console

Monitor amp Racks

Effects and EQs

12. THERE IS NO CHANNEL EQ ON A TYPE II MONITOR SYSTEM

While this system is considerably more difficult to operate, it is lacking some of the features of other systems. The most important of these is the channel EQ for the monitor sends. They receive signal from the gain stage of the mic pre and before the EQ and the output fader adjustments. This will prevent changes made to the EQ or output level during the mix from affecting the monitor signal. Each monitor mix still has a graphic EQ, but the individual channels don't. So when you ask for some EQ on your voice in the monitors, chances are very good that you will only get a slight adjustment from the graphic EQ for that entire monitor send, which will affect the tone of everything else in the mix. If it's not feeding back, don't mess with it!

There is a notable exception to this rule when a dual-purpose console (i.e., live and studio) has a pair of post-EQ/prefade auxiliaries for two monitor sends. In this case, these sends share the channel EQ's adjustment before going to the monitor send ahead of the fader adjustments. Overzealous adjustments during the mix can cause the monitors to feed back, so often the tone of your FOH mix signal has to be compromised to keep this from happening. While it does give the engineer some control of your monitor tone, it does so at a price. Since there's only one console and it shares the gain stage with everything, a compression setting that works out front may cause some problems with the monitors. Once again, there's a compromise with a Type II monitor system, and you need to know this.

Burleigh Drummond—Drums
Ambrosia/Tin Drum
Mighty Mo Rodgers
www.ambrosiaweb.com

COURTESY OF TIN DRUM WEBSITE

"On smaller systems, you have to give up some of your low end; you're not gonna hear your kick drum the way you like it because small monitors can't handle the bottom end, so you have to rely on your natural sound. Other times, the monitor can be cockeyed in the way it sounds; let's say you've run out of time and maybe patience with the monitor guy trying to dial in the sound, so you go through the show and imagine the drums sound good as opposed to what you're actually hearing. You just have to suck it up, go for it, and play like it's all there! Especially when you're an opening act and you've got 15 minutes to get it all on stage. It's incredible what some of the monitor guys and sound guys can pull off, and the monitors can make or break your evening, but vocally it can kill you! It's amazing how a bad sound can just beat you up; it's just physically exhausting trying to battle with it. It's like you're in a wrestling match and you're losing!"

In most Type II systems, there are four physical *areas*: stage right, upstage, downstage, and stage left. Practically speaking, there should be a monitor zone for each. Fig. 3.5A shows the zones and a monitor for each area. It is here on a Type II system that zones become more important and useful. If you have used the setup suggestions properly, you should have a pretty good instrument balance and should mainly need vocals and instruments from the other side in the monitors. This type of system isn't going to give you a full "stage mix" like you would have at a big show, but it will get you to a point where you can hear everything reasonably well. The two outside zones, stage left and stage right, are somewhat larger and allow more setup options, but this system will sound totally different from the Type I system you may be used to in rehearsals.

Fig. 3.5A.
Controlling
monitor
zones

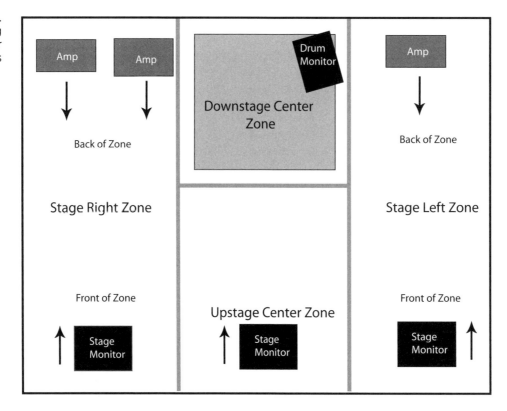

13. MONITOR LEVELS ARE CRITICAL IN FLOOR WEDGES

It is on this type of rig where you will begin to see floor wedges in the system. This is where the monitors start to behave differently, since you no longer have "channel EQ" and you are replacing elevated speaker cabinets with floor monitors that are close to the mics and stands. There can be no doubt that this type of system will not only sound different, but behave differently as well. Your monitor levels are a lot touchier when they are pointed directly at the mic from a close distance. The proximity of the monitor wedges to the microphone and the fact that the wedge is on the floor right next to the stand makes the interaction of the two much greater than elevated cabinets from a distance. Because a Type II system doesn't have the individual channel EQ to help detail the source, you will also find that EQing the wedge is much more critical. After all, it's your only EQ. Most clubs have graphic EQ on their wedges; it's an essential feedback tool.

You will not get as much side-to-side coverage as you do with elevated cabinets; however, a Type I monitor system shows up again in the form of sidefills in larger systems. It is an effective wide-range technique called "broadcasting." This technique is great for many different kinds of sounds in the monitors, but the real point here is that you won't have this option in most Type II systems. Just don't expect floor monitors to sound the same as the cabinets you use at rehearsals. Try to use wedges as much as possible or whenever you can in rehearsals, as this will be what you see most of the time onstage. By using them, you may be able to find and solve a stage level problem before it becomes an issue where it matters most: onstage! It really doesn't matter how good it sounds at rehearsal if you can't do it at a show.

14. EACH ZONE REQUIRES A SEPARATE MIX

Regardless of how many mixes are being sent back to the stage; that is how many monitor zones you will have. Each zone requires a separate aux send, EQ, amp, and monitor cabinet, so you can see why most small clubs cut their monitors to the bone. In a Type II system, the typical number of separate stage mixes is two to four. In the following examples, you will see a typical four- or five-wedge monitor system, with the zones in different shades for all three configurations.

If your system has two mixes, then expect a frontline mix and a drum mix. Fig. 3.5B shows an example of this. Everybody will get everything in the front mix, so make sure it's essential. Only the drummer will have his own mix. In some cases, the second mix is brought out front and the drummer gets nothing at all.

If the system has three mixes, you will get "left and right" or "middle and sides" and a drum mix. Fig. 3.5C shows an example of this. There is less of a compromise with this configuration than the previous one, but it is still not completely independent.

If the system has four mixes, you will get left, right, middle, and a drum mix. Fig. 3.5D shows an example of this. This is where all four performers can get their own mix. If your band needs more, you'll have to group players with similar needs in their monitors.

You need the ability to control each performer's needs individually, and a lead vocalist will need more vocals than a drummer will; a guitarist will need more instruments than a vocalist will. Having separate mixes allows players to have what they need in their wedges. Since these are the only monitors on the stage, you have to make them work for you regardless of how they sound. A Type II system will allow you to get most of what you need, just don't ask for EQ: it isn't available. In the rare instances when it is, it is being shared with the FOH mix, and there has to be a balance between eliminating feedback in the monitors and sounding good out front. You'll probably wind up settling for whatever comes up on the wedges. It's important that you have good sounds going to the PA, because there isn't much control over the tones once they're in the system. Personal stage amps with graphic EQs can really be effective for getting good tones where you need them.

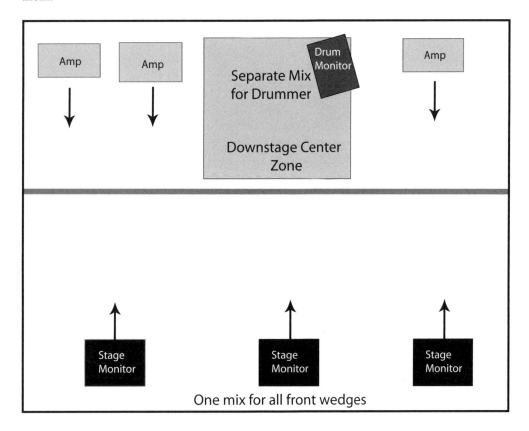

Fig. 3.5B. Two monitor zones

Amp

Amp

Drum Monitor

Separate Mix for Drummer

Downstage Center Zone

Amp

Stage Monitor

Stage Monitor

Stage Monitor

One mix for all front wedges

Fig. 3.5C.
Three
monitor
zones

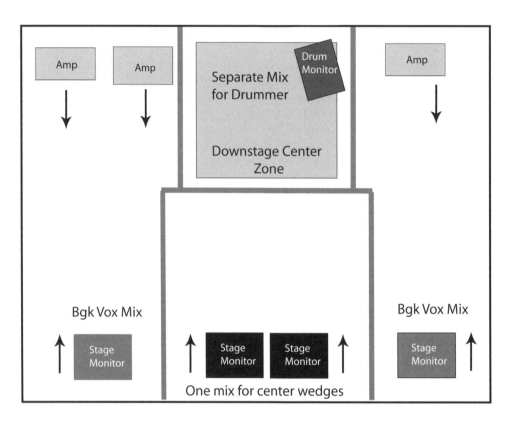

Fig. 3.5D.
Four monitor
zones

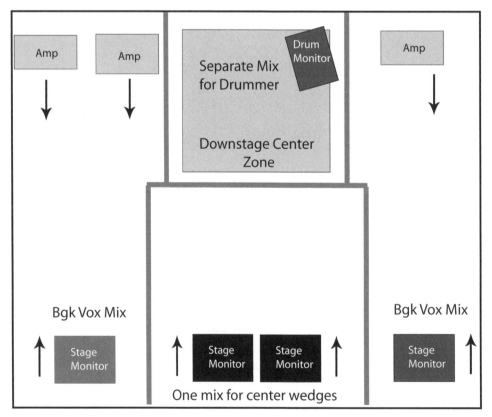

Atma Anur—Drums
Richie Kotzen/Tony MacAlpine
Jarek Smietana/Cacophony
www.myspace.com/atmaanur

"Honestly, I hate monitors, but in large venues you have no choice but to use them. First rule is, Get to be the monitor guy's friend! If you're lucky, the band's stage volume will make sense so that the monitor mix can have everything to make it seem like you are playing in the rehearsal room. If not, good luck!

You should rely on monitors as little as possible. This means setting up so that each band member can hear everybody else and use the monitors for the vocals and maybe kick drum. Also, if you don't play too loudly, everyone can pretty much hear each other acoustically on stage. High volume is a sad illusion.

I don't like in-ear monitors; for me the natural ambience is important to my basic feel. I prefer an actual monitor speaker, but when there is a click involved, I use open-back headphones. For drummers, the monitor should be next to the hi-hat and slightly angled to the back to stop the snare and hi-hat mic from feeding back."

15. REPOSITION UNUSED MONITORS

For a vocalist who also plays an instrument, it is important to set up a single small area that is effectively balanced. The monitors should be focused on where the singer's mic is. For a guitarist who moves around and doesn't sing, the monitor can be moved around to where it is most effective onstage for her needs. If a musician doesn't need a monitor at all and the frontperson needs *more,* then you could move the unused monitor toward the frontperson. Use one monitor for the frontperson's vocals and the other for his or her instrument; don't try to load both monitors with the same sounds.

Bjorn Englen—Bass
Soul Sign/Yngwie Malmsteen
Robin McAuley/Quiet Riot
http://bjornenglen.com

"I'm one of the few people who can play without almost any monitors at all. I'm pretty immune to bad circumstances, and sometimes I don't even realize that I didn't hear something until I speak with the rest of the band after the show. Part of this is wearing earplugs that block out most of the overtones and noise so I can focus on the pitches that I need to hear, especially for my vocals. But it really comes down to knowing the songs: even if you can't hear anything at a particular time, you still know the songs. You still know the melody and you still know the arrangements. *You can never overpractice.* This is how you can do a good job under any circumstances, and that will most likely keep you working for as long as you want!

I don't really care for in-ear monitors; it's hard for me to find a set that's comfortable, and even when I do, the mix often seems to change from show to show. *I prefer to hear the blend from the stage.* I try not to go too heavy on the low end; I like to stay in the middle of the range, especially live. My tone is going to the console post-EQ, and that makes a lot of engineers nervous, but I try to keep my EQ as flat as possible—I like a natural tone."

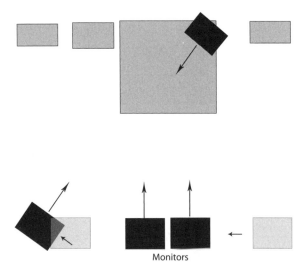

Fig. 3.6A.
Monitor
placement
option #1:
vocals/
instrument

Monitors

Fig. 3.6B.
Monitor
placement
option #2:
shotgun
setup

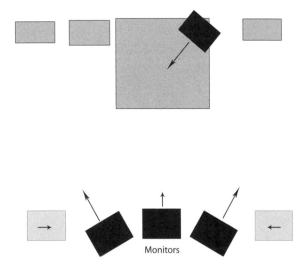

Monitors

Fig. 3.6A shows an example of this. The stage left monitor has been moved over to the lead vocalist's area, and the stage right monitor has been repositioned. The point here is to think outside the box at every step. The wedges should become part of your setup, not the other way around. There is no law that says you can't move it or point it in the direction it is needed. Your only limitation will be the length of cable that is powering the monitor cabinet.

The previous example is a good option for situations where the lead singer needs more from her wedges than some smaller systems can manage, but it also requires that the member on a side by himself doesn't need a wedge. Since this isn't always the case, a conventional monitor setup works well when one player from each side needs a wedge; however, there are other methods to consider. When stages are small, the monitor line can take up a lot of room up front. Setting up the monitors in a "shotgun" layout can open up some stage space. (See Fig. 3.6B.)

The shotgun setup is an alternative for highly animated performers who need a little more room on a small stage. It does have the potential for feedback, especially at higher levels, because the monitor is closer to the coverage pattern of the mic, so be cautious with your levels. Some guitarists need their pedalboard out front, or keyboardists could get their key rigs farther up front; this method opens up room for that. This is also an interesting setup for a solo vocalist who likes to move around a lot during his performances. The outside monitors still get some level to the outside performers on the stage without taking up that space. This may come in real handy if you have chosen an unusual setup from chapter 2. It's just another tool at your disposal. Remember to use L-F-B (Location, Focus, and Balance) to make any adjustments you need to get the monitor and stage equipment in their most useful positions.

Fig. 3.6C shows the monitors in an "M" configuration, which is really a variation on a conventional setup. Certain stages have their own characteristics, and occasionally a conventional setup just doesn't sound right. The "M" has its own personality, which may or may not suit your needs. This type of setup requires some detailing in regard to correctly focusing it, but can be an alternative when stage conditions aren't right for other setups. Reflective walls, low ceilings, or pockets around small stages can dramatically affect the acoustics onstage. This configuration can sometimes open up a dead area, or one that is particularly washed out with ambience, and bring back definition simply by changing the projection point of the acoustics. From a technical standpoint, this setup could leak monitor level into the mics due to its angular focus, but if it happens to be pointed toward the ear that hears best, then it's a fair trade. This problem can be reduced by slightly focusing the mic away from the monitor; this makes the best use of the rejection range of the mic, which will be discussed in Chapter 4: Input Sources.

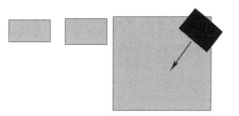

Fig. 3.6C.
Monitor
placement
option
#3: "M"
configuration

Monitors

Wyzard—Bass/Vocals
Mother's Finest
Stevie Nicks
www.myspace.comwyzard1

"When you are the headliner, more things are at your disposal—you can add more to your personal mix. When I was on tour with Stevie Nicks, the stages were so big that I needed players in my monitor who were like a mile away from me! I almost never have my bass in the monitors; I like the sound coming from my stack behind me—it always sounds more animal-like!

When Mother's Finest was headlining, we would run any loops through sidefills, although I still kept things as simple as possible: the magic always came from the sounds blending together. Playing together is always the key—listening to one another. [Vocalist] Glenn will always tweak the hell out of the monitors—rearranging monitor positions, but it seems to pay off at showtime!

In today's technology, in-ear monitoring is very popular, but I find it sterile for heavy music; a little too clean and disconnected from the source. But some players live by it. I like to have one old-school yellow foam earplug in my ear; it helps me hear my pitch from inside my head so I can sing better."

COURTESY OF ARTHUR USHERSON

TYPE III MONITOR SYSTEMS

This type of system is what you will find at large clubs and arenas. It is distinguished by the fact that there are *two* engineers, *two* mixing consoles, and usually more than four onstage mixes. You should also see sidefills onstage that resemble the rehearsal systems you have worked with before, but are sometimes much larger.

16. A TYPE III SYSTEM HAS A SEPARATE MONITOR CONSOLE

This is the "big time," and you will be able to get almost everything you need in your monitors at this point. Fig. 3.7 shows an example. You will have an engineer onstage who should be watching the stage for monitor cues and react quickly (most of the time!) to them. You will get "channel EQ" on every mic that only affects the monitors, and usually the quality of the equipment is much better than on smaller systems. Having EQ on the channels doesn't mean that you can EQ each channel differently in each monitor; it means that each channel has an EQ for *all* sends simultaneously. This can really help a signal when it is touchy in the monitors. Some signals, like acoustic guitar pickups, bass DIs, and line inputs, don't always sound that great flat, so adding some EQ to sweeten them up and remove troublesome frequencies is a good thing. While removing feedback is more often the purpose of EQ in monitors, emphasizing certain frequencies can allow you to bring the level down and still hear the signal, as each instrument has a prominent group of frequencies. Emphasizing frequencies that aren't there is often a waste and can induce feedback. Overboosting frequencies will also bring up background noise.

Fig. 3.7. Type III PA system

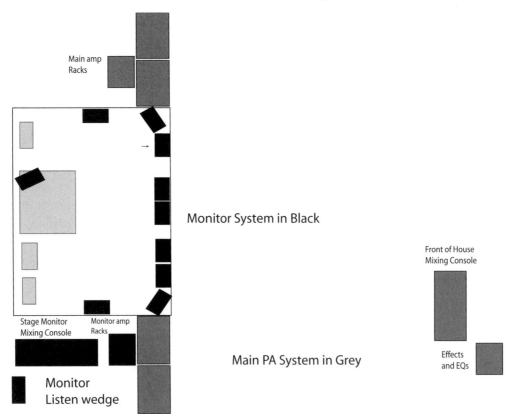

Main amp Racks

Monitor System in Black

Front of House Mixing Console

Stage Monitor Mixing Console

Monitor amp Racks

Main PA System in Grey

Effects and EQs

Monitor Listen wedge

Frankie Banali—Drums
Quiet Riot/Wasp
Billy Idol/Hughes-Thrall
www.myspace.com/frankiebanali

COURTESY OF FRANKIE BANALI

"Generally, I like to have only my drums and a little of the lead vocal in my monitors, but this is based on a perfect world where I can hear the balance of the instruments acoustically. *The more instruments you add into your monitor mix, the less control you have over hearing your drums.* And whatever level the guitar and bass might be at, this will change as the set progresses and they decide that they are not loud enough and start turning up. Let's get ready to sound-level rumble! Hey, it's true; you know it and I know it.

There are times when no monitor is better than a bad monitor. Case in point: about five songs into a Quiet Riot date, my monitor kept feeding back. No matter how nicely I had my tech ask the monitor engineer to change the EQ to stop all the feedback, it was to no avail. I finally asked to have it removed, and found the experience of playing without feedback very liberating!

One note that I feel should be mentioned: *the positioning of the monitor is critical*. I really prefer to have my monitor at ear level and directly behind me. This will make your lead singer hate you, but he's mobile; the drummer is not. If you prefer your monitor either stage left, stage right, or both, the closer it is, the more you will hear it. A distant monitor will have to be driven harder for you to be able to hear it as well; easy physics when playing loud music. The hidden danger here is that if your drums are not tuned properly and/or if the mic positioning is not favorable, it will add to the creation of feedback. Oh, in-ear monitors? I never use them; they promote hearing loss if you are in a loud band. But hey, that's only my opinion, and I've yet to get a call back from the surgeon general on the subject!"

17. TYPE III SYSTEMS ARE MORE VERSATILE

In systems of this nature, all of the wedges and monitor cabinets are EQ'd to sound similar, including the "listen wedge" at the monitor console. Engineers use this to get an accurate idea of what they are sending so they can make adjustments to levels and EQs by using the very same thing you're listening to. This listen wedge also serves as a backup for any other wedge that develops a problem during the show. It is here that you will need a monitor cue sheet, and this will be discussed in Chapter 5: Getting Organized.

All of the previous aspects of setting up your gear, setting up your monitors, adjusting your stage levels, and being in the right spot onstage will become slightly less critical. You will not be able to ignore the principles of Location, Focus, and Balance, but you have much more to compensate with. In most cases, you will get a soundcheck at these shows. Nobody likes surprises, and the PA is just too expensive to take chances with. Besides you've got two consoles to dial in. Even if all you get is a line check, it will be a much more thorough one. While this may appear to be the best of both Type I and Type II systems, it is a whole different level than the previous systems and has more personnel to operate it. A Type III system is much more versatile and the engineers at this level are often very proficient.

By now, it should be quite apparent that each level of monitor system is exponentially more expensive and complicated than the previous one, so it's easy to understand why most small clubs opt for a Type II system rather than a Type III or IV. It's also understandable why most professional venues insist on a Type III or IV system. When dealing with national acts who demand more from a monitor system, these offer full control over almost every parameter a band could ask for.

18. A TYPE III SYSTEM HAS COMPLETELY INDEPENDENT SIGNAL PATHS

Fig. 3.7A shows a flow chart for a single microphone, although a very simple one. Often there will be two or three times as many output routings for both monitors and mains. Every channel that hits the mic snake is split into two signals: one for the monitor console and another for the main console. This takes place before any gain, EQ, compression, or effects, so both consoles have completely independent signal paths. Adjustments to the FOH will not affect the monitors.

Fig. 3.7A. Type III flow chart

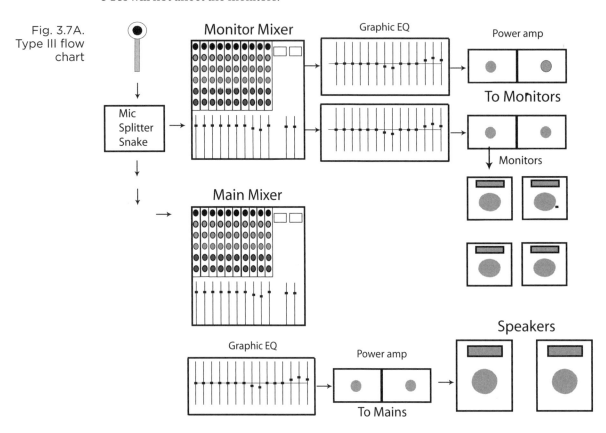

You can EQ the monitors without affecting the mains, you can compress the main signal without affecting the monitors, and you can gate the monitors without chopping off the signal in the mains. This illustrates the importance of signal flow and gain structure. If either console affected the signal in the other console, you would wind up with both engineers working against each other. Even though this still happens to a certain degree when the monitors are so hot that they affect the FOH signal, each console still receives its own unprocessed signal to work with.

One unavoidable interaction between the mains (FOH) and the monitors concerns feedback; any feedback on either system will show up on *both* systems. The reason for this is simple: feedback is a result of a microphone hearing too much of its own signal. *Because it happens at the source* and before the split, the result will be distributed to both consoles simultaneously. This can often make it very difficult to determine who is too loud or too generous with an EQ setting; however, in many cases it is monitors that cause the majority of feedback since they are directed back at the performers.

19. A TYPE III SYSTEM OFTEN HAS SIDEFILLS

Generally speaking, most Type III systems have sidefills, which, as their name would suggest, project from the side. Unlike most wedge-type monitors, sidefills resemble the Type I systems you work with in rehearsals, but are a bit larger and have full mix capability because all signals are present at the consoles. Being further to the sides gives them a different perspective than rehearsal systems. These are versatile monitors to have onstage; they have a completely different broadcast perspective and are often far enough away from mic sources to be run fairly hot. While you may not notice them as much from center stage, they really make a difference when you start moving around toward the sides. They can also be used as a zone mix when additional players are located near them.

20. SIDEFILLS ARE GREAT TO SEPARATE MIXES

Sidefills really excel at broadcasting instrument mixes across a wide stage area, and allow the floor wedges to be used primarily for vocals. Since most instrument mics are further back, there is less chance of feedback at higher levels.

Rob Marcello—Guitar
Danger Danger
Marcello/Vestry
Twenty-4 Seven
www.myspace.com/dangerdangerrob

"I point my monitors slightly away from my face. I want to hear my vocals mostly. I don't like having the cone right in my ear, and I hate guitar in the monitor; it just doesn't sound like my amp—it's all tinny and trebly. All I need is a blend of vocals in the wedges and a little drums and bass in my sidefills. I want it to sound like it does at rehearsal, that sweet spot. I'll move around onstage at soundcheck looking for that spot where my solos sound comfortable.

On the outdoor stages, I don't mind having some guitar in the sidefills. The sound moves around so much outdoors, and sometimes it's hard to hear yourself. When I'm at rehearsal, I don't have a big monitor blasting my face off, so it's not something I can ever get used to. I know what my amp sounds like, and that's what I want to hear onstage."

Trying to squeeze everything in a single floor-wedge mix is akin to listening to a stereo mix with one ear. By separating the locations of groups of sounds, distinctions can be heard much better and less actual levels are required ("It's so loud I can't hear anything!").

Fig. 3.7B shows an example of the zones in a Type III system with sidefills. While this may resemble a Type II system, the sidefills make it far more versatile and effective. In the example you can see that each side of the stage contains all three instruments in different shades: bass (dark gray), stage right guitar (medium gray), and stage left guitar (light gray). These are balanced by using stage amps and sidefills. The sidefills should contain the instruments that are *not* on that side of the stage. This works for both sides. The floor wedges are primarily used for vocals (black). Notice how these zones overlap near the vocal line. There is interaction between the stage amps, sidefills, and floor wedges, but the vocals are primarily center stage. Having multiple projection points makes everything on stage easier to distinguish and control. By not loading down any particular projection point with everything, each sound source becomes more effective and controllable. For smaller stages, having drums in the monitors isn't always necessary, but for larger stages it may very well be. Drums would also be placed in the sidefill monitors to create distinction and to keep them as far away as possible from the drum mics.

This example of zone management makes dialing in your monitors much easier. In chapter 5, we will be looking at organizing show data like this to speed things up and make it more accurate. This is a prime example of using Location, Focus, and Balance to your benefit!

Fig. 3.7B.
Type III
monitor
zones

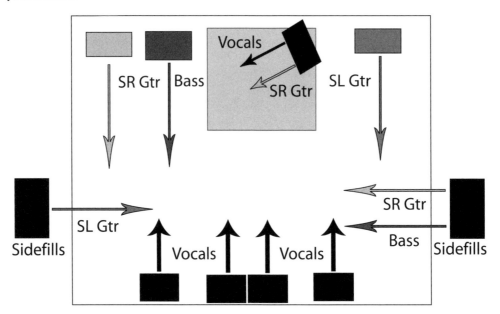

The previous example of zone management on a Type III system works well for bands that require six or fewer zones, but some of you are in bands that can have as many as eight members or more onstage. It is at this point that zone management becomes extremely important, and the correct approach is more philosophical than demonstrable. Obviously, your band would need a stage large enough to be able to create these zones and enough monitor mixes and wedges to supply them with signal, but the real trick is in properly locating the elements to cut down on zone violations. Let's have a look at a large-format band on a Type III system.

Fig. 3.7C shows an example of the zones in a large-format band; in this case, eight separate zones with a real possibility of an additional zone directly in the middle. The instrument and vocal zones are in different shades and include a floor wedge for each area. It is here where Location, Focus, and Balance become very specific to a small area and avoiding competition with other zones. The musicians will be highly dependent on a comprehensive monitor mix.

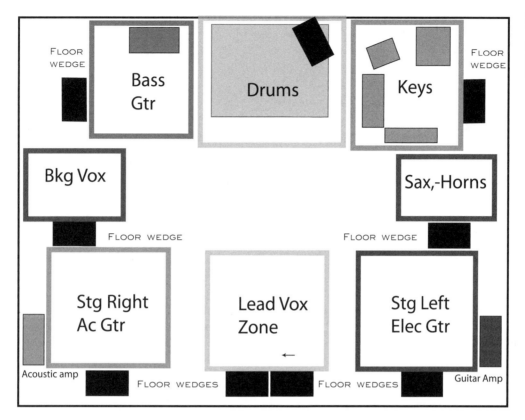

Fig. 3.7C. Type III monitor zones large format #1

Bass Gtr

FLOOR WEDGE

Drums

Keys

FLOOR WEDGE

Bkg Vox

Sax,-Horns

FLOOR wedge

FLOOR wedge

Stg Right Ac Gtr

Lead Vox Zone

Stg Left Elec Gtr

Acoustic amp

FLOOR WEDGES

FLOOR WEDGES

Guitar Amp

Alex DePue—Violin
Steve Vai/Chris Cagle
DePue de Hoyos
www.myspace.com/alexdepue

COURTESY OF MICHAEL MESKER

"I prefer to play from the left side of the stage due to the natural projection of the violin itself; however, I can play from both sides without a problem. I don't have many problems with conventional monitors, but it requires a good monitor engineer to EQ the right frequencies of the violin to keep it from being annoying. My spot for conventional monitors is right in front of the wedge, but I haven't used them for years. We use in-ear monitors, which eliminates a lot of problems right out of the gate, including some rather loud stage volumes.

I'll take one of my in-ear monitors out so that I can hear the live drums behind me. I find that it helps the energy onstage for me. One of the bass players I worked with had a platform that vibrated to the frequencies of his bass without [him] having to be loud onstage. It was an incredible experience to stand in his spot and hear the difference!"

COURTESY OF REISEG & TAYLOR PHOTOGRAPHY

Mindi Abair—Sax
Backstreet Boys/Duran Duran
Mandy Moore/Lee Ritenour
Josh Groban
www.mindiabair.com

"As a saxophonist, I try to get it as real as I can in the monitors. I test the system over and above what I use. As I play, I'll play right into the monitors onstage . . . try to get them to feed back. I'll also walk around to the other guys in the band who have monitors I can hear and adjust my volume level in their wedges. I want to make sure they can hear me as I walk around onstage during the show. It allows me freedom on stage instead of being chained to a monitor. I also test my vocal mic with my saxophone mic on. This usually creates some feedback, and once we can get that under control, I know we're in for a pretty solid performance. Feedback between the saxophone and vocal mics can wreak havoc on a show. I don't want a lot of reverb or delay, because 1) it causes feedback problems, and 2) it can cover up the reality of what you're playing. For me, *I want my monitors fairly dry to show me exactly what I'm putting out of the horn. The effects can be added by the house engineer.*

I always ask for my vocal sound to be thinned out in the monitor. I have a loud backing band, and so my vocals need to cut through that. A full sound is great and real, but doesn't cut through onstage. I usually ask to lose many of the lower mids of EQ, and if I'm still having problems hearing and we've got the volume cranked, I'll ask to have 1–2K boosted just a bit to give it an edge. Too much and it will be just that . . . too much. This is something I've learned over the years: *Put your vocal sound in a different place with EQ so you can hear yourself apart from the band.* Make sure they both have their place in your monitor mix so you can hear them and know what you're doing tonally."

The illustration's shaded layout helps keep the zones in perspective. While this example may seem to be quite simple and logical, we should take a look at how this would actually work onstage by examining the elements of the layout. These principles turn up in every aspect of stage sound I've worked with. Always keep the 5.1 Surround Sound Theory in mind!

▶**Zones.** A proper zone has been created for each instrument and vocalist and includes a monitor. This is the primary objective when designing a stage setup. You have to be able to coordinate a stage zone with your monitor zone to be as effective as possible. The more instruments onstage, the smaller the zones have to be, which means keeping the volume down. This is very important, because there are even more microphones onstage now! If everyone is balanced evenly, things will blend nicely onstage and the monitor mixes become simpler for those who actually have a monitor. For all intents and purposes, they are shown here, but many smaller stages won't have this many mixes onstage.

▶**Location.** The players at the front of the stage have their amps crossfired nearby to not only reduce the level they need for them, but to prevent them from encroaching on other zones. The bass guitar and keys are located on each side of the drums, allowing them to hear each other with some reasonable monitor levels. This also places instruments of equal dynamics close to each other and creates room for the instruments with less actual volume. The Sax/Horns and Bkg Vox are placed toward the outside of the stage and directly in the center of the other zones. Not only is the stage balanced from an audio perspective, but also from a visual perspective. There can be no doubt that the visual is an important consideration, but balancing the stage visually at the expense of the audio is highly counterproductive.

▶**Focus.** Each instrument, amp, and monitor is focused to not interfere with other zones, yet still be as effective as possible for the intended performer. This allows each player to get a comfortable level onstage. There are many ways to set up incorrectly, so be careful when locating and focusing monitors and amps onstage.

▶**Balance.** In most cases, we have used the term "balance" in reference to individual volume levels, but in this example the term "balance" is being applied to the whole stage setup in general. In almost every stage area, there is a dominant source, an intermediate source, and a passive source. If you look at stage right, you will see a dominant source (electric guitar), an intermediate source (bass guitar), and a passive source (background vocals). Looking at stage left, you will see a dominant source (keys), an intermediate source (sax and horns), and a passive source (acoustic guitar). While the center stage has only dominant (drums) and passive (lead vocals) sources, were you to add another zone in the center, it should be an intermediate-level instrument rather than a dominant or passive one. When the instrument is being amplified, it can be adjusted to be either a dominant or intermediate stage source; however, voices and natural instruments will often be passive because they require more microphone level to be heard properly. This is the litmus test in determining whether a source is dominant or passive; how much PA system mic level is required to produce a good stage volume? If it is a naturally loud instrument, it will be dominant. If it is adjustable, it can be either dominant or intermediate, but rarely passive. If it is a softer sound like vocals, bells, and chimes or low-level percussion, it will almost surely be passive, because those instruments require a microphone and their levels to be pushed up in the mixes. The more PA system level that is required to make an instrument work onstage, the more critical its location is; it needs to have a monitor as well!

Georg Voros—Drums
eVoid/Black Star Liner
Jimmy James and the Vagabonds
The Stu Page Band
www.georgvoros.com

"I never asked for reverb in my monitors to 'fatten' my immediate sound perspective. I found that I preferred to have an untreated drum (and music) mix in my onstage monitors, as this made me play tighter, especially in halls or theaters, which had a lot of natural reverb. The last thing I wanted was my immediate processed reverb competing with the natural acoustics of the venue. Those of you who have played venues with a high roof, or where you get a vicious slapback off the back wall, will know exactly what I'm talking about. Incidentally, I have the same approach when recording in that I don't want any effects (especially delay) in my cans, as this often makes the mix muddy and harder to find the pocket and lock in. But saying that, do bear in mind that what might be a nightmare for one person may be a dream for another. However, achieving an inspiring and balanced onstage mix I believe is one of the most challenging areas in sound reinforcement, as there are usually so many variables involved—unlike the studio environment, which is much easier to control!"

Another look at the zones of a large-format band could include a slightly different setup if it was more important to have background vocals and horns/sax out front. Keeping the visual perspective in mind, it's still imperative to any stage setup to make sure that the audio issues are considered. In Fig. 3.7D , when these two instruments swap locations with the guitars, the zones remain relatively intact, and in some instances this may work better. Now, all of the front line is either passive or intermediate stage sources. This type of dynamic grouping can make the frontline floor wedges more effective by isolating these zones from the dominant stage sources. Notice that the monitor wedges have been moved to the outsides of the stage for the guitars and the wedges are used for the vocalists and horn/sax players. This opens up more stage room for your show, and if there weren't enough stage monitor mixes to do all this, the sidefills could easily serve as monitors for both guitar zones. Without actually relocating the sidefills, they could simply be refocused toward these zones to achieve the same effect. Put the right sounds in the right place!

While correct examples are very helpful in laying out your stage setup, sometimes an incorrect example can be equally as effective in getting the point across. By looking at what you shouldn't do and why you shouldn't do it, the contrast of principles becomes crystal clear. Let's have a look at one of these no-no's. Fig. 3.7E shows a prime example of this.

At first glance, this appears to be similar to the previous examples, but you can see

Fig. 3.7D. Type III monitor zones large format #2

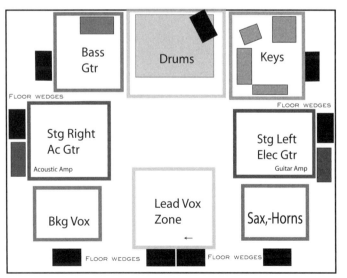

that the shaded zones are now overlapping. There is a passive background vocals zone right in the middle of both the bass and electric guitar zones! The primary reason why these two zones are so much larger is that the amps have been placed at the back of the stage while the players are at the front of the stage. And a vocal zone is haphazardly placed directly in the middle! On the stage-left side, a percussion kit that often requires three to four mics is placed directly in front of another guitar amp. You'd be surprised how often I have seen this kind of setup. Essentially, it is a large rock band setup, with the addition of background vocals and percussion, with little regard to where they have been placed onstage. This is a very common mistake.

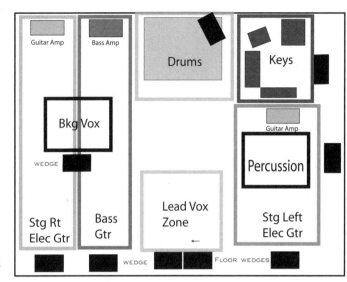

Fig. 3.7E. Type III monitor incorrect zones

Monitor zones are extremely important to manage, and a common misconception is that the stage monitors can overcome such a disparity.

Couldn't you just turn the stage amps down and put them in the monitors up front? The answer is both yes and no.

Yes: You could turn the stage amps down and jack up the monitors, but the proximity to the vocal and percussion zones would require you to render them practically useless onstage. What would be the point of having them there? Crossfiring the guitar amp would solve its *location* problem, but wouldn't work for the bass; you'd want the bass player near his amp. This would bring you back to the prior examples that do work.

No: The *focus* of the amps is still directed in the path of another zone. Now, not only are the amps too far away from their players and violating other players' zones, but they are also being blocked by the intermediate zone itself. This kind of setup is a train wreck no matter how you try to compensate for it. Why create problems for yourself? Put the right sounds in the right places!

Having the extra capabilities of a Type III system will not overcome the principles of Location, Focus, and Balance. You're not just mixing levels, you're also mixing *locations*—5.1 Surround Sound Theory. These principles will only work within a properly designed zone. Trying to ask monitors to solve a problem your setup has created is exactly why this book has been written: *to prevent you from placing obstacles in front of yourself.* In some cases, literally!

The differences between the zone layouts just shown are small, yet tremendous. Simply adding another zone to a setup may cause you to completely change the entire stage layout to make it work. If you can get it to work with minimal zone interference, even a slightly compromised setup can work; however, if it's a direct zone violation, it probably won't. Always consider the locations for anything that is going on stage: Will it block any other sounds? Will it pick up nearby sounds? Usually anything that blocks a sound will pick up that sound. Sometimes it's really difficult to envision everything in your head, so drafting stage plots will allow you to look at things objectively, rather than just moving stuff around to see if it will work. In Chapter 5: Getting Organized, we will be looking at organizing the stage data that can make your live show a consistent success. A stage plot is just one of the many aspects you will want to keep track of. Things like this will become very important when working with Type III systems and pro stage personnel; any head start you can give them will be appreciated. They can only be as organized as you are.

COURTESY OF BRYAN BASSETT

Bryan Bassett—Guitar
Foghat/Wild Cherry
Molly Hatchet
www.myspace.com/bryanpbassett

"I don't play too loud (heh heh), but I do play loud enough to get a 50- to 100-watt amp into its operating range so I can open it up and get some sustain, but still be able to turn the guitar down and get a nice, clean rhythm sound. *If there's an issue with the stage volume, I'll use some guitar in the monitors, but I try to avoid this as much as I can.* If I have to use a monitor feed, I'll have the monitor engineer roll off the frequencies above 3–4K so I don't get all the top-end string and slide noise.

So far, I'm not a fan of in-ear monitors; I like to hear the response between the cabinets and my guitar at about the 10-foot range. With in-ears, you're hearing the sound of a mic two inches from a speaker, and it's kind of harsh sounding to me. When we travel with our own monitor rig and monitor engineer, that may become an option at some point, but for most fly dates we have to keep it simple and basic. I know some guys are using ambient mics onstage and mics for crowd noise to embellish the sound of their in-ears, but this takes a talented monitor mixer and a consistent monitor system to work properly gig to gig. From my limited experience with in-ears, I feel disconnected from the stage and audience, but frankly I haven't worked on a state-of-the-art in-ear system enough to form a permanent opinion.

I like a minimal stage monitor mix. I try to get a natural balance of the band onstage and maybe add some kick and snare in the sidefills for tempo reference. On a big stage I need some guitar monitor send, because if you take two steps in front of the drum riser, you basically lose your amp sound; Marshalls and most amps in general are very directional. I don't like depending on monitors for my main stage sound, but I use them for some onstage presence for when I'm out of position, like hanging off the front of the stage for show fun. I may run some guitar in the sidefills on a bigger stage, but my sweet spot is about five feet in front of the drum riser and 10 feet in front of my amp. I also sing background; all I need for that is my own voice in the wedges. Our lead singer is powerful and very much on key. I can hear him in the house and pitch off that. Kick and snare in the sidefills, maybe a little bass, and that gives me enough band playback to find my spot for a good stage balance. Even on big stages, I prefer it to be an expanded bar band sound; I don't need a full-on house mix in my wedges or have it sound like a stereo up there on stage. I just want the sound of the band in a good small environment translated to a bigger stage."

TYPE IV MONITOR SYSTEMS

Advancements in radio technology have made in-ear monitors a practical solution to a lot of monitor problems. They are mobile and can follow a performer all over the stage without any loss of level or quality of mix. They don't have the feedback problems that conventional wedges do, and they don't take up space onstage. Another benefit of in-ear monitors is that they often sound relatively identical from unit to unit, or at least more so than conventional wedges do. As the market for them has increased, the price has become more affordable and the quality even better. Type IV systems use in-ear monitors primarily, but not always exclusively.

21. A TYPE IV SYSTEM USES MOSTLY IN-EAR MONITORS

The distinction of a Type IV system is that it has more in-ear monitors than conventional floor monitors; otherwise it is simply an in-ear system being used in whatever the primary monitor classification would be otherwise. Adding in-ears to a Type II system will *not* make it a Type IV system. Type III systems are the ones most likely to be used in combination with in-ears, making them a hybrid system. Only if there are more in-ear systems than conventional monitors would it be a Type IV monitor system.

When you add up the price of a quality EQ, high-wattage power amp, and a professional monitor wedge, in-ear monitors have become very practical alternatives to conventional monitor systems, especially when you consider that they will fit inside a small case and can be taken anywhere. The time required to physically set them up is minimal compared to a conventional wedge, but they require more time to dial in on the console. In-ear systems are not for everyone, however; some people like the feel of conventional monitors, but some people refuse to use anything else but in-ears! This is something you should decide for yourself, just not at a show; try them out at rehearsal a few times. They may seem a little strange at first, but you may really like them. One of the drawbacks of in-ear monitors is that they tend to lack the low-end impact of a conventional system; the kick and bass don't sound as fat as hearing them off the stage.

Before you go out and buy one of these wireless systems, there are a few things you need to know about them. In-ear monitor systems are not all created equal. The good ones are still pricey, and many of the cheaper ones are sometimes not worth using.

There are input considerations every time you decide to use in-ears in a live show, and a variety of adapters are necessary to make them work with different systems. We will have a look at this next.

22. KEEP IN-EAR TRANSMITTERS IN THE LINE OF SIGHT

Any wireless system works best when its receiver is directly in the line of sight with its transmitter. This shouldn't be a surprise. Keep the transmitters in the line of sight for best results. Keep them away from high-voltage/high-current AC units, which may cause interference.

If you can see the transmitter, it's in the line of sight. Sure, it may work without doing this until you get into a room that has a lot of broadcast interference. There'll be times when in-ears have problems all on their own; hiding the transmitters from the receivers just doesn't make any sense to me.

23. IN-EAR SYSTEMS WORK BEST ON TYPE III/IV PA SYSTEMS

Some systems are better suited to run in-ear monitors than others, and Type III and Type IV formats are the best choice for wireless monitors. Type I and Type II systems don't have a dedicated operator that can make the correct adjustments when needed, and they also don't have EQ on each channel, which really makes a difference in your ears: it's not always about the level, sometimes it's about the *tone*. However, they will work on any system with varying results. If you're gonna use them onstage, be sure to use them at rehearsals!

COURTESY OF DUG PINNICK

dUg Pinnick—Vocals/Bass
King's X/Living Colour
The Mob/Poundhound
www.kingsxrocks.com

"When I used conventional monitors onstage, it was a battle to get my mix right with 3,000 watts and six bass cabinets behind me. I had to use every resource I could get onstage to hear myself and everyone else. Essentially, I just had to dial out every frequency that squeaked and get them as loud as I could. Ty and Jerry never really needed monitors because they said they could hear mine . . . I probably suffered some hearing loss from that, lol!

I run my own monitor mix from the stage as well as the mixes for the whole band. It's a great sound and I'm very comfortable with it. I use in-ears and try to get my voice a bit nasally in them so I can hear the nuances better. *If I get too much low end in my voice, then I can't find my pitch.* Now that we all have in-ears, my mix balances are pretty even with the exception of my voice, and my bass is a bit louder in mine, but when I'm playing it seems balanced. If it's too much, then I start singing to myself in another key, lol! Ty's voice is on the left, Jerry's is on the right, and Ty's guitar is in stereo for pitch and lots of drums for timing.

I've used several different types of in-ears. I like a special Shure in-ear monitor that isolates really well and doesn't sound thin. The monitors are like the yellow earplugs, and they're perfect for me onstage. The whole band is using them, and we have backup units for them as well. I use a hardwired mic, but don't have a particular model; our engineer usually specs this out. My voice has a wide range of frequencies: when I sing low, it's deep; when I scream, it's got a lot of high end, so the mic has to be able to compensate for both, because it's pretty drastic. Lately I've been using Beyerdynamic.

I don't use any effects or compression in my monitors. I'm sure they do in the FOH, but it'd probably throw me off onstage. It's a good thing, because you're playing live and you need to monitor it live as well. I tried to use ambient mics for the in-ears, but my tech would forget to turn them off between songs, so I just gave up on this."

24. IN-EAR MONITORS WORK WITH REASONABLE STAGE VOLUMES

If your stage is very loud, you are going to have problems regardless of what monitor system you use, but even more so with in-ear monitors. They just don't push as much SPL as conventional wedges, and there is a bit of compression in the transmitting process. While the earpieces cut stage levels by effectively blocking some of them when they are worn, they require careful attention to levels and cues. They don't allow you to hear the stage as well as you would with conventional monitors, but this can also be a good thing at times. These systems are best used in a Type III/IV PA format where there are two engineers and more options.

A Type II system wouldn't be a great place for a full in-ear monitor system because the engineer has his or her hands full with the FOH and monitor mix, but you could probably get away with using a single set for the lead vocalist. These smaller systems often don't have enough aux sends to run very many in-ear monitors. If the club is set up for conventional monitors, then you would need to unplug the outputs and replace them with sends to your in-ear transmitters, unless there was a spare auxiliary send available. You couldn't run them both, because you may need *much* more level to the transmitter than a conventional wedge, and they would either be unbearably loud or feed back onstage, even if you could split the output. You would have to turn the amps down to prevent this. Some places are not going to want to do that in the middle of a show. A Type III/IV system would be able to turn down the outputs of the wedges without affecting the in-ear monitors.

25. KEEP A VARIETY OF ADAPTERS FOR YOUR IN-EAR MONITORS

You would also need to know exactly what type of outputs the venue's console is sending to the amp racks. Fig. 3.8 shows examples for settings of all types. If your transmitter inputs are Hi-Z and the console outputs are Lo-Z, then you will need the correct matching transformers to work properly. Sending a Lo-Z signal to a Hi-Z input would drive it to distort even at moderate levels. Sending Hi-Z signals to a Lo-Z input would not give you enough level. There is quite a bit of difference between these two operating levels, so the impedance of the connection is not the only concern.

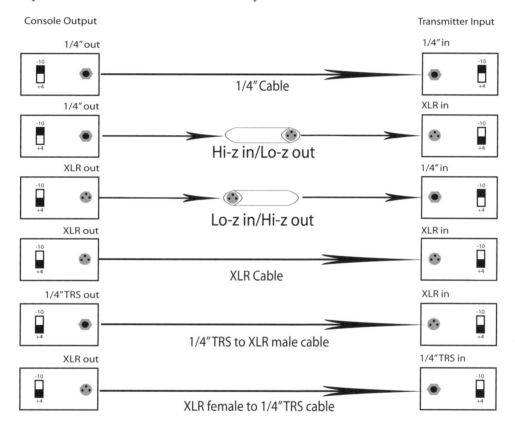

Console Output   Transmitter Input

Fig. 3.8. Matching outputs

In-line transformers not only have the right connections, but also match the signal levels. In some wireless systems, there are –10/+4 dBV switches on the ins/outs. It is important to set them correctly in order to have the right gain level at the connection. Others have two separate ins and outs for both –10 dBV and +4 dBV for multiple connections.

Now you can see why it isn't really a great idea to carry around four or five in-ear systems to use at venues with a Type II monitor system. One of these in-ear systems would be quite enough to deal with for someone who isn't an engineer and needs to focus on their show. If you really want to use one of these in-ear systems, I recommend you use it for the bigger shows and bigger stages where there is a Type III/IV system. Generally, they will have an extra aux send available on the console for your in-ear monitors. Often these mixes could stay set from soundcheck and you will not have to worry about charting the settings. On a Type III system, you will have a backup system, because the conventional system is still in place and ready to go. Quite a few big names use both at the same time. This is typically referred to as a *hybrid system*.

Pawel Maciwoda—Bass
The Scorpions/Genitorturers
www.myspace.com/stirwater

"With the Scorpions, we use in-ear monitoring, which is very comfortable (when you have a good and fast-reacting stage monitor engineer). Personally, I prefer monitor wedges on stage, but you need a soundcheck for them and we don't always get one. Depending on the room we are playing, I sometimes take one in-ear piece out, because I like to hear the stage and the audience as well. I can usually hear myself, so it really doesn't matter where I am onstage; the Scorpions are all about the stage show! Naturally, being in front of my bass cabinet is the best option. On smaller stages, I make sure I'm standing on the hi-hat side of the drummer, because when they go for the ride cymbal, your ear can go deaf!"

COURTESY OF MACIEJ RUDZINSKI

HYBRID SYSTEMS

This will be the most common system for in-ear monitors since it is rare that you will see an all in-ear Type IV monitor rig until you reach the national act level. Among the obvious examples of in-ear applications, the lead vocalist is most likely to be the one who uses them, however, there are times when in-ear systems are better suited to other players. Since the lead vocalist is usually accounted for in most stage layouts, there are generally enough monitors in the right place to get the job done. It's the additional players that often don't get enough monitors, like sax/horn players, background singers, and percussionists.

If I were to pick the player that most needed an in-ear system, it would definitely be the percussionist. These players typically have several miked instruments with a wide variety of dynamics, and that makes things very critical in a conventional monitor mix. Having an in-ear system would greatly reduce the potential for feedback in a situation like this. Another reason I suggest in-ears for percussionists is that there is often little room for a conventional wedge to work properly; some percussion kits can be rather large, and it can be difficult to place them anywhere without being a problem for softer sounds.

Since monitors often include a mix of other stage instruments, the leakage they create could contaminate delicate chimes, djembes, xylophones, and glockenspiels, which require more input level at the consoles. As noted in chapter 2, these instruments should be placed away from the loud stage zones created by other instruments, and the same applies to monitors.

Let's take a look at some not-so-obvious examples of where in-ear systems could make a difference. Fig. 3.9A shows a crowded stage with multiple zones similar to the example in Fig. 3.7C. The in-ear systems are being used for the background vocalists and horn/ sax players. Not having the floor wedges frees up valuable stage space and allows better mobility onstage for everyone. An added twist to this setup would include wireless mics for the performers, with in-ears to allow total freedom onstage.

In addition to having both in-ear and conventional monitors on the same stage, some players could benefit from using both at once. A prime example would be a lead singer/ drummer, à la Don Henley/Phil Collins. By using the conventional wedges primarily as instrument monitors and the in-ears primarily as vocal monitors, the distinctions would be much clearer for each group of sounds. This offers a few advantages that haven't been considered yet. When you think about the logistics of having both a passive (vocalist) zone and a dominant (drums) zone in the same location, you can see the immediate conflict. There are multiple mics in a small area, and they are balancing completely different elements. Here are some of the common conflicts associated with conventional setups:

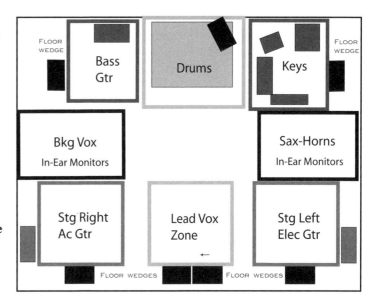

Fig. 3.9A. In-ear monitoring option #1

▶ **The vocal mic will pick up the drums.** There's very little that can be done about this other than being very careful about the drum dynamics. Lighter hits will help prevent the vocal mic from being overpowered by the snare and cymbals in particular. Since the vocal mic is being run rather hot and has a different EQ setting, this is very important.

▶ **Conventional wedges will leak into the drum mics.** High levels of drum wedge mixes can often pollute both the vocal mic and to a limited degree the drum mics. Since the drums are naturally louder than the vocals, it is often the vocals that are run hot in the wedges. At higher levels, everything turns to mush! Separation is impossible and the feedback potential is very high.

The solution? There may not be a perfect one, but there is certainly a better approach than what we just looked at. While the above approach has been used successfully before, it can work only with great caution, and even then with very inconsistent results.

What if you were to use the dominant/passive approach with the monitors as well? Let's think of wedges as dominant devices and use them on dominant sounds, i.e., drums. To follow suit, let's perceive the in-ears as passive devices and use them for passive sounds, i.e., vocals. This will create separate monitor zones within a single stage zone area. While the problem of the drums bleeding into the vocal mic is still a real possibility,

Fig. 3.9B. In-ear monitoring option #2

you should be careful with the snare and cymbal dynamics to reduce this phenomenon; however, using in-ears with conventional wedges for this situation does keep the drum area from being one big "hot zone" of multiple mics and high-level monitors.

Fig. 3.9B shows an example of this technique. The in-ear monitor is being used in the opposing ear, allowing the other ear to hear the drum wedge. This reduces any conflict between Location and Focus that would occur if done otherwise. Since most people hear better out of one ear than the other, it would be better to use the in-ears with that ear. This may or may not correspond to the drum wedge's location, so be prepared to use either ear if you need to.

26. IN-EAR MONITORS CAN HAVE MULTIPLE RECEIVERS

Each in-ear system can have several receivers, so three or four players can have the same mix. I would recommend that anyone who owns an in-ear system have at least one extra receiver since this is the part (and the earpieces) that will most likely fail first. The backup unit could easily be used for an additional performer when needed. If multiple in-ear systems are being used in a band, use the same type for all performers so that they can be shifted as needed by simply resetting the receiver designation to the correct transmitter.

This presents another option for hybrid systems: *using in-ears as vocals-only monitors for the entire band.* The wedges could be used for instrument mixes. Many players will remove one earpiece when working with both, or simply just to hear the stage levels. Right in your ear is almost always the best place for touchy vocal monitors.

Glen Sobel—Drums
Elliott Yamin/Sixx A.M.
Beautiful Creatures/Impelliteri
P.I.T. Instructor
www.myspace.com/drummerglen

COURTESY OF GLEN SOBEL

"I've been in situations where there are in-ear monitors with a house monitor engineer on every gig. This is the best-case scenario. It can be comparable to sounding like the recording studio, but onstage. If there is an in-ear monitor situation, then usually there needs to be a subwoofer on or near the drum riser, so the bass drum actually sounds like a bass drum. It can't always be this way with in-ears, but it's beautiful when it is."

In Fig. 3.9C, you will see an example of this idea. This is an alternative for bands that do a lot of three- and four-part harmonies and need a careful blend. While the idea of everyone sharing a single mix is a bit of a stretch, the harmonizing vocalists could have their own mix, because most lead vocalists require a different blend. This could be offset by pumping the additional signals in the lead vocalist's wedges. While it's not quite the same, you could do this in emergency situations. This illustration shows a separate mix for the lead vocalist. The lead vocalist's zone is shown in gray and the harmonizing vocalist's zones are shown in black.

**Fig. 3.9C.
In-ear
monitoring
option #3**

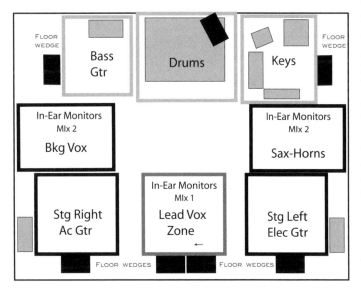

This requires not only two in-ear mixes, but five receivers; four of which are on the same receiving channel. Again, this is another example of Location, Focus, and Balance that can help you hear yourself better onstage. While this setup is not exactly for beginners, it's not that difficult to operate once you get used to using in-ear monitors. You will find other instances where in-ear monitors can work very well with conventional monitors, but the real trick is to open your mind to this possibility. With these systems just now coming into common usage, it will be up to you to push the reality envelope. When you have a problem hearing something onstage, ask yourself: "Could in-ears solve the situation?"

Tollak Ollestad—Harmonica
Don Henley/Michael McDonald
Kenny Loggins/Jewel/Seal
www.tollak.com

COURTESY OF KEYVON BEHPOUR

"A lot of harmonica players use the bullet mic, but I've been playing on [Shure] SM58s, which are fairly standard vocal mics. They're very honest, and they cover the range I'm looking for. For my style of playing, I think my personality comes out more when I don't cover it up with a lot of effects. I can hear the nuances in my playing with this mic. *I like to tone down some of the very high frequencies of the harmonica, because it tends to be rather sibilant in nature*; you'll have less problems with feedback and it'll sound less shrill. If you're using your own amp, you can control that from the stage; if you're running through the house system, you want to work on that at soundcheck.

I share a vocal mic with my harmonica, and sometimes this gives engineers a fit because there's such a level difference between them. There's definitely a science to playing a harmonica live, and you can feed back rather easily, so I have a strong awareness of how I approach the mic. I cup it with my hands, and I ease up to it so I can gauge by the monitors where I need to be. Usually the level that works for my voice is pretty close to where my harmonica level should be, and I can tell when I hit it too hard.

For monitors, I'll have very little other than what's really necessary in my monitors; if it's a bigger stage, I'll want to have kick, snare, and hat, maybe a little bass, but as little as possible to get in the way of my voice or harp in the monitors. My voice likes certain EQ characteristics, so I'll boost some bass and some upper mids to get a little cut in the wedges. I've used in-ear monitors, but personally I don't like them because it doesn't feel live anymore. If I'm playing live, I want to hear the sound bouncing around, and when I have in-ears, I don't get that at all. It feels like I'm listening to a CD, which is exactly what some people like about them. *It's all about whatever makes you play better onstage.* You need to find your own comfort level, and once it's showtime, focus more on your playing and less on the aspects of the sound you have no control over."

MONITOR CUES

27. ESTABLISH HAND SIGNALS FOR MONITOR CUES

Communication is important to any successful performance. There is an art to giving the monitor engineer cues as to what you need. I use the term "art" because it's very subjective; there could be many different ways to do this, but make sure that your whole band is on the same page with hand signals. Before soundcheck, take a minute to go over your monitor cue sheet. Tell the engineer what visual cues to watch for. If you don't get the chance, then use common sense when giving signals. At least two hand signals are needed to send a monitor cue, and sometimes three hand signals for certain situations. So let's say that in the middle of the show you need less guitar in your monitors. First, point to the guitar, then point downward; but not at the monitor, as that could be perceived as *more* guitar in the monitor. It should be apparent when you point at the guitar and then downward that you are referring to *your* mix zone. The person needing the adjustment should be giving the signal, but there are times when you can't stop playing to give the hand signals.

Erik Norlander—Keyboards
sia featuring John Payne
Lana Lane
Big Noize w/Joe Lynn Turner
www.eriknorlander.com

"I've used stage monitors for my stage levels, but with an electronic keyboard there's nothing onstage to listen to, and if the wedges go down or the monitor guy's out to lunch, you're absolutely screwed! For this reason, I always like to have some kind of combo amp, or a pair of them; this is in addition to stage wedges and in-ears (one ear only) to be able to hear a variety of sources, including the levels from the stage. I'm actually using four different sources for levels onstage. The trick is to set up your sources in a way that allows you to hear everything and not impose on the rest of the stage. I like to hear the sound of a guitar cabinet and the smack of the drums; I want to feel the thunder of a rock 'n' roll band! It makes a huge difference in the way I play. *Using one in-ear with a floor wedge gives me the low-end and punch that just in-ear monitors don't deliver.* Strictly in-ear systems seem foreign to me; almost like wearing a space helmet or something, lol!

If you make monitor adjustments onstage, you need to have very clear signals that aren't contradicting; the really confusing one is "thumbs up," because you could perceive that as either "turn up" or "I'm good!" That's a very dangerous signal to use. I'll point at the instrument that needs adjustment with my index finger, then up or down for the level; when it's right, I'll give the A-OK sign or simply the "stop" hand sign. In the middle of a show you only get a second to give them the right information, so it has to be very clear or you can wind up with something worse."

They would have to verbalize the adjustment on a busy stage to someone who could get that signal to the engineer, or wait until the song was over and go from there. If you are giving signals for another player, then you should point at the guitar, then at the person's wedge with one hand and downward with the other hand *at the same time*. This is where three hand signals are needed. While these three signals could be done in succession, chances are that the monitor engineer will be making adjustments according to the second hand signal and may miss the third signal altogether. You should develop this system or one that makes more sense to you (and the engineers) and practice it. Use it at rehearsals so that everyone can be familiar with it.

LOOPS AND FLIES

Most of you already know what loops are, but the term *flies* may be a bit less familiar. Let's have look at each of them and establish the differences.

LOOPS

A loop is a prerecorded section of a rhythm that repeats itself in time. While this rhythm can be percussion-, electronic-, acoustic-, or industrial-based, it most definitely has a timing, and usually has its own beat. Loops don't always require click tracks for this reason. Many bands are using loops in their shows; it lends a fullness to the mix without complicating the performance or crowding the stage. There is a certain consistency to loops that adds feel to the song.

Flies

A *fly* is a section of sound that appears occasionally and/or has little rhythmic information to be able to play to, but still requires impeccable timing in order to sound correct. It could consist of sampled background vocals, ambient noise tracks, or carefully timed special effects tracks. The term "fly" comes from when sampled vocal tracks were "flown" to tape in studios, meaning that a perfect chorus was sampled and then punched in to replace all the other less than perfect choruses.

Flies require click tracks to be used during the song, but there are exceptions if the fly starts the song or if the timing isn't critical. For more complicated flies like huge choruses and timed breaks, click tracks are essential. This is why most bands are more comfortable with loops than flies, but you'd be surprised at who's using them!

In most cases, loops and flies are operated from the stage via a CD player or other playback device such as a laptop, iPod, small workstation, or even a sampler. And while it would be tempting to go into how that is done here, the various methods on how to set these devices up can be found in chapters 4 and 8. Since we are discussing monitor applications here, we will simply look at the possibilities for monitoring loops and flies onstage. You need to be able to hear them—otherwise how will you know when they're working?

The vast majority of loops and flies are run through a PA and listened to through the stage monitor system. When you get a soundcheck, this method is usually quite acceptable; however; without one it can be very hit or miss. Since it's really hard to tell if your levels are right if you don't actually get to soundcheck them, you are really putting a lot of responsibility in the hands of the engineer. This gives you very little control once the signals hit the house PA system, and requires that the FOH/monitor engineer distribute the levels onstage. What if there were some way to run your own levels onstage and not have to depend so heavily on an outside factor in your show? Let's have a look!

28. use a type I system for loops and flies

Here is a trick that can help you in situations where you may be having problems hearing your loops and flies onstage. Sometimes there just aren't enough resources to go around for larger bands playing smaller shows. If you own a rehearsal PA system, in particular a Type I system, you could use that for sidefills to project your loops and flies onstage. "All-in-one" type systems are perfect for this: you simply plug in one power source, the loop/fly inputs, and the speakers. I'd seriously recommend using speaker stands for these; otherwise they may not get enough level where you need them and too much where you don't!

This method doesn't interfere with the regular monitors, and you are in complete control over the levels and EQ, which is very important to a band with a relatively high stage volume, or larger bands that need a lot of coverage. Not everyone uses loops and flies, because they require a good bit of work and attention, but this can help make things a bit simpler. Fig. 3.10 gives an example.

Fig. 3.10. Type I PA for loops and flies

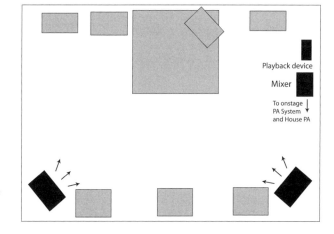

Playback device

Mixer

To onstage
PA System
and House PA

29. use a type I system for sidefill monitors

For those of you who need several onstage personal monitors for acoustic guitars, keyboards, and/or loops and flies, you could use *one* small PA system rather than several combo amps. This could save you time and money as well as give you the ability to consistently control a variety of stage levels from one source. You can easily mark your settings (or take a picture with your smartphone) from rehearsal and simply use the master volume to give you more or less level onstage, as every venue will need some adjustment. The pan control allows you to place the signals where they are needed onstage, and the EQ gives you adjustments over each instrument's tone, which is very important. Many times, it's either the level or the tone of house monitors that make them unsuitable for some instruments. *This technique is exactly the same as using sidefills on a much larger stage, with a single exception: you have control.* That's what this book is all about!

This is a good choice when a large area needs coverage, but the lead vocalist may not get as much of his or her instrument without being comparatively loud in the mix, as s/he is farther away than the two outside performers. For situations where there are two frontpersons, this is great.

IN CONCLUSION

Understanding monitor systems and how to make adjustments to them is the key to a successful show. You have very little control over what is out front unless you hire a personal engineer, and even then a certain amount of trust must be placed in his or her hands. What should really matter the most to you is that you are able to hear and play comfortably onstage. By using Location, Focus, and Balance to get comfortable onstage, you should be able to develop solutions to most situations that will change from show to show. There is a certain Zen to finding solutions: Examine the problem and choose the simplest method. It isn't always about turning something up; sometimes it's about turning everything down. The more options you have to consider, the better choices you can make.

The 5.1 Surround Sound Theory is the underlying concept to balancing your stage sound. It's not just about how loud it is: it's where you put it, where you point it, then how loud you run it. One size *does not* fit all! Creating zones for both your stage instruments and the monitor wedges and coordinating them effectively is your primary objective. This is how you can take control of your stage sound and get what you need to hear in the place it needs to be. Be aware that monitor levels are always critical and have a "ceiling"; they will only get so loud before they start feeding back, but listen for the rollover point for your vocal monitors. You will have to adjust your stage levels to make the monitors effective once they are maxed out.

James Kottak—Drums
The Scorpions/The Cult
Montrose/Kingdom Come
Warrant/Kottak
www.jameskottak.com

"I generally won't do a drum check until the instruments are set and ready. *You can check drums all day long, but it doesn't matter until you hear them with the amps.* Then if I need to make an adjustment, I'll do it then. I use an "Asskicker," which is two small speakers mounted on the bottom of the drum stool, so when you hit the kick drum you feel it like a real monitor, while the in-ears carry the rest of the signal. The Scorpions went all in-ear in 1998–99, but before that I essentially had a club PA behind me cranked up while wearing earplugs! The problem with that is it killed my FOH sound, and none of that made any sense.

I'm singing on almost every song, so I sacrifice a bit of my drum monitor sound to be able to sing clearly. I have to have a real fine blend between Klaus and my vocals, so I have a small mixer that I can use to adjust the balances between vocals, guitars, and click. I always keep a lot of Rudolf in my mix, who's one of the best rhythm guitarists in rock 'n' roll, and it's really not so much that everything's loud as it is balanced. When you soundcheck in an empty hall and then come into a huge show, things change! This way I can make my adjustments on the fly. It's very simple and there's not too much to mess with all night.

Sometimes we play with an orchestra, and six of our songs are to click; my in-ears are completely closed off so I can hear the click track. It's all linked up with video and lights, so you need the click to make it all work right. Our bass tech/keyboard guy runs our click tracks for us, or when we're with an orchestra, the conductor gives the signal to start the click. Our intro tape has a lot going on, so we just start with a click track right off the bat."

COURTESY OF JAMES KOTTAK

Let's have a look at what we have covered in this chapter:

1. A Type I Monitor System Is Really a PA System
2. Identify the Zones of the System
3. Use Location, Focus and Balance to Get What You Need
4. Set Up Your System Properly
5. Set Gain Controls to Center with the Master Down
6. Start with Your EQs Set to Flat
7. Adjust the Graphic EQ to Control the Output First
8. Adjust the Channel EQ to Control the Input
9. Avoid EQ Contradictions
10. Avoid Gain Contradictions
11. Use the Same Equipment at Rehearsal That You Plan to Use at the Show
12. There Is No Channel EQ on a Type II Monitor System
13. Monitor Levels Are Critical in Floor Wedges
14. Each Zone Requires a Separate Mix
15. Reposition Unused Monitors
16. A Type III System Has a Separate Monitor Console
17. Type III Systems Are More Versatile
18. A Type III System Has Completely Independent Signal Paths
19. A Type III System Often Has Sidefills
20. Sidefills Are Great to Separate Mixes
21. A Type IV System Uses Mostly In-Ear Monitors
22. Keep In-Ear Transmitters in the Line of Sight
23. In-Ear Systems Work Best on Type III/IV PA Systems
24. In-Ear Monitors Work With Reasonable Stage Volumes
25. Keep a Variety of Adapters for Your In-Ear Monitors
26. In-Ear Monitors Can Have Multiple Receivers
27. Establish Hand Signals for Monitor Cues
28. Use a Type I System for Loops and Flies
29. Use a Type I System for Sidefill Monitors

Getting the Right Signal to the Monitors and Mains

INPUT SOURCES

The purpose of this chapter is not to teach you how to run sound, but how to get your sounds into a PA system properly. You should have an idea of what an engineer needs, and you may have to make some adjustments in order to get the sound you're looking for. As with anything, it's always a good idea to take first things first and then work in order. We have covered your instruments, your setups, and your monitors; now it's time to look at input sources.

What is an input source? This is the device or process that is used to send a usable signal to the mixing console. Four out of five times, it will be a microphone, but since there are many types of mics and various other input sources like direct boxes and mixer outputs, we will examine them all. Included with microphones are stands, clips, cables, and wireless systems. You need most of these to get through a show, and they affect your tone as well; you should know what to expect when you use them.

The Logic here is to streamline getting your sounds into the mains and monitors as quickly as possible and with the best results. You won't actually be mixing, but you have to know what the engineer will need when it's time for soundcheck. You may have to provide some options for them if you have something unusual or unique. Remember that you will need to be able to hear what you are playing; provide what you need for monitor signals, and get what the engineer needs for the mix: *They can only mix what you give them, so give them options!* You are not just giving them options; you are giving yourself options, and this is where you can take control of your sound. While no one is asking you to bring your own mics to the show, there are some very specific elements you can bring to the party to give your band the advantage it needs. Issues like finding shortcuts to complicated miking situations, providing direct inputs to monitor applications, and having the right mic for a specific tone will not only speed up your stage setup and allow you to hear yourself better, but will give you a better-sounding mix in the end. In this chapter, we will take a much closer look at the various input sources that are available and their advantages and disadvantages. Some will be better suited to your particular situation. You may be surprised at just how easy it is to get better sounds into the console and save time in the process.

MICROPHONES

Microphones are used on sounds that either don't have an electronic output, or when the tone you're after is an acoustic one. An example of this is a guitar cabinet: while the amp may have a direct output, it doesn't capture the tone of your amp pushing a 4×12 cabinet with vintage speakers in it. Another example is the human voice—where would you plug that in? Other instruments like acoustic guitars and violins can have contact mics/pickups and microphones, and direct signals are your preferred method for monitor applications. Even if you don't use both signals all the time, you will still have a choice. No contact mic/ pickup? No choice!

For now, we will be looking strictly from the microphone's perspective. Mic stands, mic placement/focus, and mic types all have a bearing on your end result, and these factors will also be considered in this chapter.

Microphone Types. For most live sound applications, there are two main types of mics: dynamic mics and condenser mics. And while there are other types such as ribbon mics, boundary-layer mics, and bullet mics, these rarely find their way to the stage, and only then are used for a special purpose. Microphones also all have a specific range of frequencies and coverage that divide them even further. While looking at a microphone's specs and graphs won't tell you how it will sound on a particular instrument, it will tell you if the mic is suitable for that application. How a mic is used and on what instrument is another animal altogether. A lot more on specs is covered in Chapter 8: Technical Aspects.

1. USE DYNAMIC MICS FOR DYNAMIC SOUNDS

Dynamic mics are simple, durable, and affordable. They seem to be the choice for most sounds. They don't require 48V "phantom" power and can handle some normal abuse without a problem. Dynamic mics work best on "dynamic" sounds like drums, guitar cabinets, and other fairly loud sources, but can be used on *any* sound. There isn't any miking application where a dynamic mic can't be used, so in the absence of a suitable condenser mic, use a dynamic.

Dynamic mics work by sound vibrating a diaphragm attached to a coil positioned in a magnetic field. They are less sensitive to subtle nuances than a condenser, but they handle rough transients better. There are two different kinds of dynamic mics—wireless and wired—and different types of coverage patterns, like cardioid and hypercardioid, but dynamic mics are rarely omnidirectional. This will all be examined in this chapter as well.

2. USE CONDENSER MICS FOR COMPLEX SOUNDS

Condenser mics are slightly more sophisticated; they require phantom power (48V) and are more sensitive to abuse than a dynamic mic is, but they are also more sensitive to nuances than a dynamic mic. Never plug or unplug a condenser mic without removing the 48V phantom power from its channel! It will cause an ugly pop in the PA and monitor system. If the channel is at a high level when this happens, you'll take out drivers—more than likely monitor drivers. These mics are also very sensitive to nearby monitors, and should be used with caution in this regard. Condenser mics work best on complex sounds like pianos and violins, but can also be used in almost any application that a dynamic mic would be. While they may not behave like a dynamic mic, they will get the job done when there's no other option; however, they don't do well in the hole of a kick drum—the air movement is just too strong for the diaphragm.

A preamplifier is used to raise the signal to a usable level. Condenser mics can also be wireless or wired, have different coverage patterns and different diaphragm sizes. We will examine these variations as well.

3. CARDIOID MICS ARE SEMI-DIRECTIONAL

Coverage patterns determine a mic's suitability for a specific purpose. There are three main choices for live sound applications: cardioid, hypercardioid, and omnidirectional. Cardioid mics have a coverage pattern that looks like an upside-down heart; hence the name "cardioid." They sound best on axis, but will pick up off-axis sounds as well. How well sound is picked up is determined by the specific "polar pattern" given in the mic specs. Cardioid mics have a fairly wide range of coverage that picks up most of what is in *front* of it. They will pick up very little from behind. This wider range of coverage is great for vocalists who move around a lot. It means that the signal will not disappear when they are not directly on axis. Cardioids will pick up nearby sounds in a tight situation, but can also be adjusted by focusing them away from the unwanted signal. You can see in the illustration below that the mic picks up very little sound from the back.

4. HYPERCARDIOID MICS ARE UNIDIRECTIONAL

Hypercardioid mics are very similar to cardioids, except they have a narrower and more focused range of coverage. These mics will pick up some sound from the back, as a figure-8 mic would, but not as much. They also pick up less "wash" from the sides, but require that you properly focus them; the sweet spot is a bit smaller. While their pattern appears to be narrower than a cardioid mic, they can have a greater effective distance which is handy if you can't get right on top of a source.

5. OMNI MICS PICK UP SOUND FROM ALL DIRECTIONS

Omnidirectional mics are designed to pick up sound from all directions in a somewhat equal manner. These mics are great when you need to cover several sounds with a single microphone. They also work well on pianos that have a wide range of focus. Each string of the piano occupies a different space, and an omnidirectional mic will pick up all these sounds better than a cardioid, especially a hypercardioid.

6. KEEP OMNI MICS AWAY FROM MONITORS

Omnidirectional mics have a couple of drawbacks that should be considered in live sound applications: they pick up nearby sounds, and they will also pick up the monitors! If you place an omnidirectional mic near a stage monitor and bring it up high in that monitor, expect some feedback. If you have a few dynamic sounds close to an omni mic, you will not be able to stop the mic from picking them up. For these reasons, omni mics are used for very specific applications in live sound, and are kept away from the local monitor or not assigned to one at all.

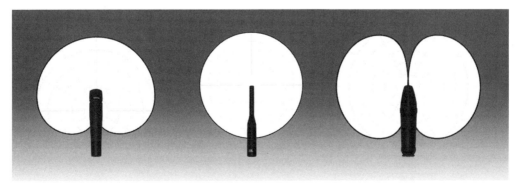

7. RIBBON MICS HAVE A FIGURE-8 PATTERN

Another type of omnidirectional pattern is called figure-8. It is identical to omni, except that the back side of the mic is out of phase with the front side. This will cause some background noises to be canceled out; especially the sides. Because the sides are common to both diaphragms (which are opposite in polarity), they cancel each other out. We'll take a closer look at phase relationships in Chapter 8: Technical Aspects. The figure-8 pattern is rarely used in live sound, but lately some high-end modern ribbon mics have done a great job on sounds like guitar cabinets and horns/brass. Ribbon mics are always figure-8 by design and naturally roll off higher frequencies, making harsh sounds smoother. Ribbon mics perceive sound similarly to the way your ears do. It's the nature of their design. They are expensive (usually) and a bit more fragile than condenser mics. They should be considered as an option when conventional mics aren't performing well. Being a form of omnidirectional mic, they don't do well in nearby monitors either.

8. USE VOLUME/MUTE PEDALS FOR BULLET MICS

"Bullet"-type mics look totally different, but are often just dynamic mics in a different casing. These are used for harmonicas, juice harp, and other mouth-driven instruments. There are two ways to use a mic of this type: an XLR input directly to the console gives a cleaner result, but when plugged into a small combo amp that is miked up, you get that "old school" honky-tonk tone that most people are looking for in the first place. Should you choose this method of using a "bullet" mic, be aware of the possible feedback that can occur if it is placed near the amp or left open during the show. It needs some sort of mute or volume control and some actually have one. For those that don't, a guitar volume pedal works perfectly in this instance and even helps with the dynamics and tone of the source.

9. MOST UNBALANCED MICS ARE CHEAP TOYS

Other Types of Mics. You will see a few other types of microphones in various places, but other than the ones mentioned above, they will be typically be suspect regarding their suitability for stage use. In particular, Hi-Z mics with ¼-inch plugs on them are generally toys. Some of them may resemble high-quality units, but if there's not an XLR output on the mic, it will be of little use in a PA system.

The primary exceptions to this are bullet mics that are run to a stage amplifier. Guitar and instrument amps generally have ¼-inch inputs, and an XLR-type mic would need an adapter cable to work. The only reason you would ever need a mic with a ¼-inch plug would be for use in an amp, so be aware of this distinction.

10. MEGAPHONES WORK WELL ONSTAGE

Megaphones pop up every now and then for "special effects," and are a great approach; they provide a visual effect as well as an audio effect. I recommend using one if that is the sound you are looking for. The results are generally *much* better than using an effect processor to simulate it. Spending a lot of money on one of these would be a waste; you are actually looking for a "cheap" sound! Some singers will simply cup the ball of the mic to make a nasal-sounding effect, but the results fall short of what is intended and create serious problems. Using a bullhorn or megaphone gives you control over when it's used. In the case of a performer who is playing an instrument and needs this effect, then your primary choice is to use an effects processor at the console and have the engineer bring it in; however, I have seen them duct-taped to a mic stand. This effect doesn't need to be in the monitors, or it could create a potential feedback problem. They produce enough level to be heard onstage. Try to hit the mic at an angle, not directly into it.

Todd and Troy Garner—Vocals
Lenny Kravitz (bkg)
The Seventh Hour (lead)
www.myspace.com/theseventhhourmusic

Todd: "We learned a long time ago how to work with a mic and a mic stand, which is a prop and can be used to your advantage. *You have to sing directly into the mic*; you can move around, but that mic has to stay right with you and be focused on a particular spot. I can be jumping up and down, but that mic stays in the same position relative to my voice. It's important for people to hear what I'm singing, and it's my responsibility to keep that mic in a position to deliver that."

Troy: "You also want to find a mic that suits your voice best; my choice just happens to be a Shure SM57, but that may not work for everyone. You need to like the sound of your voice in your mic, whatever you choose. Don't just go buy a mic, because we've heard really expensive mics that sounded like crap, and some lesser mics that sounded much better. The wireless mics give us more freedom onstage, but since we use the same mic technique for both types, it really doesn't matter. Personally, I like the corded mics, but I can work with whatever is there. It's a rock 'n' roll show—just make me sound good! For soundchecks, my objective is to be able to hear myself while the band is playing, so there's a balance between the band and the vocal monitors. *We let the band get settled in first before we start making adjustments; otherwise it's wasted time.*"

Todd: "It's important as a singer to learn the terms that musicians understand as well as terms the engineers understand, even if you don't know how to read music or engineer. The idea is to blend everything onstage as a unit, because that's how we play. We use a lot of dynamics, so it's important for our stage sound to follow our song dynamics. We'll start with our heaviest song for soundcheck, and then work on our acoustic based-song to see how it translates. When we have that, we're good to go!"

COURTESY OF DERON REED

Wireless Microphones

Wired and Wireless Mics. Most mics will be wired. They are simpler and can operate in conditions that wireless systems would have problems with. They are less expensive, but often sound better and more consistent than their wireless cousins. Yet while they don't require batteries, transmitters, and receivers, they also don't offer the mobility that wireless mics do. In a live show, having this mobility can often make a huge difference. For vocalists and instrumentalists who are highly animated onstage, wireless systems would be the only way to go. For most stationary instruments like drums and cabinets, wired mics will be your choice. However sax and horns would definitely benefit from having a wireless mic. Here is a comparison of these two designs that shows the advantages of each. Each category shows the preferred type. You can use this as guide to deciding which mic you should use in any application.

Dynamic range	Wired mics
Frequency response	Wired mics
Reliability	Wired mics
Gain before feedback	Wired mics
User mobility	Wireless mics
Range of use	Wireless mics
Stage appearance	Wireless mics

While I'm sure that everyone would prefer the reliability and performance of a wired mic, the mobility factor of a wireless mic is very compelling. Be aware that having a large number of wireless mics may become a problem if there is an unusual amount of interference in the area. Limit your wireless systems to the most essential elements.

11. WIRELESS SYSTEMS HAVE LESS HEADROOM

Wireless Systems. We have briefly gone through certain elements of wireless systems, but now is the time to examine them closely. They do have the distinct advantage of being mobile, but that doesn't come without a price. It really doesn't matter what kind of system you buy; the wireless version of a mic will never sound quite as good as the wired version. Most engineers will tell you the same thing. The problem lies in the radio transmission electronics and in the broadcasting process in general. Wireless mics also offer less headroom and gain before feedback. You almost *never* see wireless systems in the studio. Nonetheless, they still do a pretty good job for most live shows, and it's very unlikely that anyone in the audience would be able to hear the difference. The only place you would really notice a lack of gain is on a very loud stage.

12. SOME WIRELESS SYSTEMS ARE BETTER THAN OTHERS

There are different types of wireless systems, and the distinctions lie in the method of transmission rather than in the microphone itself. In most cases, a wireless mic is just an ordinary mic with a built-in transmitter incorporated into its body. VHF is probably the least reliable system. Its frequencies are comparatively lower than other types and are more prone to interference. UHF uses a higher frequency range; the shorter waves don't penetrate walls as easily, and that means less interference from outside the area. Interference works both ways. *Diversity receivers* can switch frequencies to find the best transmission. *True diversity* and *digital diversity* receivers transmit on two channels simultaneously and always use the strongest signal. Like diversity receivers, true diversity receivers search for strong, clear frequencies.

Rob Marcello—Guitar
Danger Danger/House of Lords
Marcello/Vestry
Twenty-4 Seven
www.myspace.com/dangerdangerrob

"I like it simple and clean, so I just use a chorus and delay pedal. I also use a tuner that mutes my acoustic so I can have some control, and a volume for my leads on electric guitar. *I believe the less stuff you have, the better!* I'll let the sound guy add what he thinks it needs, but a lot of it depends on the room; if it's real dry and dead-sounding, then I want a little ambience, a little bit of vibe. I want to get my tone from the amp because *I think the amp is just as important as the guitar*. If you think about it, it's like a violin and a bow; they work together.

Some guys like their amps really close miked, but I like mine at a 45-degree angle to the cone. Not every speaker sounds the same; so you gotta listen to them and pick the best one. I even put a taped square right where I want the mic. I don't know how much all this really matters in a big room, but to me it does because I know that it's there. I make sure the guitar is perfectly set up as far as intonation, action, and pickup height, so I'll have someone do all this for me. I change strings before every show or recording. *New strings, good cables—everything you do matters*. Each little point may not make that big a difference on its own, but when you add them all up *it does!*"

13. MAKE SURE YOUR WIRELESS IS IN THE LINE OF SIGHT

"Line of sight" is a term for the transmitter having a direct path to the receiver. They work best when they "see" each other. Since the freedom allowed by wireless systems is often used to its fullest, line of sight will keep the signal stronger when the singer is turned away from the receiver and moving around quickly. They will work without line of sight, but occasionally (and unexpectedly) they may lose some signal or drop out. Especially if the battery isn't as strong as it should be; this brings me to my next point.

14. USE FRESH BATTERIES FOR EVERY SHOW

It really wouldn't be a revelation to mention fresh batteries again in case you missed it earlier in this book, but use a fresh battery for *every* show! That goes for any battery-powered device that is critical to your performance. If you were playing several shows a week, I could see getting through one or two with the same battery, but if you are only playing out once a month, use a fresh battery every time.

15. HEAVY-BASE STANDS PICK UP STAGE NOISE

Mic stands, clips, and cables are essential for getting the mic in the right spot, but they can affect your sound more than you may realize. In some cases, they can affect your ability to perform as well. Making the right choice can improve your ability to pick up the right signal and ultimately improve your mix and monitors. Some mic stands have a tendency to pick up stage noise from the floor. Heavy, round-base stands pick up lots of subsonic frequencies from bass and guitars.

16. BOOM STANDS PICK UP STAGE NOISE

A boom is often needed to place the mic in a usable spot, but adding boom attachments to stands can adversely affect your sound; booms can amplify stage noise. A mic on a fully extended boom will pick up much more stage rumble than a mic on a straight stand without a boom. It's a matter of simple physics: leverage. While shockmounts help reduce noise, there is a much better choice we are about to take a look at below. Using a shockmount on a boom stand is fine in the studio, but very cumbersome onstage.

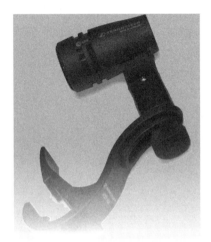

17. CLIP-ON MIC STANDS AND MICS ELIMINATE NOISE

Clip-on mic stands and mics are more stable and less likely to be knocked around or vibrated away from their location. Some people place sandbags over conventional mic stand bases to keep them from moving, but this really adds to the noise that they pick up. This is often the case with kick drum mics; they have a tendency to move around a lot. Internally mounted mics are probably the best choice, but a shockmount can be used with a conventional mic to cut down any extra noise. You will want to own the mic for it as well. Clip-on mic stands are very effective for getting your mic in tight spots on drum kits and percussion kits, but have other advantages as well. They take up less room onstage, they pick up less stage noise, and while they do pick up sound from what they are mounted on, often that is the sound you are after anyway! Double bonus! They also have another obvious advantage; they move with the instrument they are miking. If a tom slips on its mount or is relocated during the show, the mic goes with it and stays focused.

A mic clipped to the bell of a sax will follow the sax player's every movement without any dropouts. You certainly could shake it off if you tried, but normal, smooth stage movements wouldn't be a problem for a clip-on mic and would be a problem for a conventional stand. The only real disadvantage to clip-on mics is that you lose the ability to "work the mic" the way you can with a mic/stand combination. Conventional stands are always prone to being knocked around, slipping, or breaking. They also take up more precious setup time and stage space, and require more adjustments. Bell-mouthed instruments use different types of clip-on mics that are lighter. Most often they are condensers, which are better suited for the more subtle sounds they produce, while drums are complemented more by dynamic mics. The higher SPL levels could damage or distort many condenser mics in a close-miked application. In both cases, clip-on mic stands are smart alternatives. Use the right one!

18. INTERNAL MICS WORK BEST IN TIGHT SPOTS

Internally mounted microphones are an option for those who can afford them, but they're really not that expensive. Acoustic guitars, drums, percussion, and pianos are some examples of instruments that would benefit from them. There is an advantage to having the mic premounted correctly; it keeps your sound consistent and predictable. Remember, this book is about taking control, and consistency is your friend! Internal mics do require a bit of time and money to install, but can really cut down on your setup time. They reduce stage noise, improve isolation from other sounds and monitors, and are practically invisible. Once mounted, they never get lost or stolen and are protected better than setting them up and tearing them down every time you play. Look into your alternatives if you are having problems getting good sounds or having problems with monitor levels.

Mike Hansen—Drums
Tribe After Tribe/George Lynch
Souls of We/Leif Garrett
The Pointer Sisters/Paula Abdul
www.myspace.com/cymbalcrasher1

COURTESY OF ALEX SOLCA

"I use the May internal shockmounted miking system. You can pick any mics you want for this system, so you have a variety of tones. I prefer the AKGs, but some of the jazz and funk guys like the Sennheisers. They're a little more cutting edge, a bit cleaner and have less low-end, but it's more of a personal choice at this point.

I haven't used triggers in a long time, but I learned a lot about them. I would make my own from piezo microphones at Radio Shack. I'd put a ¼-inch jack on the ends, take a piece of Velcro and strap them in the shells of the drums. Another way to run triggers is to split the signals from my internal mics—send one to the house and the other to my drum module. This works much better than most cheap drum triggers; it's more sensitive and dynamic. I never had a problem with this technique; there is nothing to break when it's inside the drum. Not only is it isolated inside the drum, but it also picks up the concussion of the shell.

Occasionally I'll hear something weird in the house PA, and I'll work that bottom head to get it to sound right in the system. With the internal mics, you're tuning the shells and not the heads, so it becomes more critical. When the FOH guy has my drums up in the system, I can hear what's going on in the house. If I hear frequencies that sound 'off,' then I'll start tuning the shells to get rid of them. You need to be on top of your game; you don't want to leave the guy all by himself on this! When you hear something acoustically vs. magnified by a microphone, there's stuff you don't hear until it's up in the system. Get your sound right acoustically first, then make adjustments if you need to. Take a good listen to what you sound like in the PA. If it's not right, work it!"

19. USE THE SMALLEST STAND THAT WILL WORK

Always use the smallest stand that will effectively work for each situation. Don't use a boom if you don't need it. Use a clip-on mic/stand in tight spots or a wireless for high-mobility instruments. When you do need a very stable mic stand and a heavy base to keep it from being moved around, use a shockmount to eliminate stage rumble, a clip-on variety or internally mounted mic. Shockmounts are available for just about every type of mic made, but you may have to look around for them. Internal mics are specialty items, and you may have to search for the right ones, but they are always worth the investment. As mentioned in the beginning of this chapter, the purpose of this book is not to teach you how to run sound, but to help you take control of your sound and provide options for you to do this. Thus far, we have looked at a lot of elements that you don't typically control. You don't own mics, you don't own stands, you don't set them up at shows, *but you could!* This is where thinking outside the box can really pay off. Drummers, percussionists, brass and reed players would benefit greatly from having their own clip-on mics or internally mounted mics. There are a few instruments that aren't named here, but anything that can be pre-miked and set up in advance will save you time and give you a more consistent end result. Guitar and bass cabinets don't really need them, but lead vocalists should own and maintain a good quality wireless system if they move around a lot. Don't expect the venues you play to have the specialty items you need and in the quantities you need them—invest in success!

20. USE A SHOCKMOUNT FOR HEAVY-BASE STANDS

As we looked at earlier in this chapter, heavy-base stands can really pick up stage noise. The same goes for light-base stands with sandbags or other weighted materials placed on their bases, as is common with kick drum mics that like to move around. Another similar situation that would be good for shockmounts is when a mic is on a very resonant stage or near several dominant sound sources. It doesn't really matter what kind of stand you use; if it's in a highly resonant area, a shockmount will reduce some of the stage noise and keep it from causing a problem. By now, you can understand why feedback and microphone bleed are such omnipresent occurrences in live sound. It seems like everything from mic bleed to monitor noise, stands, and resonant stages is out to screw up your sound; it will if you let it! Just keep this in mind if you're having a problem with excessive signal contamination.

This is why you must take the initiative and make the right choices to help reduce the effect of these evil gremlins. What to do about it? Let's look at some situations and your alternatives as this will help you make good decisions about miking choices. While most engineers are doing the best they can with what they have, sometimes it isn't much. Take control of your stage sound and *provide them*. Let's take a look at other aspects of microphones and inputs.

21. ALLOW SPACE FOR MICROPHONES

It's very important for each microphone to have an adequate amount of space to do its job *without interference* from other sound sources. While this applies mainly to drum kits and percussion, it can also be a problem when a passive sound is set in front of a loud guitar cabinet. If you have a background singer, don't place them directly in front of the lead guitarist's amp! Two things will happen when you do that:

►The singer's mic will pick up almost as much guitar as it does vocals; AND

►You are blocking the sound coming from the guitar cabinet, which will almost surely cause the guitarist to turn up even further! End result: way too much guitar, not nearly enough vocalist in that channel. And it doesn't have to be a vocalist; it could be a percussion kit, or even an acoustic guitar that just happens to be very sensitive to that frequency range. One of the worst things you can do onstage is block the sound coming from a cabinet with a source you want in the PA system. If you have a loud guitarist and really want to deflect some of his level, use a stage prop that won't have a mic on it.

Generally speaking, allow a clear path from those higher-level sounds to reach their players, *or* use one of the setup alternatives in chapter 2. The solution is to either relocate the loud sound, or relocate the not-so-loud sound. This is just another example of things to watch out for when setting up your stage. Zones apply to mics as well, so don't create any problems for yourself.

22. GET THE MIC IN THE BEST LOCATION YOU CAN

Not only is allowing room for mics important, but so is getting the mic into the right spot. Snare drums can be hard to reach with a conventional mic and stand combination. Using a clip-on mic or an internally mounted mic will take care of this problem.

Internally mounted snare mics are your best alternative, especially if the snare placement is very tight. They also reduce the level of mic bleed in these tight spots. Even if the rest of the kit is conventionally miked, an internally mounted snare mic will always be a benefit. The fact that there is no microphone in the way of your playing should be reason enough to consider one. Clip-on mics and internally mounted mics work well for djembes and congas that need a mic on their bottoms. With any sound source for which you have a problem locating a mic correctly, try to find a permanent solution for this problem or it will still be there waiting for the next show.

Speaking of getting the mic in the right spot, focusing the mic is another very important skill you should be aware of. Close-miked sound sources can be very finicky about mic placement. Since the mic is so close to the source, it needs to be in the right spot to sound good. If you don't believe me, go put your ear about 2 inches away from a drum being played! Understanding what you are miking is the key to great results. *Examine the source and determine where the sound you are looking for is coming from; then position the mic in the middle of that area.* This is usually the best place to start as you can easily adjust it either way.

James Kottak—Drums
The Scorpions/The Cult
Montrose/Kingdom Come
Warrant/Kottak
www.jameskottak.com

COURTESY OF JAMES KOTTAK

"*A simple rule for drum tuning is tuning the top for feel and the bottom for tone.* So the top head doesn't always have to be higher or lower than the bottom head. A lot of people go by that rule, but for me it's more whatever it feels like. I tend to play loud, and even when I'm playing the toms, I'm hitting rim shots and get a bit more volume with this technique. You have to remember that you're competing with thousands of watts of amps, even when you're miked up. I use Ahead drumsticks. They never break, they're loud, and they keep your joints from hurting so much. I get a special sound out of them; I can't even play with regular sticks. I use Aquarian snare heads, and they last a few shows. It makes no sense to use a thinner head when you're essentially beating it with sledgehammers.

One of the biggest things to keep up with is maintenance: *Change the parts on your drums before they break.* You know your snare strainer is gonna let go at some point, you know your snare head's gonna wear out; change it out before it goes. Autograph it and sell it at the show!

I've tried both internal mics and clip-ons for live shows. I use clip-on mics for the snare and toms. For the kick, I use the Kelly SHU; it's like a spider web, and you can adjust it to move the mic wherever you need in the drum. I don't miss the mic stand sticking out in front of the drum that singers and guitarists love to trip over, lol!"

If you are miking a speaker cone, place the mic halfway between the inside cap and the outside rim. Moving the mic toward the inside will give you more top end; toward the rim will give you less top end.

Fig. 4.1 gives an example. Occasionally, a sound will come up perfectly on the first try, but unless you move the mic around to see, how will you ever know that it was "perfect"? Simply go back to that spot if it was really the right place. When you have a basic understanding of what you're doing, you should never be afraid to experiment. This is how you learn.

Snare drums and toms should have their mics pointed halfway between the middle of

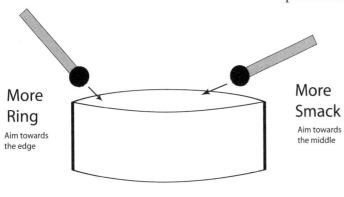

Fig. 4.1. Miking a speaker

Lows

Lows (highs) Lows

Lows

More Highs | More Lows

the head, or "strike point," and the outside rim. Aiming the mic toward the strike point will give you more smack and less ring; aiming it toward the rim will give you more ring and less smack, which is very useful if you need something extra. Because the mic is so close to the drum head, even slight angle adjustments can make a noticeable difference in the tone. If you can get your mic to sound "right" (whatever that is!) without having to adjust your EQ, you will be eliminating any background noise that will be emphasized by EQing the sound.

23. FOCUS MICS TOWARD THE BEST TONE RANGE
Start in the middle of the range and see what comes up first. You can tune your sound by simply moving it and without having to go to the EQ immediately. Once you have found the correct balance of smack and ring, you can use the EQ lightly to polish it up some. Remember that the more EQ you add to a channel, the more mic bleed you will have in that frequency range. With drums, it's better to remove unwanted frequencies than to boost the ones you want, but often you have to do some of both. Make most of your mic placement adjustments without using any EQ. This philosophy should be applied to any source that is miked (see Fig. 4.2). The last consideration when focusing mics is the *rejection range* of the mic. A cardioid mic picks up sound from the front, and rejects sounds from the back. So this end of the mic should be aimed toward any nearby sounds that may bleed into that channel. There is a fine line between where the mic sounds best and where it rejects sound best. Fig. 4.3 shows two guitar cabinets placed next to each other with examples of correct and incorrect mic placement. The correct mic placement would be

More Ring

Aim towards the edge

More Smack

Aim towards the middle

Fig. 4.2. Miking a drum

to use the far-side speakers, with the mic pointed away from the other cabinets. The incorrect mic placement shows each near-side speaker being miked with the mic pointed toward the other cabinet.

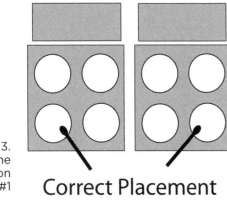

Fig. 4.3. Using the rejection range #1

Correct Placement

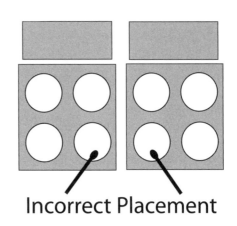

Incorrect Placement

Bruce Bouillet—Guitar
Racer X/The Scream/DC 10
Epidemic/Bottom Dwellerz
Grammy-winning producer/engineer
www.myspace.com/brucebouillet

COURTESY OF BRUCE BOUILLET

"Watch the brightness of your tone; you'll get a lot more definition out of a beefy tone with fewer highs, even if it's not natural for you. I'd much rather have the engineers add some highs as opposed to completely pulling them out of the mix. And make sure it's not feeding back like a maniac when you're just standing there.

I see a lot of people putting their heads on their cabinets, but they would have to run cable 35–40 feet back to their amps on the larger stages. On the G3 tours, I saw guys putting their heads on the side of the stage, and they were able to use shorter input cables to get a better tone; you're losing a lot of signal on that long of a run.

Pedalboards are another thing that people get caught up in. You go to a lumber store and get a board cut large enough for your pedals and small enough to fit in a gig bag or guitar case. Cover the whole board with Velcro and your pedals with the hooks, get some zip ties and lock the thing down. You don't have to rebuild your setup whenever you travel—it's almost indestructible! And don't get cheap on the cables, either; you lose more money trying to save there! When you have problems onstage, a minute seems like an hour, lol!"

24. USE THE REJECTION RANGE OF A MIC TO REDUCE STAGE NOISE

While incorrect mic placement will often work with fair results, correct mic placement will help reduce phase cancellation, mic bleed, and stage rumble ever so slightly. If you can cut a couple of decibels of noise from each channel, theoretically you could end up with 48 dB less noise in a 24-channel mix than you would with a careless setup. Using the far-side speaker will reduce the floor noise that leaks into the opposing mic stand. This will also help the monitors, but to a lesser degree, because there aren't as many sources assigned to them. In any case, a reduction in mic bleed and background noise is always a plus!

Another example of using the rejection range of a mic can be demonstrated with rack toms closely mounted together. Fig. 4.4 shows the correct and incorrect mic placement for this setup. Here, the difference will be much more noticeable, and every ounce of isolation and rejection will help clean up your end result. There is a very good chance of phase cancellation with the mics pointed at each other in the incorrect example. Any time two mics are less than 18 inches apart and pointed in the same direction, you have an increased possibility of phase cancellation.

Fig. 4.4. Using the rejection range #2

Splitting toms is a technique used to stretch the PA when resources are slim; i.e., there are not enough mics and channels. It's a compromise, but it will work in a pinch. It does require some "detailing," so be prepared to move

Correct Placement

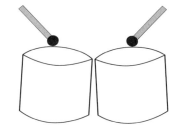

Incorrect Placement

the mic if one tom is weaker than the other. There is no way to adjust two sounds in one mic without actually moving the mic. They are sharing levels and EQs, so it's important for them to sound pretty close.

Fig. 4.5. Splitting toms

The general idea is to get the mic in a place where it can hear both *sweet spots*. Close

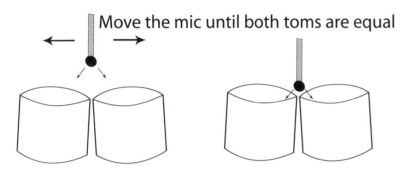

Move the mic until both toms are equal

miking doesn't quite do the job; you have to back the mic off some. When the mic is too close to the drums, it stays focused on the ring zones of the heads. When it is backed off, it will allow more of the smack zone into the central axis of the pickup pattern. Fig. 4.5 shows the correct and incorrect mic placement for this setup. This is where it really helps to have some "space" for the mics, as mentioned earlier.

How to *not* split toms is another subject altogether. There are many times I have seen drummers with three toms who only had two tom mics/channels to work with. The most obvious miking technique is the wrong one! I know it sure looks good with the mic on each side of the center tom, but it is the surest way to get phase cancellation or an imbalance in your drum mix! The truth is, you can only split *two* of the toms, and the third should be close miked with the rejection range toward the other two toms. It really doesn't matter if you prefer the first tom close-miked and the second and third toms to be split as long as you use the rejection range of the mic to "focus out" the other two toms. Isolate the tom that is played the most or needs the most work to sound right. Conversely, split the two toms that sound very close to each other.

COURTESY OF NICK MENZA

Nick Menza—Drums
Megadeth/Marty Friedman
Deltanaut
www.menza.com

"Having the right setup and getting a great sound is important to having fun onstage; if it's not fun, it'll come out in your playing. I didn't start playing because I thought I could make money at it, I play because I love it! I'm also trying to get the drums to feel right as well, because it's just no fun to play a kit that doesn't feel right, regardless of how it sounds. You can play pretty effortlessly if it's set up right.

I leave space in my kit for mics, because if you have the cymbals too close to the toms, then you'll have problems mixing. *I keep my kit pretty tight, but you still need some separation for the mics.* When you use triggers live, you want to get your acoustic drums to sound pretty close. You want to be conscious of what you're lacking in the sound, so work your tone to get it right.

Playing outdoors is tough because there's no walls to work with and it all sounds a little thin. The tone is just crap, so you have to know that you still play good and rise above it. Let's face it, people pay to come see you play, and you've got to deliver the best possible performance you can and step out of that muck. Whatever aspect you're involved with, you do the best you can and have fun with it!"

Fig. 4.6 shows the correct and incorrect mic placement for this setup. While these last considerations of using the rejection range are helpful tricks in some severe situations, you should try not to compromise the first two principles of Location and Focus just to reduce something that may not be a real problem. In other words, don't cause two problems trying to fix one. When the situation calls for you to make use of these

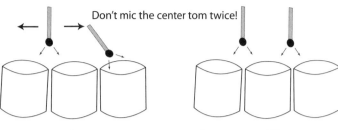

Don't mic the center tom twice!

Correct Placement   **Incorrect Placement**

Fig. 4.6. Splitting three toms

techniques, help yourself. If things are tight and balancing the rejection range compromises the sound of the source you are after, it's hardly worth it. It really depends on just how loud the nearby sound is in relation to the intended sound. If the unwanted sound is very loud in comparison to the intended sound, you may have to relocate one of the sounds to get the separation you need. Now, let's look at these three principles and see how they work together from a microphone perspective:

Location. This is the specific area where the mic should be placed. In most cases, it should be close to the source you want to mic, but there are times when it doesn't sound right. Try to get it as close as you can and still sound good. Location is the primary point to consider in any miking situation.

Focus. This is the specific range of sounds you are trying to capture with the mic. Miking directly "on axis" will generally yield the best results, but miking off-axis can make things sound warmer. Correct focusing will give you the clarity or ambience you are looking for. Focus should be the second point you consider.

Balance. This is the focus point of the rejection range of the mic. It should be aimed away from unwanted sounds when possible. This will be the last point you consider in a miking equation, and it will be the least important one. *These principles apply to your instruments, your amps, your monitors, your mics, and even your position onstage.*

Burleigh Drummond—Drums
Ambrosia/Tin Drum
Mighty Mo Rodgers
www.ambrosiaweb.com

COURTESY OF TIN DRUM WEBSITE

"I tend to tune my snare bottoms very tight, but that's just the way I like it. Then I can usually crank one lug of the top head up or down for control. If I take it down, it'll give me a fat sound; if I take it up it will give it a cut for like a "Police" kind of tone. *For toms, I always tune the bottom heads lower than the top so that the pitch dives.* It will sink to the lower pitch; that's how you get that diving tone. I usually tune the front head of my kick drum low, where it's barely tight enough to have a pitch. I like the bass drum to be the bottom of the band.

The thing I know is that you can tune a drum and it can sound great to you on the stage, but you've got to hear what the mic is doing. Depending on the mic they're using or how they're miking it, there can be some frequency that doesn't sound right and it may not be audible without a mic on it. Live on the stage it may sound great, but when you hear it in the PA, you can sense whether it's happening or not. First I tune for myself on the stage with what I hear, then I may have to retune to make it work in the setup. It's not automatic that just because it sounds good to you that it's gonna work."

LINE INPUTS

Now that we have covered microphones and the principles you should be concerned with, it's time to look at other input sources like line-level signals and direct-input devices. Here you can make a difference in your stage sound and your mixes by providing good choices of line inputs to the PA system. Even when a source can be miked, it should have the option of a line source for monitors, and both personal and stage mixes. While contact mics and pickups are not completely free of problems, they have some advantages that microphones don't. They aren't quite as prone to feedback, they pick up less background noise, and they move with the instrument onstage. They offer a backup to conventional mics in the event of a mic problem, they provide an alternative signal to the monitors, and they have a completely different tone than a mic would. They often have more highs and lows than a traditional mic would produce, and when used in combination, the two sound great together in the PA system.

Without this, your options will be limited. Keyboards, CDs, and other self-generated sound sources have *total* isolation from other sounds and are virtually feedback free, except for turntables; they can get low-end feedback at very high levels. The needle is attached to a rubber-padded contact mic, and is one of the reasons why they sound so warm.

25. USE CONTACT MICS AND PICKUPS FOR PERSONAL MONITORS
Contact Mics and Pickups. I have mentioned throughout this book just how important it is to have a personal monitor, and it is with these types of mics and pickups that you'll be able to get acoustic instruments into your personal monitor and the stage monitor system. Contact mics are small transducers that can be mounted or taped to violins, cellos, guitars, or anything that resonates through its body. Typically these are Hi-Z outputs that should be run to a direct box to be converted into a professional line-level signal. Some will have mounts for jacks that allow the instrument to be plugged in with a standard cable. In any case, there are always a couple things to consider when using contact mics/pickups: volume level and mute. While a volume control will turn the output completely down, a mute of some form is always needed between the DI and the instrument output. If you are switching instruments while plugged into the direct box, you will need a mute to prevent any unwanted noises in your mix.

A mute will allow silent instrument changes without that nasty "pop" that happens when you unplug and plug in to a hot channel of a "live" PA system. Be sure to have a personal monitor for your instrument and use the pickup for the monitors, even if you use a microphone for your out front sound.

Acoustic Pickups. These transducers are *very* similar to contact mics and serve a similar purpose: they allow you to send a direct electronic signal to other devices.

Having some way to control the volume and mute for your rig as well as a personal monitor applies here as well. This also goes for internally mounted microphones, which often sound very good, but can still be touchy in the wedges.

26. USE DIRECT BOXES BEFORE THE AMP
A *direct box* or *DI*, as it is often called, is a small transformer that converts a high-impedance (Hi-Z) signal into a low-impedance balanced signal that is compatible with the inputs on a console. It's not that the console won't accept Hi-Z or unbalanced signals, it's that the cable run distances back to the console would cause a significant loss of level and pick up a considerable amount of noise if the signals were unbalanced. DIs also

serve another purpose: as a line splitter. You can plug into a DI, and then run another cable from the DI to your amp. This allows you two signal paths; one to your stage amp or personal monitor and another to the PA system that is completely free of the subsequent signal chain. Placing the PA feed at this point rather than behind the amp's electronics means that if the amp or anything else *after* it in the signal path fails, the PA will still receive a usable signal. If the instrument or cable that is *before* the DI fails, then all signals will be lost. This also makes it very easy to find the problem, as there are only a couple places there could be a problem. Placing the DI here in the signal chain also allows a clean signal to the monitors, which will generally result in less feedback problems than if it were elsewhere. This signal is also free from any EQ changes you might make from your personal monitor amp and provides an easily recallable soundcheck setting that will help keep your show consistent.

Earle Dumler—Woodwinds
Frank Zappa/Barbra Streisand
The Beach Boys/The Carpenters
Three-Time Grammy Award–Winner

COURTESY OF DAVID PALMER

"On a wind instrument, the room itself is part of the sound. My sound will change in every room I play. The louder I play, the more some rooms open up and get bigger. You do not mic my instrument at the bell, because it sounds like wax paper on a comb; all you get are highs! All woodwinds are best miked close toward the left hand, but you can use contact mics on sax and flute. While [these are] not as good as a quality mic, it gives the mixer the opportunity to isolate the signal. *Good mics tend to pick up a lot of peripheral noise, which contact mics don't at all;* but for double reeds, they don't work as well as an actual microphone. It inhibits your movement, but you can control the tone by changing the angle. If the mic comes straight on toward the keys, the sound will have more lows; if you turn slightly to the side, you'll get more highs. I can tell how I want to approach the microphone by what I'm hearing back in the monitors. It doesn't matter whether it's live or for a recording, it's the same thing. People use [the words] *bright* and *dark* meaning 'good' and 'bad'; *bright* to me means 'vibrant' with a lot of ring, and *dark* means 'dull,' a little on the dead side. I want a combination of that. I want a full sound that has a lot of ring in it."

DIs usually have a wider frequency response than an ordinary mic and are not subject to the same feedback potential as a traditional mic is. DIs are also free from a large portion of the background noise that would normally bleed into a microphone. So for many reasons, you should be using DIs on a wide variety of inputs. Acoustic guitars, electric basses, violins and cellos, mandolins and banjos all benefit from having a pickup/contact mic, volume/mute control, DI, and a personal monitor amp with tone-shaping abilities. Even a graphic EQ could be helpful in reducing feedback or troublesome frequencies. As you can see, an entire system is required to be able to get a consistent stage sound from gig to gig. While it is much simpler to just use a mic, doing so will eliminate your ability to take control of your sound. *Without the right tools to control your tone and volume, you simply have no choice but to settle for whatever you get.*

COURTESY OF CARVIN; USED WITH PERMISSION

Bjorn Englen—Bass
Soul Sign/Yngwie Malmsteen
Robin McAuley/Quiet Riot
http://bjornenglen.com

"I like to send a mic and a DI signal to the board so the engineer can have a choice. While the DI is more truthful, the sound of the cabinet is part of my tone, so I want to hear that. My DI is post-EQ off my amp, and I don't do too much with my tone after I soundcheck that would jack up the level. It's frustrating for most engineers. Slight changes are okay, but if you do something drastic, it could be a problem. I adjust my sound to the band I'm playing with to fit in the frequency spectrum and by using a pick or my fingers and where I'm playing on the strings, not just the EQ. You have a lot of options to work with to get the right tone!

I'm not a big effects guy; I use a little bit of compression, but I try not to practice too much with it. You can wind up depending on it in your playing. So far, I haven't found a wireless system I've been happy with from a reliability perspective. I'm not obsessed with this point and I'll eventually have to use one, but I'm still looking.

One of the hardest things to control is sitting in with a band on someone else's amp and it's terrible. That can be *brutal!* Bringing a good preamp can make things easier to deal with."

27. USE DIRECT BOXES AFTER VOLUME AND MUTE CONTROLS

Acoustic guitars, electric basses, violins and cellos, mandolins and banjos all benefit from having a pickup/contact mic, volume/mute control, personal monitors and a DI. As you can see, an entire system is required to be able to get a consistent stage sound from gig to gig. Fig. 4.7 gives an example of a professional setup that will yield the best results. This illustration shows a guitar tuner with a built-in mute switch. The output is muted when the guitar is being tuned. You can use this function when plugging in or out or changing instruments. When there is no mute or volume control between your instrument and the DI box, always unplug your cable from the DI first, then your instrument. This will reduce, but not eliminate, the popping in the PA system. When you plug into a hot system, plug in your cable into the instrument first, then plug into the DI.

Fig. 4.7.
Volume
and mute
controls

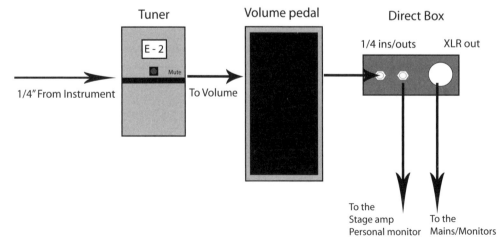

Tuner — E - 2 — Mute

1/4" From Instrument — To Volume

Volume pedal

Direct Box — 1/4 ins/outs — XLR out

To the Stage amp Personal monitor

To the Mains/Monitors

It's also handy for simply muting your instrument when it's not being played, which is something you will want to keep up with during your shows. You could mark this on your set list so you don't forget. You can see that the DI is located *after* the volume control and tuner, where they can mute signals when the instrument is being unplugged from the system. If it were located before the tuner and volume control, you would hear the instrument being tuned in the system at full volume. By placing the DI after the volume pedal, the main PA system will receive the correct volume levels when using the pedal to control dynamics. If your instrument has an onboard volume control, you could eliminate the volume pedal, but it is still a very useful item to have. If you are working with a contact mic or passive pickup, you will surely want some dynamic control. Having the volume pedal will give you options if feedback happens to creep into the show. It will also allow hands-free adjustment.

Direct boxes or DIs are not all created equal, but they all do the same thing: they turn high-impedance line-level signals into balanced low-impedance signals that can be run hundreds of feet to a console without picking up noise. Some are very simple, with just a pair of parallel in/outs, and others can be complicated battery-powered active units with gain controls, ground switches, phase-reverse switches, and input pads. Let's have a closer look to see which one may best suit your needs.

Simple DIs. This unit is a passive transformer that converts a high-impedance signal to a low-impedance balanced output. It will generally have two parallel ¼-inch inputs and one XLR output. The two ¼-inch inputs will often be labeled "in/out" because they are most often used that way. Neither one is actually an "output"; it simply jumps whatever signal is applied to it over to the next jack to be used as a connection to a stage amp or personal monitor. It can also be used to combine two signals from a stereo unit into a single mono sound source.

The only real "output" is the XLR connection. This DI can also be used to run a pair of inputs to a single channel, as would be the case with a stereo keyboard, CD, turntable, effects, or whatever doesn't need to be run to an additional amplifier. This signal will be a single mono output, but it will accept a stereo input. Fig. 4.8 shows both examples: with and without a stage amp.

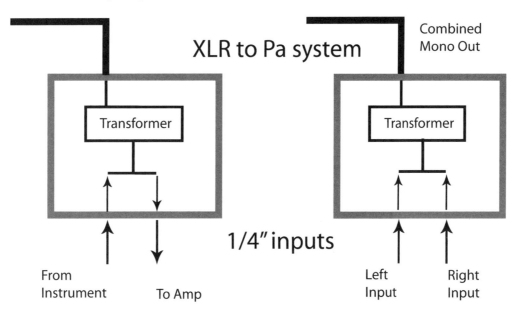

XLR to Pa system

Combined Mono Out

Fig. 4.8. Simple DI box

Transformer

Transformer

1/4" inputs

From Instrument

To Amp

Left Input

Right Input

Phantom-Powered and Active Direct Boxes. While most DIs are quite simple, they can range from battery-operated units to phantom-powered devices with gain, phase, attenuation pads, ground lifts, and multiple impedance-matched outputs. If you are considering purchasing one, I would probably recommend one in the midrange category: a passive DI with a ground lift and input level pad. It's simple and reliable, but has the most common features that would make it useful.

Fig. 4.9.
Active DI box

Active direct boxes also bring in keyboard signals, tape/DAT/CD, DJ equipment and anything else that doesn't have an XLR output. Some of these setups aren't quite as elaborate as others, but keyboards can get into a world of their own when it comes to being complicated. Even a medium-size three-tiered keyboard rig can get sloppy. It has always been my philosophy that the simpler things are, the more reliable they are, and this would be no exception. Active DIs can add gain before the signal is sent to the console and reduce the amount of noise that is picked up on the way, which is why most engineers prefer them for low-level signals. Fig. 4.9 shows an example of this type of DI box.

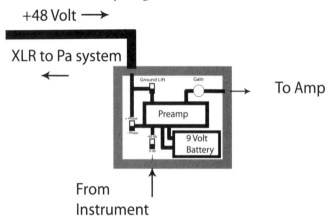

+48 Volt →

XLR to Pa system
←

Ground Lift   Gain

Preamp

+ Phase
- Phase

9 Volt
Battery

To Amp →

From
Instrument

COURTESY OF DUG PINNICK

dUg Pinnick—Vocals/Bass
King's X/Living Colour
The Mob/Poundhound
www.kingsxrocks.com

"For my bass, I have two signals: one goes to the high-end amps and the other goes to the low-end amps. I use an EQ before both preamps to focus each sound. The high amps get mostly highs and the others get mostly lows, but I don't use a crossover or it'll eliminate the overlap between them. I also compress the low end heavily so that no matter where I go on the neck, my low end always comes up; the high end always seems to be there regardless. This allows me to have the best control for each. I do the same thing going from the preamps to the amp just to get rid of anything I don't want! *One of the things I'm looking for in my tone is sustain, so it needs to be loud enough to carry some sustain.*

If you're not a tone chaser, then you'll never have a good sound. You really have to work on this. Some guys just plug in, and the engineer can't put them in the mix because they don't have any idea. Bass is a very difficult instrument to mix in with a band. You have to understand frequencies and balances to get it into the mix correctly. If it's not in your ears and your hands, you're not going to find it in the amp. This is why it's important to be a tone chaser and tweak your sound until you find something incredible. *You need the low end to give it some bottom, but it can't drown out the kick drum. You need midrange to give it definition, but not too much or you'll cover up the guitar, and you need high end, but you can't make it too live or it just hurts!* You have to really stand out there and listen to see how it couples with the rest of the band.

To get my bass tone to balance with the kick, I'll turn them up and start dialing out frequencies until I can distinguish the two and have them blend. I'll do the same thing with the high end of my bass and the cymbals. When I can distinguish both, the rest is easy. You have to go after your sound, and if it's got knobs, I'm tweaking them! I think that bass players especially should have some kind of understanding of this, because bass is the hardest thing to mix."

Geoff Nichols—Keys
Black Sabbath

COURTESY OF ADRIAN CHARLES

"My own rig for years was two Peavey 1,000-watt full-range cabinets with anything from a 1,000-watt amp up to a 1,800-watt stereo with my own 16-channel stereo mixer. I did of course have to sometimes use the monitors provided by the PA company: some were great, some were crap, but as the old saying goes, "The show must go on"!

In the early days it was one mono or stereo mix from a mixer straight to the outfront desk via DI boxes, but as keyboard players' rigs became more complex, with samplers and computers and the like, nearly all the instruments went in separate DI boxes, which sometimes became a problem with all the grounding for each instrument, trying to eliminate all the hum and strange buzzing sounds.

At one point with Sabbath, I had 10 separate keyboards, including the Mellotron to recreate all the sounds, because there was no time to change the settings quick enough, but the sound it got was fantastic! For that, I built a special rig into a flight case; by removing the lid and hard-wiring all of the keys to a snake, it was quick and easy to connect to the amp and speakers. Ready to play!"

28. CHOOSE KEYBOARD DI LOCATIONS FOR YOUR NEEDS

Fig. 4.10 shows a couple of examples of how the DI box can be placed in the signal path. Each has an advantage *and* a disadvantage. In Example A, the DI is placed between the volume pedal and the onstage keyboard mixer. This will send a *separate* signal for each keyboard sound. This is very helpful for both the FOH and monitor engineers; it gives them control over the EQ, compression, panning, and individual levels of each sound. The disadvantage is that the signals will likely be mono. Also, having two direct boxes for each keyboard can really rack up some channels in a large keyboard rig. Another disadvantage to this method is that the keyboardist loses control over the blend. If there are some subtle elements in the performance that the keyboardist is going for, they may be lost if the engineer isn't aware of exactly what the keyboardist wants. Also, placing the DI after the volume pedal means that the main/mons will have the same dynamics as the onstage sound. If the keyboardist fades a keyboard out, it will fade out in the house PA the same way. Since the gain structure in the keyboardist's stage monitor will be somewhat different from the house PA gain structure, it may not always translate perfectly, but should work for most applications without any serious gain deviations. This is how the majority of accomplished keyboard players run their rigs; however, national touring acts may have a few more options at their disposal than most club acts would.

In Example B, the stereo outputs of the keyboard mix are used to feed the DIs. This will send a *combined* stereo signal to the mains/mons, and there will be no way to separate it in the monitors or the mains. The advantage here is that the keyboardist regains control over the mix.

Fig. 4.10. DI locations

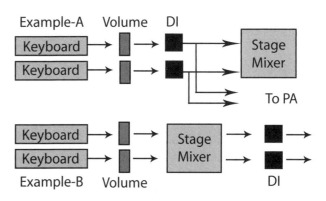

145

The disadvantage is that the engineer loses control over the tones and levels. When using the DIs on the keyboard mix, the keyboardist has to be fully responsible for his or her levels and balances. No one can pull up a single sound from a "blend." If a bright piano is mixed with a dark Hammond, there will be no way to change the EQs. Most of the time, I see this method of sending signals to the console rather than the individual keyboards in the DIs, but it is important to know that you have a choice.

I would like to point out that *under no circumstances* should the DIs ever be placed *before* the volume pedals in the signal path. Any adjustment to the signal volume made by the keyboardist would not be reflected in the PA and would create a problem for the sound engineer, who has to constantly attend the volumes of the patches. This is not the place for a DI.

LOOPS AND FLIES

Tape, CD, and DAT. There are a few styles of music that will run "loops" and "flies" along with the show. A *loop* is a track that usually has drum beats or some other type of rhythmic quality to it. It often starts the song, and then the band plays along to it. Sometimes there will be a click track that should run only to the monitors or a set of headphones so that the band or just the drummer can keep time with it. This part can get a bit tricky. Fig. 4.11 gives a couple of examples.

Fig. 4.11.
Setting up
loops

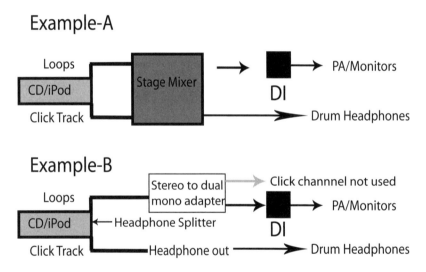

Example A shows a CD player/iPod with a click track on one channel and a mix of the loops on the other channel. Both channels run to a small stage mixer that allows the drummer to control what he is hearing onstage and provides additional headphone gain for loud stages. The loops are routed to a DI box that goes to both the FOH and the stage monitors. The click track is routed to the headphone output of the mixer that feeds the drummer's headphones. This is the "preferred" method of the two examples. It gives the drummer precise control over *exactly* what he needs to hear. While the click is the more important of the two, he may want some loop in his mix to be able to stay with the feel. A small stage mixer will be able to do this *and* provide a hotter signal to the headphones.

Example B is a simpler version that can work for smaller gigs. All you get is a simple headphone output with the loop and click on different sides of the headphones. Notice that there are some splitters and adapters required to make this work correctly. There will be very little control over what you get; it either works or it doesn't. The headphone outputs offer marginal level, so this won't do well with open-back headphones and higher stage levels. For most small, intimate gigs with simple setups, it will do just fine.

Loops can be recorded on tape, CD, or anything else that has at least two channels. The loop can be recorded on one channel, and the tempo track or "click" can be on the other channel. It should have a four- or eight-count intro. Someone will need to operate it so the click can be sent to just the drummer, who counts it off for the rest of the band, or it can be sent to the monitors and run at low levels, but you risk missing the count-in. This technique can vary considerably, depending on the skills of the person who is creating the loops and the equipment that is being used. ADATs, laptops, and MiniDisc recorders are capable of sending multiple channels to the PA, thus giving you separation in a stereo mix or even individual sounds on each channel. Using a stage mixer to control what you hear is essential if you're using headphones for this.

Erik Norlander—Keyboards
Asia featuring John Payne
Lana Lane
Big Noize w/Joe Lynn Turner
www.eriknorlander.com

COURTESY OF KEVIN MERCHANT

With Asia, I use five or six keyboards, all with different ranges of voices. It's a challenge getting the right sounds finely tuned for each song. I may wind up using five to eight different sounds that cascade within a single song, not just one sound to the next. It's really not as complicated as it looks; each module has a variety of pianos, and another has organs, synths, etc., so that I can have a full range of sounds all at once. This keeps my patch changes down to a minimum and I can focus more on playing and not pressing buttons. I use a Mac laptop to make multiple patch changes on all keyboards at once for each song, rather than having to change each one manually and hoping for the best, lol! If I do need to make a patch change in the middle of a song, I'll set it up in a logical system that allows me to press one button; like going from patch #27 to patch #37. I also use particular groups of patches for specific bands. One band may get patches 1–40, and another may get 41–80. This way I can copy programs and change them to suit the band without overwriting the sound for another band. Take the time to name your edits, too! If you use a bit of discipline, this can really help you out.

I use a one-space digital mixer that has an EQ and effects processor that is tied into my laptop so I can see my adjustments and assignments on the screen. It has spectrum analyzers, phase meters, and a few other items for diagnostics. This is really handy on tour; you never know what's going to happen, and having a toolbox like this is really important. The PA system gets a premixed stereo pair for both mains and monitors.

When hooking my gear up onstage, I have a procedure: AC power first, MIDI cables, then audio. I use about eight power cables, six MIDI cables and 22 audio cables. I'll always bring a couple spares, but my goal is to never need them. I do wind up using some spare footpedals for the keys quite often. *If you hook up randomly, it's easy to miss something and not find out until it's too late. If you have a logical system, it becomes easier to keep up with it all."*

Here's something you may want to think about when setting up loops and flies for your band: create them in the correct order that you will play them. Intros, outros, and any other show effects can be added in the correct order and will simplify this process somewhat. Of course, this means you'll have to decide on a song order and stick to it, but that's not a bad idea in itself.

You will also have to create this for each show you play, but it definitely cuts down on the number of false starts and wrong tracks if you do. This is actually quite easy if you are running tracks from a CD: simply create a playlist and burn it. For tracks on a laptop or iPod, it's even easier. For multitrack loops with more than two channel outputs, it's a completely different story. This requires a considerable amount of planning and execution to get right.

29. AN 808 SHOULD HAVE ITS OWN OUTPUT TO THE CONSOLE
This is particularly useful if you have an 808 kick drum running. The balance on an 808 is very critical: not enough and you can't feel it; too much and it distorts. Having it on a separate channel will allow the engineer to properly blend it with the rest of the mix and in the monitors (see Fig. 4.12). This example shows a four-track device with the click on one channel, the 808 on another channel, and a stereo loop mix on the other two channels.

Fig. 4.12. Multichannel loop setups

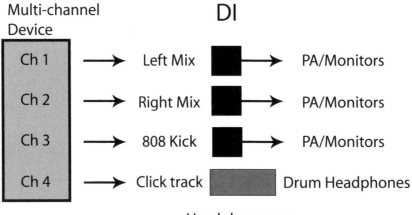

30. FLIES NEED A CLICK TRACK ON A DIFFERENT OUTPUT
Flies are similar to loops, but are intended for enhancement rather than as a backing track. A big vocal chorus, strings, or even industrial noise coming in at a particular spot are all examples of flies. A loop generally will run most of the way through a song, but flies will typically come in at certain places. It is very important that they come in at the right place. Click tracks are always used for flies. You need a click track to play to so that the flies come in at the right spot. You will want to create a CD or recording for flies the same way you would for loops; you will want to put the flies on one side of the stereo mix and the click track on the other side.

Frankie Banali—Drums
Quiet Riot/Wasp
Billy Idol/Hughes-Thrall
www.myspace.com/frankiebanali

"Clicks are the occasional 'necessary evil.' Rule of thumb: If you hear the static click track while you are playing along with it, you are probably already off the click. *Feel it, don't hear it*. Loops are easier to deal with because it's like playing along with a percussionist of sorts. I love old-school rock 'n' roll bands, because there are no loops, prerecorded background vocals, or the plethora of prerecorded instruments that may have been on the CD that you are promoting. But if that's your gig, learn to work with the click.

Miking the drums? It's pointless to wax philosophical about using this or that microphone in the studio or live, because none of the variables will be equal. That is, every engineer likes certain mics, not all engineers have the same mics, not all studios have the same mics, not all boards have the same EQs and mic pre's, etc. Get the picture? Then add to this the fact that no two performance venues or studio live rooms have the same acoustics, and it becomes the impossible dream. Trying to apply the same mic configuration, application technique, and acoustics from a previous effort to any other random effort is the definition of failure, purely because unless you only play one venue or only record in one studio, there is always change. And change is good!"

David Garfield—Keys
George Benson/Boz Scaggs
Natalie Cole/Smokey Robinson
Karizma/Los Lobotomies
www.creatchy.com

"I generally use two keyboards onstage and a MIDI volume controller for each of them. Analog pedals create other issues with noise and gain structure that don't happen with MIDI controllers. There's less to go wrong, and I can place my DIs directly off the keyboards because the volume is controlled from the keyboard itself. My bottom keyboard has my piano and Rhodes, which are my primary sounds and stay relatively the same, but the top keyboard has my strings, synths, Clavs, and organs, and *I use the volume pedal to blend them together*. If resources are limited, I'll use a mixer and send a pair to the system, but in larger situations I like to send both stereo signals to the house over four DIs so the engineer can have more control over the blend."

COURTESY OF GEORG VOROS

Georg Voros—Drums
eVoid/Black Star Liner
Jimmy James and the Vagabonds
The Stu Page Band
www.georgvoros.com

"If you're playing music where the drum sounds don't vary too much sonically, then you simply need to get the best mix of 'your' acoustic drum sound; in other words, that which sounds good to *you. A set of good drum mics would be the first option for me.* Or what about triggering electronic sounds to beef up the acoustic kit level? Maybe you need different snare drum sounds, tight high-pitched toms and also thunderous deep tom sounds, a compressed tight kick sound but also a rounder, jazzier sound with resonance? The answer lies in electronics! Bear in mind that these are merely starting points and every situation is unique, but you need to resolve your personal choices in a manner that works for everyone, whatever the end result may be. *However, the option of considering an in-ear monitor system should be taken very seriously; not only do they give you a clear mix directly into your ears; they also cut out excessive outside volume and therefore double as ear defenders.* Sounds like a win-win situation to me! I believe the more we know about the technicalities of our respective instruments and related areas, then the better for us, as knowledge = power!"

IN CONCLUSION

No one is asking you to actually run sound; you just need an idea of what will be the best option for *your sounds.* This chapter is here to inform you of these options so you can spot a solution to a problem that most musicians might miss from behind their instruments. The more preparation you put into your setup for microphones and DIs, the better you will sound onstage and out front. The engineer can only work with what you give him, so make sure that you are giving him the best signals and a few options to work with them. More important, give yourself something to work with, and this includes proper signals to the monitors as well. And no one is asking you to go out and buy a whole set of mics, but if you need a particular mic or input device for your band, then you need to integrate that into your setup and learn how to use it properly. Find a way to make it trouble-free, or at least low maintenance. It's not just about getting better tones, it's also about finding shortcuts to things you do every time you play. It's even better when you can do both. Always remember that your primary objective is to control your stage sound, not the FOH mix, but these two elements work together to form one amazing mix. Don't let your stage sound control you!

I would be very skeptical of any situation that required you to completely sacrifice a stage sound you're comfortable with in order to make things "perfect" out front. *Perfect* is such a subjective term that it really can't be used at all. While the audience didn't come out to hear a bad mix, they really came out to see you having fun, and when it's not good onstage, it's not fun. A live show has more elements to it than just the "mix," and if your stage sound is working for everyone, the performance will be better, and that's something even a Neve console can't make up for!

Here are the things you should consider when examining input sources for your stage sound.

1. Use Dynamic Mics for Dynamic Sounds
2. Use Condenser Mics for Complex Sounds
3. Cardioid Mics Are Semi-Directional
4. Hyper-Cardioid Mics Are Uni-Directional
5. Omni Mics Pick Up Sound from All Directions
6. Keep Omni Mics Away from Monitors
7. Ribbon Mics Have a Figure-8 Pattern
8. Use Volume/Mute Pedals for Bullet Mics
9. Most Unbalanced Mics Are Cheap Toys
10. Megaphones Work Well Onstage
11. Wireless Systems Have Less Headroom
12. Some Wireless Systems Are Better Than Others
13. Make Sure Your Wireless Is in the Line of Sight
14. Use Fresh Batteries for Every Show
15. Heavy-Base Stands Pick Up Stage Noise
16. Boom Stands Pick Up Stage Noise
17. Clip-On Mic Stands and Mics Eliminate Noise
18. Internal Mics Work Best in Tight Spots
19. Use the Smallest Stand That Will Work
20. Use a Shockmount for Heavy-Base Stands
21. Allow Space for Microphones
22. Get the Mic in the Best Location You Can
23. Focus Mics Toward the Best Tone Range
24. Use the Rejection Range of a Mic to Reduce Stage Noise
25. Use Contact Mics and Pickups for Personal Monitors
26. Use Direct Boxes Before the Amp
27. Use Direct Boxes After Volume and Mute Controls
28. Choose Keyboard DI Locations for Your Needs
29. An 808 Should Have Its Own Output to the Console
30. Flies Need a Click Track on a Different Output

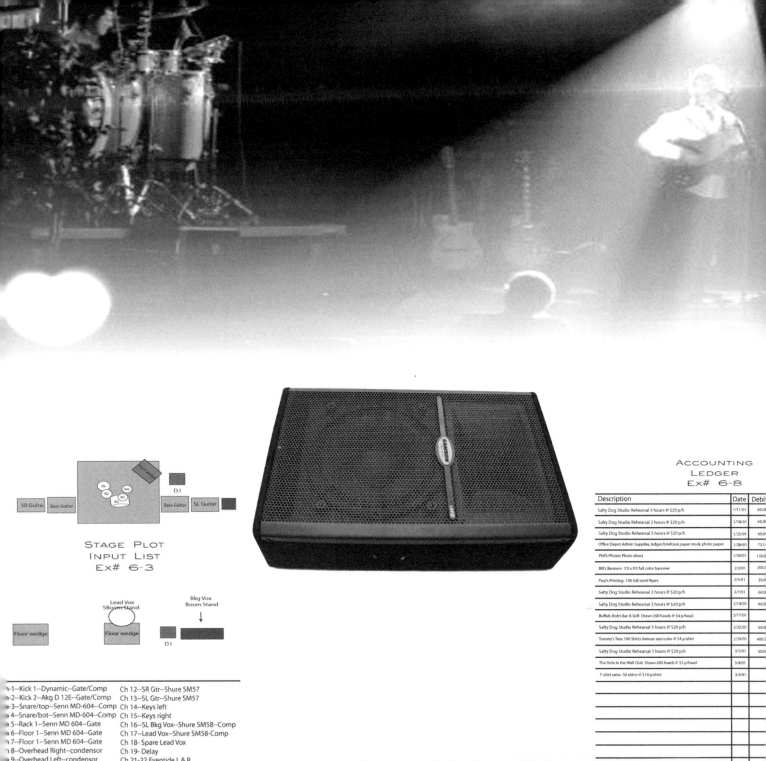

STAGE PLOT
INPUT LIST
Ex# 6-3

SR Guitar | Bass Guitar | Bass Guitar | SL Guitar
D I

Lead Vox
SBoom Stand

Bkg Vox
Boom Stand

Floor wedge | Floor wedge
D I

Ch 1--Kick 1--Dynamic--Gate/Comp Ch 12--SR Gtr--Shure SM57
Ch 2--Kick 2--Akg D 12E--Gate/Comp Ch 13--SL Gtr--Shure SM57
Ch 3--Snare/top--Senn MD-604--Comp Ch 14--Keys left
Ch 4--Snare/bot--Senn MD-604--Comp Ch 15--Keys right
Ch 5--Rack 1--Senn MD 604--Gate Ch 16--SL Bkg Vox--Shure SM58--Comp
Ch 6--Floor 1--Senn MD 604--Gate Ch 17--Lead Vox--Shure SM58-Comp
Ch 7--Floor 1--Senn MD 604--Gate Ch 18- Spare Lead Vox
Ch 8--Overhead Right--condensor Ch 19- Delay
Ch 9--Overhead Left--condensor Ch 21-22 Eventide L & R
Ch 10--Bass Cab--Shure SM52 Ch 23-24 CD Player
Ch 11--Bass DI

ACCOUNTING
LEDGER
Ex# 6-8

Description	Date	Debit
Salty Dog Studio Rehearsal 3 hours @ $20 p/h	1/11/01	60.00
Salty Dog Studio Rehearsal 3 hours @ $20 p/h	1/18/01	60.00
Salty Dog Studio Rehearsal 3 hours @ $20 p/h	1/25/01	60.00
Office Depot Admin Supplies, ledger, briefcase, paper stock, photo paper.	1/28/01	73.10
Phil's Photos Photo shoot	1/30/01	150.00
Bill's Banners- 3'0 x 9'0 full color bannner	2/2/01	200.00
Paul's Printing- 100 full sized flyers	2/5/01	20.00
Salty Dog Studio Rehearsal 3 hours @ $20 p/h	2/7/01	60.00
Salty Dog Studio Rehearsal 3 hours @ $20 p/h	2/14/01	60.00
Buffalo Bob's Bar & Grill Draw=200 heads @ $4 p/head	2/17/01	
Salty Dog Studio Rehearsal 3 hours @ $20 p/h	2/25/01	60.00
Tommy's Tees 100 Shirts Various size/color @ $4 p/shirt	2/29/01	400.00
Salty Dog Studio Rehearsal 3 hours @ $20 p/h	3/1/01	60.00
The Hole in the Wall Club Draw=200 heads @ $5 p/head	3/4/01	
T-shirt sales- 50 shirts @ $10 p/shirt	3/4/01	

Assembling the Tools to Make Your Show Consistently Great

GETTING ORGANIZED

Playing in a band should be fun, and it'd be great if all you had to do was show up and play. Sure, there are some people who can appear to pull this off for the most part, but you're not seeing the incredible amount of preparation that has gone into this ability. Chances are good that they've spent a lot of time working on the songs so that it all feels very natural. Even when they don't actually know the particular material, they have spent enough time on other similar songs that it's simply a matter of adjusting the chords and changes to match the feel. When you have gotten to this point as a musician, it can really be fun, but it takes a lot of hard work to get there.

This same ethic also applies to the organizational side of the music business. Just as you had to train your fingers and hands to automatically know what to do, you will have to train your mind to keep up with the multitude of information that goes into a professional live performance. It is here where even great musicians can be a bit lackadaisical and undisciplined. Just as you should work out all the arrangements to your songs, you should also work out all the arrangements to your show. Most bands simply prepare for a show by promoting it and working on a set list; the rest will take care of itself, right?

Other bands put an enormous amount of time and effort into appearances and stage props, but fail to coordinate the lights and stage layout that will give these enhancements maximum effect. It would be of little use to place something onstage that couldn't be seen properly or that had a negative effect on the show. The logistics of getting everything to and from the gig, storing these items properly between soundcheck and showtime, and getting it all on and off the stage can be very taxing! Since experience is the best teacher, most bands don't think about these logistics until they have bitten off more than they can chew and something becomes adversely affected.

Even when these aspects are properly managed and accounted for, a good many bands fail to keep the business aspects of a band under control. There are more ways for a band to lose money than to make money. If you aren't keeping up with the finances, you may never realize this until it's too late. CDs, merchandise, and promotional material can greatly enhance your offstage appearances, which are just as important as your show. Unfortunately, everyone's situation is different, and life's lessons don't always come in the correct sequence. *The reality is that music is fun, but business is work.* There are some things you can do to keep up with most aspects of your show because they happen every show. Let's have a look at some of these logistics and see how they can help you make your show consistently better.

The Logic: If you want your band to be successful and become progressively better with every show, then you will need some way to keep up with all the information it takes to run a band. Keeping up with the things you are doing is the best way to figure out what is working . . . and what is not. Regardless of who actually winds up in charge, it is still each member's responsibility to be individually organized. And even if each member is organized, that doesn't necessarily mean that the band as a whole is organized, but it is a start. If each member went through these lists and wrote down what he or she needed to do, it would be fairly easy to compile this information and rectify any conflicts. Here are some of the aspects that often get overlooked by most bands:

> ▶**Band Inventory:** Do you remember everything you brought to your last gig? What if something was missing? Do you have a serial number to verify it if it were found?

> ▶**Stage Plot/Input List:** A picture is worth a thousand words. Having a stage plot makes your set changes faster. An input list helps your engineer set up faster. Having these lists for a busy show can cut five minutes or more from your changeover.

> ▶**Monitor/Instrument Cues:** Even when you are okay with turning the engineer loose on the mix, you are still going to need the right blend in each of your stage monitors. This is a great way to speed things up. Instrument cues tell the engineer when to anticipate an instrument change.

> ▶**Sound/Lighting Cues:** You could literally run out of breath trying to describe everything you want in your show. Trying to do so just before you go on is ridiculous! Even if you could, who'd remember all that? Put it down on paper and you may stand a chance of it actually happening.

> ▶**Show Plan:** Showing up, setting up, and kicking butt doesn't always work; if you're not prepared, it may be your butt that gets kicked! Each new venue will have different circumstances that require advance planning, like transportation, addresses, soundcheck and showtimes, set lists, promoting your next show, merchandise booths, etc. Not every club does things the same way every time, or with the same accommodations.

> ▶**Promotionals:** This is optional if you are not serious about being a professional; however if you are serious, *it is not optional!* Phone numbers, addresses, e-mail, press clippings, promo packs, business cards, flyers, T-shirts, and CDs should all be available when you need them. In most cases, you can create an "electronic press kit" or EPK in PDF format that fits on a CD or DVD and that can be e-mailed as well. Smartphones can store your info and send it out anytime, anywhere!

> ▶**Accounting/Business Records:** You need to be able to keep up with the money coming in and going out. Money problems have broken up many bands. This will cover your rear end in *both* directions. Copyrights, publishing splits, and business licenses are also part of the equation. After all, it's the money that will keep your band going!

Some of these things are optional; it just depends on how serious you are about being successful. Even when you don't feel the need to do some of these things, they will still need to be done. One person doesn't have to keep up with all of this; these responsibilities can be shared among the band.

Even though you don't *need* an inventory list, you still keep one in your head . . . sort of. You think about what you need before the show because you have to load it into your vehicle. You think about it while you're setting up, tearing down, and loading out. How many times have you stopped to think, "Have I forgotten something?" How many times have you actually forgotten something?

Even though you don't *need* a stage plot/input list, the engineer or stage manager is still going to ask you most of these questions. The engineer needs to know so he or she can set up the equipment while you're setting up yours. Even though you don't *need* monitor cues, at some point your engineer is going to ask, "What do you want in your monitors?" Wouldn't it be nice to have this available when you start?

I really shouldn't have to go on about why you need these things; enough experience will do that quite well. Most of this is already in your head, and each person generally knows what they should be doing, but a large part of this information is for the benefit of the other people who become involved in your show. They may have never worked with your band before, and even if they did, it would be highly unlikely that they would remember all the details of *your show*. They would spend as much time asking questions as they would actually being productive. Since most people can read faster than you can talk, a quick glance at a cue sheet can save a minute or two on just about everything and provide a point of reference during the show when they can't ask those questions. Having cue sheets will allow you to direct two different aspects at the same time: the monitor engineer can be setting up the mics while the FOH engineer is dialing in assignments. There's a lot going on in a show, so let's take a look at each section separately.

INVENTORY

Personal Inventory. Begin with your individual inventory sheet by writing it on a sheet of paper or as most people do today, by creating a spreadsheet in your computer. Either way doesn't matter, but the computer is much neater and easier to organize. It should have *at least eight* columns for each item, although you are welcome to include more. Having a detailed sheet for each major piece of gear you own wouldn't be a bad idea, either.

▶The first column should be a short description of what it is.
▶The second column should be the make; what company it is made by.
▶The third column should be the model. Be as specific as you can.
▶The fourth column should be the color; you may have a few similar items in different colors. Insurance companies and the police will ask this question in the event of theft. It is the most important visual clue for them.
▶The fifth column should be the serial number—a very important piece of info to have.
▶The sixth column should be for "Notes." This is a miscellaneous column that can be used for anything from repair/maintenance to loan/borrow information.
▶The seventh column should be labeled "In," and you would put an X here if you load it up for the show. If someone loans you a piece, this column should reflect that. If it goes out for maintenance or repair, then this column will be used to show that it's back. You can specify which category it falls under in the "Notes" column.

▶The eighth column should be labeled "Out." You would put an X here if you have loaded it out of the club. If you loan a piece, then you mark it here. If it goes out for repair, also mark it here.

Your personal inventory sheet should be the very first list you create. Take your time and be thorough. It may take you a week or two if you have a lot of gear, but do it. After you have gone through all of your main gear, list your backup gear as well. Include all cords, power supplies, extension cords, adapters, tuners, cases, and even small items like picks and sticks. Put your name and the date at the top. Once you have listed everything and double-checked it for accuracy, then you should make a few copies. If it's on a computer, then just change the date and print as you need to. You can even edit the list to include only what you take on a particular night. Make a point to add new equipment as it comes in. If you have a digital camera, take pictures of all your gear. Keep it in a folder with all of your equipment data, either on your computer or in hard copy. Fig. 5.1 shows an example of a personal inventory list.

Now would be the time to not only make your personal inventory list, but to also take a look at what you are bringing to your shows and see if you have adequate backup items, like cords and cables, batteries and power strips, drum heads and snare bands, cymbal screws and footpedal parts, and anything else that could be important. In addition to keeping track of model/serial numbers, it would also be a great idea to mark your equipment in both an *obvious* spot and a *not-so-obvious* spot. Mark it so that it is not easily removed.

Fig. 5.1.
Personal
inventory list

Description	Make	Model	Color	Serial #	Notes	In	Out

1. ASSEMBLE A BACKUP KIT FOR YOUR GIGS

While you don't necessarily have to carry all these backup items into your show, at least have them in your vehicle in case of an emergency. Keep them in a separate case or box that you can spend as little time as possible moving around. If it's a small case, you could easily leave it in your vehicle permanently so that you always have it. If you keep your backup items separate, there will be less chance of losing them at a show, or simply leaving them behind. You may want to keep an inventory sheet just for this case. It will allow you to mark off any used items so that you can restock them as needed. It really doesn't matter if it's your first show or if you are a touring professional: having a variety of backup items will make a difference at some point in your life. If you use something every time you play, it might be a good idea to have two of these smaller items.

While most top pros have technicians to handle these items, this is one of the things techs do to keep up with the national acts they work for. Until you can afford to hire a tech, you are your tech, and experience will teach you most of what you need to know.

Bjorn Englen—Bass
Soul Sign/Yngwie Malmsteen
Robin McAuley/Quiet Riot
http://bjornenglen.com

COURTESY OF CARVIN; USED WITH PERMISSION

"Making a checklist plenty of time before you go on tour is a great idea , as you may realize that the best deal on something is online or at a store far away. Regarding amps and cabinets: you should arrange getting these with the amp company or rental firm(s) well ahead of time, before you do anything else! After that's done, I go through everything in my head, starting with strings, guitar, cords, and lastly pedals, tuners, and preamps, making sure I have some extra stuff, and then I'll make a list from that. I like to do a lot of this myself so that I don't have to depend on my tech(s). Also, you can never have too many extra strings, 9-volt batteries, or duct tape. Bringing extra tools and screws is important, and looking at common things that happen will allow you to prepare better. Once you leave town, there's no going back! I also keep a lot of contact info and memos in my phone and my calendar and back them up online in case something happens. You never know who you may need to get in touch with really fast when you're on tour: attorneys, doctors, musicians, gear suppliers, etc.

As far as the music is concerned, I usually write stuff that's hard to remember on charts or on the set list. The goal is to not need any of this, as you often don't have much of a chance to use it in a live show. Everything goes by so fast, and there are too many other things to pay attention to (it's even difficult to read at rehearsals a lot of times!). Plus, the onstage lighting may or may not be good. Once you've played the songs enough and you're comfortable with the arrangements, you can take a better look at the details."

2. MAKE A PERSONAL INVENTORY SHEET

Why? Most equipment is covered under homeowner's insurance (up to a point), but a few auto insurance policies will cover it if your vehicle has been broken into. Even if it isn't insured, the police will need this info to start an investigation. You can't even go snooping around pawn shops unless you know specifically what you are looking for, *with serial numbers*! You can't look for them once they are gone. In most states, it is legally required for retailers and pawnshops to hold any recently purchased used items for 30 days and to clear them through the local police agency. Chances are very good that if your gear has been stolen, it won't show up right away or in one of these retailers. Keep your eyes out for private sellers on Craig's List and postings at rehearsal studios. You may find it onstage at another band's show, but have all your paperwork, including the police report, before you investigate in any way; simply let the cops handle it.

Another reason for keeping track of this data is for tax purposes. Most people aren't very good at tax issues, but if you are going to run a business you'd better be able to keep track of deductions. Even if someone else is doing your taxes, they will need this info. This doesn't mean that your band will have to file with the IRS, but if you are receiving a moderate income from shows, then you will need this information at some point. If you plan on making a living at music, you will *absolutely need to have this info!* And if your band does go "pro" in a couple of years, you can still backdate your equipment purchases and expenses for write-offs.

COURTESY OF MICHAEL MESKER

Alex DePue—Violin
Steve Vai/Chris Cagle
DePue de Hoyos
www.myspace.com/alexdepue

"When you're on the road and you have a number of successive shows, it's important to keep your own instrument maintenance in line. While your crew is there to help out onstage, you are still responsible for keeping these incidents to a minimum. If you're a guitarist or violinist, you absolutely need to have a spare instrument or strings ready to go, and especially for a violinist who only has one or two violins on the road—string changes have to happen fast . . . and I mean "sweating bullets" fast! And any fiddle, whether it's an electric or acoustic, doesn't like to stay in tune, especially when you're doing an outside show in Spain, where it's really humid. Acoustic violins don't respond well to this, and it's your responsibility to be in tune at all times.

Regardless of genre, there are a plethora of mistakes that can be made by choosing the world of music as a vocation, in particular drugs and alcohol and the whole party atmosphere that drew many people to it in the first place. *While it's okay to have a little fun along the way, make sure your love for the music is much greater than your love for the rest of it!*"

3. MAKE A MASTER INVENTORY FOLDER

Once everyone has made their personal inventory sheets, go through them and assemble a folder that has everything you typically use in a normal show, with backup items. This will be the master inventory folder, and it should be kept with the business records. This is handy for promoters and clubs that can provide a backline; it tells you just what is being used onstage. Having this inventory in your computer will allow you to send the correct info to the right people.

4. MAKE A STAGE PLOT

A *stage plot* is very important to a touring band. It requires a decent amount of graphic skills. You will need a computer to do this correctly. There are a few programs out there that can be useful, but pretty much anything will work if you can create images and text together. Using different colors can help bring attention to particular groups, like direct box locations or backup vocal mikes. Your stage plot doesn't have to include *every* physical aspect, but it should be recognizable, and the more detail, the better. The primary point of a stage plot is to show the engineers what needs to be miked and DI'd, and to show stage managers and stagehands where these items will be located onstage.

For those of you who aren't very good with computers, you can paste "cutouts" of your stage equipment onto a blank page. It is a good idea to make the cutouts to scale with the proper dimensions, but as long as the plot can be understood, it will work. Copying this cutout page will blend the cutouts together and make subsequent copying easier. (This is the "OG" cut and paste that has been around much longer than computers.) For those of you who are artistically inclined and can draw or sketch a fairly decent rendering of your stage setup, that is another option.

While these two methods will work in most instances, once you are sure which stage setup you want to use, you may want to take your hand-created stage plot to someone who can create a computer illustration and PDF file from it. Having your stage plot in digital form will allow you to send it via e-mail when you need to.

5. SHOW DETAIL IN YOUR STAGE PLOT

Start with the drums: One kick drum or two? Two rack toms or three? If the drummer sings, show a vocal mic in that location. Does the keyboardist run samples? Show the number of direct boxes needed. These items are what your engineer *really* needs to know at showtime.

Show the guitar amps, keyboard rigs, backup singers, acoustic guitars, and personal monitor amps, horns, and anything else that you normally use. Show their locations onstage. If you have a preference as to the locations for the monitor wedges, show that as well. These items can be designated with a simple box or circle; you don't need a stick figure for a vocalist; just put a square where they would stand and label it "bkg 1." You are simply looking for a way to describe what you need onstage for your band. This is *very* important for large, complex setups, but it's also very helpful for four- and five-piece bands. If you use some of the alternative setup techniques described in the book, like "crossfiring" or "doubling," it is essential for the stage manager to know this. If your setup is very large and has a lot of detail, you could use two sheets: one for the stage plot and one for the input list.

Fig. 5.2 shows an example of a stage plot. In the preceding chapters, there are a lot of tips and tricks to try out. The combinations make them exponential. As soon as you find a setup that works for your band, *make a note of it*. Once you have gotten to the point where you are comfortable with your sound and your show, you need to start logging the specifics. This is also a great place to mark your stage prop locations when you get to that point. That is what professional bands do.

6. MAKE AN INPUT LIST

The stage plot helps you set up your gear in the right place onstage. The input list helps you set up the mics onstage and get the inputs in the right place on the console. Your input list should indicate the signal source, its channel order in the console, mic preferences, mic stand preferences, direct boxes or XLR inputs, and any other pertinent information that comes up. Fig. 5.3 shows an example of an input list combined with a stage plot.

This is the way most pros do it. In smaller clubs, you will get whatever you get; in larger ones you will get some of what you ask for; in pro venues you will get most of what you ask for. What do you think you will get if you *don't* ask for it? There are two main reasons for an input list:

▶ You get the right type and quantity of inputs in the right locations. The stage manager may have to make a trip to the mic locker; make it *one trip*. S/he needs to know what kind and how many stands/cables/DIs to bring out. In some cases,

Fig. 5.2.
Stage plot

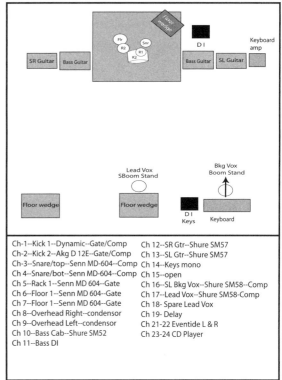

Fig. 5.3.
Stage plot and input list

Ch-1--Kick 1--Dynamic--Gate/Comp	Ch 12--SR Gtr--Shure SM57
Ch-2--Kick 2--Akg D 12E--Gate/Comp	Ch 13--SL Gtr--Shure SM57
Ch-3--Snare/top--Senn MD-604--Comp	Ch 14--Keys mono
Ch 4--Snare/bot--Senn MD-604--Comp	Ch 15--open
Ch 5--Rack 1--Senn MD 604--Gate	Ch 16--SL Bkg Vox--Shure SM58--Comp
Ch 6--Floor 1--Senn MD 604--Gate	Ch 17--Lead Vox--Shure SM58-Comp
Ch-7--Floor 1--Senn MD 604--Gate	Ch 18- Spare Lead Vox
Ch 8--Overhead Right--condensor	Ch 19- Delay
Ch 9--Overhead Left--condensor	Ch 21-22 Eventide L & R
Ch 10--Bass Cab--Shure SM52	Ch 23-24 CD Player
Ch 11--Bass DI	

you may have a couple of people working the stage, and having a stage plot and input list will allow all of them to do their jobs simultaneously and with the correct information.

▶You get the correct assignment on the snake. A group of inputs needs to appear on the console together: You don't want half of your drum channels on the other side of the board! One last-minute detail can change the whole assignment on the console or push something completely out of place. This input list helps the engineer when he or she doesn't have time to mark the inputs on the channel strips. This list also works together with your sound/light cues. I'm sure that somewhere along the way, probably in the beginning, someone will curse and say that you don't all need this. If you are a five-piece straight-ahead rock band, maybe not at first. However, I'm pretty sure that someone else will thank you for having one. Some stages, like the union stages in Las Vegas and Atlantic City, would frown on you if you don't have one. Who knows more about live shows, IATSE Local #720 or the guy at Joe's Bar? If you aren't sure *before* you play on a union stage, you will be *after* you play on one. These guys are pros; Joe's Bar sells drinks, and you are simply background music.

7. MAKE A MONITOR CUE SHEET

Your monitor mix is just as important as your FOH mix. If you can't hear yourself properly, or you can't hear the other musicians and vocalists properly, you won't be able to perform comfortably. Everyone may not get their own monitor wedge and separate mix onstage, and just because there are six wedges onstage doesn't mean that you will have six mixes to work with, because oftentimes they are "paired." This means that a single mix is sent to a pair of stage wedges to increase the efficiency and serve as a backup in case one wedge fails.

Depending on the size of the venue and the type of system used there, you will get anywhere from one general monitor mix to four separate mixes. Professional Type III and IV systems can have as many as 12 mixes onstage. Regardless of how many stage mixes you end up with, it is a good idea to list everyone's monitor preferences. If you get to a venue that has less than you need, some compromises will have to be made in the monitor assignments. Having an "overview" of what everyone is looking for makes this much easier for the engineer to make the right judgment calls. When you play in a venue that does have what you need, you will stand a much better chance of getting it *if you have a cue sheet*. The other alternative is to spend extra time on your monitor mixes at soundcheck; how often do you get to do that? This cue sheet really shouldn't be that difficult to make, and these questions are asked pretty much every show you play. If every musician lists what he or she needs in the monitors, simply combine the lists. You will learn how to adjust them for different venues.

What not to ask for in the monitors is another good thing to know *before* you make these lists. Here are two things that may compromise your monitors if you insist on having them:

▶**Effects.** Don't think for a minute that what you are listening to *is* or *should be* what is being mixed out front. Using delay or chorus in the monitors is asking for coloration that will be cyclic. The more of it you use, the more it will affect your sound. Chorus will throw your pitch off when you are singing. Flanges will probably feed back at certain points of the cycle. Delays will introduce a ton of background noise into your monitor wedges. Doubling will affect your timing, especially if there is a lot of it in the monitors. Small amounts of short reverb are acceptable, but stay away from long-tailed reverbs, or your monitor mix could turn to mush.

►Excessive amounts of drums in the drum monitors. Kick? I can understand that, because it's not in a good place to hear. Snare? You need some of that for dynamics. Toms? Here's where you start running into problems. Unless they are properly gated, you may wind up with some feedback. If you *are* having a problem hearing your own drums, you should examine the real reason why: Is the stage too loud? Are the amps too close? Once you have taken a look at these aspects and made corrections, *then* you could ask for some drums in your wedge, but you will probably need *less* than if you didn't correct the *real problem*, which is often excessive stage levels. On bigger systems that have gates on all the drums, I'd be more inclined to oblige; without noise gates properly set up, you are asking for feedback. Keep the drums reasonable in the wedges.

What you should ask for in the monitors is quite simple. After you set your stage levels to where everyone can hear themselves, then ask for other instruments and vocals in the monitors that you need to hear a bit more of. Get only what you need. Properly balancing your stage levels will reduce the amount of assignments and levels for everyone. Simpler is better!

Burleigh Drummond—Drums
Ambrosia/Tin Drum
Mighty Mo Rodgers
www.ambrosiaweb.com

COURTESY OF TIN DRUM WEBSITE

"If we're doing a major change in our show, we try to rehearse it before we go, and if we can, we try to refresh it at soundcheck, but it's a gamble if we get to do that. I'm responsible for the tempos, and sometimes we'll do a jam that leads into a song and it's open as to where it will go, but it has to come back to a particular song tempo, and that's my responsibility. *What I've learned is to have the chorus in my head before I count it off.* If the vocal is laying right, then the tempo is right; there's a very small range where that works. You really have to get that in your head. If I find that the tempo isn't right, my body will feel it; then I'll sing the chorus in my head and I'll automatically come back to it gradually. Just keep hearing that chorus.

For the mix engineer, we try to point out who's doing the lead vocals for each song because we have three lead vocalists. If he sets a balance of one lead singer and three background singers, and one of the background singers is singing lead, then it won't have the right balance. We don't request any effects other than a nice reverb, because you never know what you'll get, unless we worked with him before and he knows our stuff."

Lead vocals should be in all monitors to some degree; they call songs out, count off downbeats, and relay general information to everyone onstage. Background vocalists should have their vocals in their mix to be able to properly harmonize. Bass players should have a decent amount of drums for timing, and guitar for pitch. Keyboards are the best pitch reference for any player: they don't go out of tune!

The common conception is that drummers need a lot of bass guitar in their monitors, but most drummers are typically cueing off the guitarist for arrangements and dynamics. And while they do need to "lock in" with the bass player, it's usually the bass player who "locks in" with the drummer. The last thing I'd want is a drummer who's chasing everyone's meter around! Pay attention to what you hear the most in practice; this will give you an idea of what you will need onstage.

COURTESY OF KEYVON BEHPOUR

Tollak Ollestad—Harmonica
Don Henley/Michael McDonald
Kenny Loggins/Jewel/Seal
www.tollak.com

"When it comes to organizing your show, there are a few different stages. *First and foremost is just being really well prepared.* Nothing can take the place of feeling that you've done everything you can to know the material. It's such a simple thing, and I'm surprised how many musicians don't get it. Ironically, it's some of the better players that think they don't have to be prepared. To put it simply, always do more than is expected and you'll be amazed at how many more doors open for you.

I'll go through my set list and set out my harmonicas in the right order of keys so I can pick them right without a problem. There have been a few times when I didn't do this and wound up scrambling around with one hand on the keys . . . lol!

In other situations, even when you're well prepared, there are things that are really complicated. It's certainly no sin to use cheat sheets, so there are times when I bring my own shorthand. I don't think it looks good to have sheet music on the stage, but having some Post-It notes for tough parts can really help out. Whatever it takes to make sure you know what to do and when to do it, at least until you get it fully memorized. Experience will help your instincts for things like this. You'll learn how to think on your feet, which comes from jumping into situations where you don't know what's going to happen. *Playing in 'jams' will really help develop your instincts, and it's a very valuable skill to have as a musician!*

If you're lucky, you'll have a tour manager who'll help you keep up with the itinerary, but nowadays there's so many people doing double duty that this can slip through the cracks sometimes. The more you have your end together, the smoother things will be. You always get a copy, so you should keep up with it and make any schedule adjustments on there or you will find yourself hanging. These things are all about being a pro: showing up on time, being prepared, and having a good vibe are huge. Now that things are more competitive than they've ever been, you don't want to have even one element that's not 100 percent!"

8. SHOW INSTRUMENT CHANGES AND CUES

The second part of this list deals with instrument cues. Do you have acoustic guitars on one or two songs? Do you have loops or flies on a song? Is there a guest vocalist that sings on one song? A cue sheet will let the engineer know when to turn an unused channel on or off, because having an open mic onstage can cause feedback. These are items that a FOH and monitor engineer should know about. Most engineers will appreciate a heads-up in regard to the mix so they can be aware of when to expect these changes in your show. Unplugging an instrument in a hot channel can damage monitors and mains. If you have a properly set up mute switch, this won't be a problem. Fig. 5.4 shows an example of a monitor/instrument cue sheet.

9. MAKE A SOUND/LIGHT CUE SHEET

Sound and Lighting Cues. Every band has a vision of what it should sound like onstage, and your band may have some very specific ideas. Every engineer has a vision of what the mix should sound like out front. These two "visions" aren't always the same. Even if they were, you are limited by the equipment, and even then, most engineers have their own particular style that works for the venue. You could just get up there and hope for the best, or you could do everyone a favor and put your vision down on paper. While there's no guarantee that you will get everything you're asking for, without this cue sheet, you may not stand a chance. The same idea applies to stage lighting as well, but it can actually go much further than this. Even small lighting systems can be very effective if they are focused correctly. And a couple of special effects, like a fog machine or blinders, can really add some dimension to your show. If you're using stage props, it may be a good idea to have them "self-lit." It's been my experience that most engineers are more than willing to accommodate your requests on two conditions: 1) You know *what* to ask for, and it is reasonable; and 2) You know how to ask for it without being whiny or complaining. Now would also be a great time to whip out a small token of your appreciation!

10. LIST THE CUES IN THE SET ORDER

Start by listing your songs in the order that you will play them. If you are using an intro CD, list it first. Next to each song, make notes of exactly *what* effects, if any, you would like to have. Specific delay times and the number of repeats you would like are very helpful, but even general terms like "light reverb" or "slapback" are just fine. If there is a particular background vocalist that should be prominent in the blend, list this as well. Don't put "George," put "drummer" or "SR-Gtr" (Stage Right Guitarist) so that it is unmistakable whom you are referring to. If there are loops and flies, make a note of them and even make a blend preference like "heavy loops" or "light strings."

11. KEEP CUES SHORT AND PRECISE

Keep these notes short and precise, as they will always be subject to interpretation. Lighting cues can be on the same page directly underneath the sound cues, or beside them. Here, you will need terms like "dark on intro," "strobes on drum solo," "heavy purple" (or "Deep Purple" for those with a sense of humor). Once again, keep your requests short and you will be far more likely to get what you are looking for. *Limit lighting cues to three descriptors: 1. Intensity, 2. Color, 3. Effect.* An example would be "Bright Reds and Blues with Chase"; simple, yet very

---

Figment and the Hallucinations
Monitor/Instrument Cue list

Mix -1-- SR Wedge-- Medium Vox Blend, Medium SL Gtr

Mix -2-- Center wedge-- Medium/high Ld Vox and acoustic guitar, Medium Bkg Vox Blend, Medium SR Gtr

Mix -3--SL Wedge--Medium Ld Vox only, Medium SR Gtr

Mix -4--Drum Wedge--Medium Ld Vox, Medium/high SL Gtr, Medium Kick Light Snare

---

Song 1-- Intro CD-- Plenty in the stage monitors--No Acoustic Guitar

Song 4-- Acoustic Guitar DI up.

Song 5-- Acoustic Guitar out

Song 7-- Acoustic Guitar change, guest performer

Song 8-- Acoustic Guitar out

Song 9-- End of show, cue Outro CD

Outro CD

Fig. 5.4. Monitor and instrument cue list

Figment and the Hallucinations
Sound/Light Cue list

Order	Stage Cue	Effects	Color	Intensity	Effect
Intro CD Outro CD				Dark	Flashes
Song 1	Ld Vox	Light Verb	Red/Blue	Bright	Chase
Song 2	Ld Vox	Light Verb		Medium	Smooth Changes
Song 3	Ld Vox	Delay 375 ms Chorus only	Green/Blue	Bright	
Song 4	Acoustic Guitar	Ld Vox Slapback	Deep Purple	Dark	Fog Machine
Song 5	Drum Vox Up	No Effects		Medium	
Song 6	Drum Solo	Flange	Magenta	Bright-Dark Strobe	Strobe
Song 7	Acoustic Guitar	Ld Vox Delay 420 ms		Medium	
Song 8	SL Gtr Solo		Follow Spot	Dark	Blinders
Song 9 Encore	SR Vox Up	Long Dly/Vrb All Bkgs	Red Only	Bright	Police Lights

Fig. 5.5. Sound and lighting cue list

descriptive. Each lighting rig is different, as is each light operator, but they should be able to get as close as they can with what they have to work with. As your band becomes more successful and you play better shows with more resources, you will find more ways to improve your performance. This is a great way to get started.

Keep in mind that these cue sheets don't *require* anyone to actually follow them to the letter, but if you don't have some idea of what you are looking for in your show, then you can't ask anyone else to know. For those of you who are in a position to hire your own sound and light operators, these lists can be as detailed as you like, although you're still working with house gear.

Fig. 5.5 gives an example of a sound/lighting cue sheet.

12. MAKE A SHOW PLAN AND ITINERARY

This particular sheet contains all the information you need to know for the show. When is it? Where is it? What time is load-in? What time do we go on? Who else is on the bill? What is our set list? Who is riding with whom? Bar tab? Dressing room? Contact person and phone number? All of this is information you should have before playing a show.

COURTESY OF DAVID HAPLEY

David Garfield—Keys
George Benson/Boz Scaggs
Natalie Cole/Smokey Robinson
Karizma/Los Lobotomies
www.creatchy.com

"*To keep my band organized, I have a recording of every song we play for reference*, even if it's not exactly the same version, which would be helpful. I keep all of them in my iTunes and on iDisc. For each song, I try to have a folder with charts, sheet music, and audio files. This way I can either burn someone a disc or e-mail a file. I also carry a tub of sheet music and charts for my repertoire. While I intentionally don't play the songs exactly the same way every night, it's a great place to start from. I'd never ask one player to emulate another; this is the magic of a live performance!

I have folders for itineraries, schedules, and technical specs, but now everything is going digital, and I get so many e-mails for these that I'm moving away from folders and storing them all on my computer and phone. *I keep a list of everyone's equipment in my band so I can spec out backline and monitor requirements, along with stage plots and input lists; whatever is needed for the show.* Yet as an artist you can get bogged down with all this stuff. Larger acts will have their tour manager handle these issues, and I like to stay focused on the music."

Typically, you almost always get this information anyway, but I seriously doubt that you have it all on one page and that everyone has a copy. You may not need this when you are playing a regular gig—same time/same place—but having an itinerary is very handy when playing a new club out of your usual area.

Fig. 5.6 shows an example of this. Having a map printout with the correct address and phone number is very smart. You can figure routes and travel times for the time of day that you will be traveling. While there's no way to cut it down to the minute, expect the unexpected and you'll be okay. *I have found that by planning my day backward from the most important time, I'm able to get a much more realistic look at what it will take to make it all happen.* There's no time-saving on some aspects, but if you look at all the finite considerations, it becomes much easier to account for the variables.

Fig. 5.6. Show plan/itinerary

12-31-01 Saturday 10:30pm-12:00 pm
The Watering Hole 19654 Camelback Dr, Phoenix AZ-Guy Dude/602-333-7777
381 Miles/60 mph avg= 6.4 hours
8:00am Load Up from Reherarsal space
9:00am En Route
3:20pm Arrive at Venue
4:00pm Load in and setup
5:00pm Soundcheck
5:30pm Set Strike
6:00pm Meal, Showers Provided-Dress for show
9:00pm Set up Promo and Merchandise
10:15pm Set up for show
10:30pm Showtime
12:00pm Set Strike and Load out
12:30pm Promotion and PR
1:00am Load out Merchandise Finalize Business
2:00pm Hotel Check in

Take Los Angeles freeway 10 East all the way to Phoenix Az
Exit North on Central Ave, go approx 2 miles
Turn Right on Camelback Rd, go approx 1/2 mile
The Watering Hole on right, drive to the back of club

1 meal, 2 drinks, 1 guest per band member
Dressing Room with shower
(1) 3' x 6' merch table Club takes 10% of all merch sales
Opener/Joe Schmoe -- Support/Wasted Breath -- Closing/Last Chance Band

Dave Foreman—Guitar/Bass
Snoop Dogg/Christina Aguilera
Jay Z/Rihanna/Boyz II Men

"When I learn songs, I learn the title and lyrics of the song, and it helps me remember the arrangements so I can improvise when I need to. I can take a picture of a song in my head, and even remember the key. Since I play by ear, I rely on my ability to hear everything onstage. I don't usually run a lot of effects; I want you to hear what the guitar really sounds like. It's more interesting to me. I'll use a distortion and a wah pedal, but that's about it. I don't feel comfortable relying on effects for my vibe, and it helps me establish my tone onstage. *I've gotten used to not always having soundcheck, and this allows me to just get up there and go; I can always find my tone.*

For bass or acoustic, I prefer active DIs, because I get a warmer tone. I use my tuner as a mute to keep things quiet when I'm not playing and prevent any popping when I plug in and out. I don't use both stage amps and monitors for acoustic; it's got to be one or the other. Sometimes I'll get a little feedback if I run them both; the low end likes to just take off. I try to meet the engineers halfway at soundcheck and keep it as simple as I can. It makes things go quicker; I don't like turning soundcheck into a rehearsal. I find that a lot of engineers will show their appreciation for this. I don't like in-ear monitors *at all*; I love the natural sound of the stage balance. I don't want it too loud, because I still want to hear some of the house levels. If I can't hear any of the house, I know we are too loud onstage!"

Fig. 5.7.
Promotional
data

13. ORGANIZE YOUR PROMOTIONAL MATERIALS

This is often more than just a list, especially if you are selling T-shirts and other items. You can approach this quite a few ways as well. Some items like T-shirts can take up most of a page just by themselves. It may be a good idea to assemble a "master list" and then break the larger items down into digestible pieces. Of course, this means you will have an extra step to account for, but there's rarely one perfect document that will have everything you need to know on it.

Let's start with the "promo" items. You will need some way to organize and collate your promo, so a briefcase and boxes would be handy. Stickers, flyers, 8×10 band shots, CDs, DVDs, T-shirts, and other promotional stuff should be taken to every show. Anything that is "for sale" should have a log sheet that shows the sales for these items. It would also be a good idea to keep up with the non-sale items (see Fig. 5.7). You need to know how many of each type have come in and how many have sold. This will let you know when to reorder *before* you run out.

Promo Item	Unit Cost	Sell Price	Qty Stock	Qty Sold
8" x 10" B&W Photos				
8" x 10" Color Photos				
Phil's Photo's-818-639-4215				
CD's				
DVD's				
Electronic Press Kit				
Dan's Discs-213-324-6798				
4" x 6" Color Promo Cards				
3" x 4" Small Stickers				
4" x 10 Bumper Stickers				
Stan's Stickers-626-567-4325				
T-Shirts				
Teddys				
Hats				
Tommy's Tees-714-876-0285				

Clear storage containers with different size and color shirts are handy and let you know when it's time to restock the bin. Having band photos is convenient when someone asks for autographs, but generally they are for posting at shows. Stickers, cards, and flyers should be left on tables right before, during, or after your band plays so that you hit your audience while their memory is still fresh. Right after a great show that's had a favorable audience response is usually best. If you place them on tables too soon they will often wind up on the floor or in the "round file." Placing them too late is exactly that: *too late!* Make sure you include your website and upcoming show info on flyers, because you want your fans to know what's going on.

14. PURCHASE AND USE A LEDGER SHEET

Accounting and Business Records. There is a lot of information involved with a regularly gigging band that doesn't get organized until there is a problem. Financial records, club and promoter contacts, press clippings, advertisement info, artwork masters, and data CDs should all be kept together. This is where a briefcase or laptop really comes in handy.

One of the most important records you can keep is the financials. This should start *before* you make a dime! Did you take out an ad looking for other musicians? Log it. Did you rent a rehearsal space to audition them? Log it. Banners, artwork, flyers, strings and sticks, gas to rehearsals, anything that you spend on this band should be logged in the accounting book, *even the price of the book itself!* Fig. 5.8 gives an example of a ledger sheet. If you are selling T-shirts and CDs, you will have to pay money up front for that. You will want to see it come back, with *profit!*

Fig. 5.8.
Accounting
ledger

Description	Date	Debit (-)	Credit (+)	Totals
Salty Dog Studio Rehearsal 3 hours @ $20 p/h	1/11/01	60.00		
Salty Dog Studio Rehearsal 3 hours @ $20 p/h	1/18/01	60.00		-120.00
Salty Dog Studio Rehearsal 3 hours @ $20 p/h	1/25/01	60.00		-180.00
Office Depot Admin Supplies, ledger, briefcase, paper stock, photo paper.	1/28/01	73.14		-253.14
Phil's Photos Photo shoot	1/30/01	150.00		-403.14
Bill's Banners- 3'0 x 9'0 full color bannner	2/2/01	200.00		-603.14
Paul's Printing- 100 full sized flyers	2/5/01	20.00		-623.14
Salty Dog Studio Rehearsal 3 hours @ $20 p/h	2/7/01	60.00		-683.14
Salty Dog Studio Rehearsal 3 hours @ $20 p/h	2/14/01	60.00		-743.14
Buffalo Bob's Bar & Grill Draw=200 heads @ $4 p/head	2/17/01		800.00	+56.86
Salty Dog Studio Rehearsal 3 hours @ $20 p/h	2/25/01	60.00		-3.14
Tommy's Tees 100 Shirts Various size/color @ $4 p/shirt	2/29/01	400.00		-403.14
Salty Dog Studio Rehearsal 3 hours @ $20 p/h	3/1/01	60.00		-463.14
The Hole in the Wall Club Draw=200 heads @ $5 p/head	3/4/01		1000.00	+536.86
T-shirt sales- 50 shirts @ $10 p/shirt	3/4/01		500.00	+1036.86

15. GET A BUSINESS LICENSE

If you have a good band and you're ready to start playing shows, it's time to get a business license. Having a business license will prevent taxes from being automatically deducted from your larger gigs. It will also allow you to deduct the expenses on your tax return. You may lose some money the first year or two, and you will want to be able to deduct that. Most bands wait until they are actually making some good money before they start claiming deductions, but that would leave them holding the bag for the first couple years of losses. Another good reason for having a business license is that it automatically helps protect your band name, even if just on a local level. Registering your band name is another animal completely, and it's not exactly cheap. A business license usually costs less than $100.

16. DO A QUICK SHEET FOR BAND PAYROLL

While this is great for taxes, there are other reasons for keeping good records. It keeps everyone honest. A quick sheet keeps things fair in case someone is putting in a bit more than others, and it also shows you where the "waste" is in the spending.

It shows you how much each member should be paid, which by far is the most important aspect of this exercise. You'll want to put together a quick sheet when adjusting payments for each member. This sheet has the totals from the master ledger, the account balance, the newly acquired band expenses. and the recent show income. It shows the amount to be divided and how much each member is to receive. Fig. 5.9 shows an example of a quick sheet, and it's nothing like your pay stub from work. It keeps people from asking where it all went, or just assuming that you're skimming some for yourself. If you are running most of the business aspects of the band, then you may deserve an extra amount. That however, should be decided in advance and agreed upon by all involved. And should you accept the task of handling the business, you need to have your act together.

When it comes to paying for band expenses, make sure it's for the band and not the individual musicians. Just because there is some money in the account isn't a reason to start buying gas, strings and drum heads with it; these are your personal expenses and should be deducted against what you make from the band. Band money should be spent on things that the band as a whole is in need of, such as rehearsal spaces, photo shoots, T-shirts, etc. Of course drummers often have more expenses than singers, but that is the responsibility of being a drummer. As soon as your band starts paying for personal expenses, you've let the genie out of the bottle and it turns into a free-for-all on the ledger!

Description	Date	Debit (-)	Credit (+	Totals
Buffalo Bob's Bar & Grill Draw=200 heads @ $4 p/head	2/17/01		800.00	+56.86
Salty Dog Studio Rehearsal 3 hours @ $20 p/h	2/25/01	60.00		-3.14
Tommy's Tees 100 Shirts Various size/color @ $4 p/shirt	2/29/01	400.00		-403.14
Salty Dog Studio Rehearsal 3 hours @ $20 p/h	3/1/01	60.00		-463.14
The Hole in the Wall Club Draw=200 heads @ $5 p/head	3/4/01		1000.00	+536.86
T-shirt sales- 50 shirts @ $10 p/shirt	3/4/01		500.00	+1036.86
PAY OUT TO MEMBERS - $25 Admin (Lead Vocalist)	3/6/01	25.00		+1011.86
PAY OUT TO MEMBERS-Total/4 (Lead Vocalist)	3/6/01	252.96		
(Lead guitarist)		252.96		
(Bassist)		252.96		
(Drums)		252.96		
				+00.02

Fig. 5.9.
Quick sheet

17. KEEP DETAILED BUSINESS RECORDS

Band records are very important. You need to keep track of club contacts, promoters, press clippings, artwork masters, show flyers, band photos, bios, press kits, inventory sheets, stage plots/input lists, monitor/instrument cues, sound/lighting cues, promotional information, and the sources for all the materials you use in your band. It's not a bad idea to keep detailed information about the clubs themselves, such as stage dimensions, accommodations, policies, and even a map. When you do your show plan/itinerary, simply keep a copy for each club. If something changes, you can track the changes. How you organize all this will depend greatly on how much you have to organize and how you would like to see it. You could keep a master list for every section, or just keep all related stuff together. It's entirely up to you, after all: It's your band! I personally prefer to keep it all on computer and print it as I need it. It's much easier to change. If you decide to do things this way, be sure to burn your data to CD every couple of months and keep hard copies for reference.

COURTESY OF CINDI CRAMER

Mitch Perry—Guitar
MSG/Cher/Edgar Winter Group
Asia Featuring John Payne
www.mitchperry.com

"If I have to read off sheets during a show, I've taken myself out of that zone you're required to be in onstage, *so I learn my material well enough to lock it all in my head.* If I have guitar changes, I'll have notes for my tech, but that's about it. I try not to give myself extra work. For a lot of fly dates, we list our backline so that the venues can have that ready to go for us. It's all part of the gig rider in the contract. It's the only way we can fly in to a remote show.

The jury's still out on wireless systems for me. I did some investigating on this, but I haven't been convinced yet. If your sound is very processed, it shouldn't make that much of a difference; mine isn't. When you're soundchecking, don't play when you don't need to. *Play for your soundcheck and not to put on a show; make sure you handle what needs to be handled.* Playing too long will give you too much time to dwell on what's not right. If you know what's going on, you'll know the mix will change as soon as you get bodies in the room. *The whole point is to get comfortable onstage and let the soundman deal with what's out front.* Treat the stage personnel nice—you need them on your side!"

At the end of the year, go through your quick sheets and your personal inventory records and put together a comprehensive expense sheet for your taxes. Each member should be able to produce his or her own expense sheet from these two items. I use these records in every business I'm involved in. I can tell you that this has helped me at the end of the year more often than not.

While there are a number of important details and procedures involved with tax breaks, you still have to keep up with the information in order to use it. If you are running the business of a band, you will also want to read up on how to do this. Many publications are out there that can help you with this part.

IN CONCLUSION

There are many different aspects involved in having a successful band. This chapter may involve more work than most of you will be willing to do, and that's okay. Pick out the part that really means the most to you or that is most relative at this point and start there. Trying to assemble all these aspects at once would be a daunting task for even the most experienced organizer. Maybe someone else in the band would be willing to help with one or two elements.

Pick the right person for the task. The detail-minded player should probably assemble the inventory and the stage plot/input list. The technical-minded player should assemble the sound/lighting cues and the monitor/instrument cues. The sales-minded player should handle the promotionals, and the business-minded player should handle the accounting/business records. It's these little things that bring the band together as a team and make each member valuable. When one person does most of the work, he or she may wind up resenting it, and everyone else resents them for "overdoing" it. If everyone gets a taste of the work, then everyone appreciates what the others are doing, provided it's done well.

Let's have a look at what we have covered in this chapter:

1. Assemble a Backup Kit for Your Gigs
2. Make a Personal Inventory Sheet
3. Make a Master Inventory Folder
4. Make a Stage Plot
5. Show Detail in Your Stage Plot
6. Make an Input List
7. Make a Monitor Cue Sheet
8. Show Instrument Changes and Cues
9. Make a Sound/Light Cue Sheet
10. List the Cues in the Set Order
11. Keep Cues Short and Precise
12. Make a Show Plan and Itinerary
13. Organize Your Promotional Materials
14. Purchase and Use a Ledger Sheet
15. Get a Business License
16. Do a Quick Sheet for Band Payroll
17. Keep Detailed Business Records

Jon Butcher—Vocals/Guitar
Jon Butcher Axis
Barefoot Servants/Johanna Wild
www.jonbutcher.com

COURTESY OF JON BUTCHER

"I keep track of song info, take that into my practice room, and work on it to where all I need to do is show up with a set list. With new material, I might jot down the key on a set list, but that's pretty much it. Before I take off on tour, I'll number my equipment with stencils for the road case stuff, and the rest I have my guys keep a close eye on. As far as the rest of the scheduling goes, I have two words: tour manager! Let's be honest; it'd be really difficult to do all this and keep my head clear for the show. I've found that their expense is worth it to me. My guy is both FOH and TM; it just seems to be a combination that works well together.

I'll keep up with the merch and promo in a peripheral way, but not so much on a nightly basis. I do bring my laptop with me and pick it up on off days, but I'm more concerned with the music. *I would recommend that anyone keeping up with this have a laptop; it just makes it easier and cleaner.* There's often time on tour to go over this stuff, and someone has to check at the end of the night to make sure the tally is right, but once the tour is over, I'm *all over* those numbers. Even if nobody's stealing from you, stuff can fall through the cracks. Make sure you have a business license when you're making money; otherwise they'll automatically take taxes out on some of the bigger shows. If you're making real money, you'll want to do business under a corporate name."

Guitar   Bass   Drums   Guitar

OUT FRONT
BALANCES
EX# 7-1

↑   ↑   ↑
Less accurate   Less accurate   Less accurate

More accurate   More accurate   More accurate
↓   ↓   ↓

Guitar   Bass   Drums   Drums   Drums   Guitar
Bass   Guitar   Bass   Balanced   Guitar   Drums
Drums   Drums   Guitar   Bass   Guitar

A Systematic Approach to Consistency

SOUNDCHECKING

Everything you have read in this book so far was to prepare you for this very important part: Soundchecking. Your soundcheck actually began in rehearsal. Everything you have done prior to soundcheck will affect the outcome, which is why this book was written in this particular sequence. Your tone was the very beginning and helped shape the sound of the band from the start. Everything your band has done together as a unit will shape your future. Anything beyond the ordinary "show up and play" ethic will take you even further into the next level. Chapter 5: Getting Organized showed you how to actively go after the elements of a live performance that are often overlooked by most players as a rule. While some of you may get a handle on one or two aspects, few master them all right away. Most of them are learned through experience, one mistake at a time. *Here is your chance to look hindsight straight in the face!*

Soundcheck is the point where everything needs to come together. If you have a good soundcheck, your chances of having a great show are much better. While this is not always a hard and fast rule, most bands feel more confident when they have a good soundcheck. The more preparation you put into your show, the better your show will be. This has to include *all* of the elements we looked at in chapter 5, not just the licks and arrangements. If you have carefully considered the contents of the last chapter and worked out the most important details that apply to your band, then you should be looking forward to soundcheck, not dreading it!

For those of you who think soundchecks are a waste of time and would rather just get up and play, you are squandering an opportunity to solve a problem before it becomes a nightmare. One of the main points of soundchecking is to get familiar with the room and have a look at what may be best for your band onstage. Spending an enormous amount of time on soundcheck will usually leave you disappointed; there are just too many variables to replicate in a live show.

So when you book your next show, do your homework and put together as much information on the venue as you can. Since everyone's situation is different, you will find ways to improve the stuff that helps and eliminate the things that are not needed, but without some way of tracking your progress, you will never really *progress*. In setting a "standard" for your show, you will be able to take an objective look and see if you are on the right track. You can then make calculated adjustments without overcompensating and creating a completely different set of problems.

The Logic: There is a system to soundchecking that is really quite simple. It starts with both the mains and the monitors *off*! Just like at your rehearsals, you want to get an even balance that everyone should already be comfortable with. You want your band to sound like a band *before* the rest of the system comes up. Once this happens, you add some monitors, get comfortable with them, and then you are ready for the FOH to start soundchecking. Bands that do shows with just vocal-only PA systems know this technique well. Just because you have a full PA system and an engineer or two doesn't mean that you can stop doing things the old-fashioned way. While this sounds very simplistic, it is the best way to avoid unnecessary compensations and adjustments to overcome balance issues. A mistake that many bands make during soundchecks is being overly concerned with the FOH mix rather than the blend onstage. Spend more time on your monitors than on the mix. I'm not telling you to forget about the mix out front, but you'll be doing this in an empty room without the showtime adrenaline and the inherent moisture and temperature changes that happen when a crowd rolls in later that night. The real point of soundcheck is for the band to get comfortable levels onstage, for the engineer to get comfortable with the band, and to develop as much of the stage setup as possible. Soundchecks are standard for larger venues and higher-profile bands. You won't always get a soundcheck in a small club, but when you do, you need to make the most of it. If all you are getting is a quick line check, then you should know how to properly soundcheck so you can make some adjustments on the fly. If you kept up with your previous soundcheck settings, you may be able to use them as a starting point in another venue.

Zones will be an important focus at soundcheck. Controlling your stage equipment and its zone, getting the most from the monitor zones, and finding the right balances for each of them is the key to making your stage comfortable. Keep the principles of Location, Focus, and Balance in your mind at all times and you will instinctively be able to spot simple solutions to just about anything. Try to replicate the zones and levels that you use at rehearsals. Take a minute to examine the stage and its monitors to find the best location for your zones. Visualize your stage setup, then visualize the best spot for the monitors and start there. If you do this every time you play, you may not always be right, but your instincts will become *very intuitive*!

COURTESY OF DARLENE WARD

Bobby Rondinelli—Drums
Black Sabbath/Rainbow
Blue Öyster Cult
www.myspace.com/bobbyrondinelli

"As far as getting the best sound from your drum set, make sure your kit is in balance with itself; be sure that the cymbals don't drown out the rest of the kit. I prefer to set up a little in front of the backline so I can hear the rest of the instruments before the monitors are turned on. From there, I want my drums (no cymbals) and a little guitar in my monitors. I can usually hear enough vocals from the front wedges and sidefills.

I like to see the drum mics about 2 inches from the rim, pointing down at the drum. I don't like to use clip-on mics for the snare in case I have to change it out during the show. For the kick drum, I like an inside mic a few inches away from the head near the beater, and an outside mic for depth whenever possible. I also like to see mics for the hat, ride, and two overheads.

Keep track of what you are doing with a set list, and mark any tempos or arrangement notes you need to keep up with. It's also a good idea to keep a drum rug with marks on it for your kit placement, and a good tech is worth his weight in gold!"

1. GET THERE EARLY

But hey, aren't musicians *supposed* to be late? Yes, and that's exactly my point; if you get there "early" you may actually be on time! My apologies to those of you who typically do show up with plenty of time to spare, but a large majority of our brethren have given us all a bad rap.

The real point of getting there early is not to stand around and be bored, but to see what the conditions of the club are like so that you can make adjustments if you need to.

If it's a venue that you know well, then you should have an idea of what to expect, but even then there can be some last-minute surprises as well as a few delays in everyday traffic. If it's a club you've never played before, getting there early is essential. In any case, here are some very different reasons to be early for every soundcheck:

NONPRODUCTIVE REASONS

► Oops! I forgot the %$@#^; gotta go back and get it!
► I have to get gas/strings/sticks/flyers/etc.
► I have to pick up "Johnny." (Johnny's always late!)
► Traffic jam/flat tire/jump start/speeding ticket.
► Where the heck is this place?

PRODUCTIVE REASONS

► I can get a really good parking spot!
► I can find the easiest way to load in.
► I can see what the other bands are doing for their soundcheck.
► I can survey the stage and see what would be best for our band.
► I can get my stuff loaded in early and be ready to go.
► I need to change my strings/drumheads.
► The first band didn't show and we can start soundcheck early!

So now you can see that there are more good reasons to show up early than there are bad reasons, but there is *no* reason to be tardy! Nothing good will happen if you get there late, and nothing bad will happen if you get there early. Tardiness is very unprofessional.

Atma Anur—Drums
Richie Kotzen/Tony MacAlpine
Jarek Smietana/Cacophony
www.myspace.com/atmaanur

"Bring your own drum rug and mark the stand layout on it, mark your stand heights, and use memory locks. Having the same setup every time makes playing easier and more fun. I have been carrying a tool kit with me for almost 20 years. In it are tools for fixing and maintaining the drums, various drum keys, two kinds of tape, glue, hose clamps, oil, WD-40, files, sandpaper, Band-Aids, extra wing nuts and screws, hand cream, a flashlight, reading glasses, and aspirin.

If possible, rehearse the order of the set before the show. I also suggest a short preshow warm-up to get you lose and relaxed before playing. This also means getting where you have to be . . . early! Matching preset volumes, knowing which effects are for what song and exactly where they are in your set will help.

Having a calm, friendly attitude and keeping an open mind will get you through every unexpected situation. *Peaceful communication is the key to conflict resolution and problem-solving in the music business.* Try to at least 'appear' to be humble and grateful. I find that soundchecks are generally a waste of time unless you are headlining, but you should do them anyway. Make your needs known, but be prepared to not have them met. Headlining is quite a different story, and your soundcheck is essential to the show being great!"

2. HAVE A LOOK AROUND

"Okay, I'm here early, now what?" Find the closest parking spot to load in. Go in and have a look around. Check out the current soundcheck and see how it's going. Pay attention to the stage levels by walking right up to the stage and having a listen. It might not be a good idea to walk onto the stage during someone else's soundcheck, but walk all the way around it, front to back, side to side. Listen to how loud their amps are, how loud the monitors are and what the mix sounds like out front. This will give you an idea of what you may need to do for your band. Pay attention to how they are set up as opposed to how your band sets up. Would the difference cause a problem? Is there an adjustment from chapter 2 that would help? Is the headliner striking their drums? What is the best way to load in? Is the rest of your band here checking things out too? How about the lights? Will this work for our stage props?

Once you have a good idea of what's going on, talk to the stage manager and see where you can stage your gear and what time you can get started. If you're there early, the engineer may get you started sooner. If you're late, it means that you don't care; why should he? Even if it isn't time to start your soundcheck, get your stuff in and preassembled. Tune your drums and guitars, set up stands, and do whatever else you need to. Now would be a great time to get something to drink, hit the bathroom, smoke a big fatty, or whatever. When you can have a minute to relax and warm up your instrument, you have nailed it! It is at this point that you know you have gotten there on time. Keep pushing your starting time forward until you have time to relax and warm up. It really matters! Showing up on time is simply professional courtesy. This is for the benefit of others you'll have to work with, and will definitely help their attitude when you do. Showing up early is not for your benefit only. It may not really matter to anyone else, but it will make things easier for you in the long run.

Bruce Bouillet—Guitar
Racer X/The Scream/DC 10
Epidemic/Bottom Dwellerz
Grammy-Winning Producer/Engineer
www.myspace.com/brucebouillet

COURTESY OF BRUCE BOUILLET

"Onstage, I want to be just above the level of the drums, so I set my volume while the drums are playing. I recommend that you walk out and get ear level with your amp for a second and hear what your amp sounds like. Once I'm done, then we'll go to the bass. If I try to check my guitar while the bass is playing, it usually sounds a little thin when the bass is not there. If I get it to sound right without the bass, it sounds even better when the bass comes in! On some of the bigger tours, they'll let us dial in our show on the first day; from there we try to stay with those settings for the rest of the tour, and if we have to we'll make slight adjustments. I used to put a graphic EQ in my signal path, but now I just do it from my amp.

Anyone with a pedalboard should have at least one 30-foot cable ready in case you have a problem and need to run straight to your amp. It's just so much easier than fighting a problem onstage; that will take you right out of your game. I try to make it where there's as little room for error as possible. I have a loop effect in my rig that I use to create some atmospheric sounds in case there's a problem with anything else. I can just create some riffs and improve around them while things are getting resolved and there's not much dead time onstage."

It's been my experience that not everyone is consistently late, but sometimes there's one guy in the band who is, or a couple of guys who take turns. It is here where you should exercise discipline and be consistently early. If you decide that you aren't in a hurry and show up at their regular late time, they feel justified, and it gives them a reason to be even tardier! Set the example or forever hold your peace.

3. GET SET UP AS QUICKLY AS POSSIBLE
The next step in this process is to allow your band as much time as possible to do a soundcheck. After all, this is a precursor to your show setup, if not the show setup itself. You want to get the drums up as quickly as possible; they take the longest to get set up, miked up, and dialed in. They should be ready to go in every sense of the word possible. That means taken out of their cases, tuned up, stands pre-adjusted, cymbals pre-mounted, and racks stood in place with drums mounted. Have your drum cases put away and stacked inside each other. This alone will cut 10 minutes off your setup time. You want them as close to the stage as possible without interfering with the preceding band's teardown. (Be sure to allow them a couple of obvious lanes to strike their equipment, though.) When the preceding band has cleared the stage, *attack*! Have everyone in the band grab some drums and get them in place immediately! The average four-piece band should be able to get the drums onstage in three minutes. From there, the rest of the band can move on to their equipment. An exception to this would be keyboard players with extensive rigs; they will need a hand as well. In this case, have half the members carry in the drums and the other half carry in the keys. This may mean a little more work for everyone, but it will always be worth it. From there, the other players can move on to setting up their equipment. Once everyone's gear is in place and wired up, you are ready for the next step. For bands playing their

first shows together, you may want to time your setup and see approximately how long it really takes. This is the only way to track and improve your progress.

COURTESY OF ARTHUR USHERSON

Wyzard—Bass/Vocals
Mother's Finest
Stevie Nicks
www.myspace.comwyzard1

"My experience on tour goes long and deep; with Mother's Finest we toured with acts like the Who; AC/DC; Parliament Funkadelic; Santana; Aerosmith; and Earth, Wind & Fire, to name a few. As a bass player and backing vocalist, I liked to keep it simple; that way there was less to go wrong with my mix. What I needed most was my vocal in my floor monitor. I got my bass sound from my amp, and the drummer and other vocals from the sidefill monitors; I could always hear guitars and keys from the source.

Each venue has a different sound situation, from boomy to dry to slapback, etc., so my simple approach would get me through every situation with the least amount of time spent. Also as an opening act, the soundchecks are very inconsistent and sometimes there are none at all! It's important to be tight with your band members and work together to make the band sound great; by being at the proper volume with dynamics so you can have a great stage sound. That makes it easier for the sound man to get that sound to the people."

4. START WITH YOUR REHEARSAL SETTINGS

You should take note of what your settings are in rehearsals and have an idea where to start, but you need to be aware of the differences between your rehearsal space and the stage. Set up like you do at practice, put the amps in approximately the same places, and turn your settings to where you normally do. If you have spotted an advantage before soundcheck, now would be the time to make use of it.

5. ADJUST YOUR PLACEMENT AND LEVELS FOR THE STAGE

If the stage is deeper, then you may need more volume from your backline or to upstage it. If not, then you may need less volume or to downstage it some. *If the stage is wider*, then you can spread your backline out a bit, but for best results try to keep it pretty close to what you rehearse with. Some of the exceptions to this technique are covered in the extra chapter "Unusual Stages and Other Oddities," on the www.rockinyourstagesound.com website.

It is rare that everyone will finish setting up at exactly the same time, so as soon as you are ready you can ask the engineer for a quick line check. Even though your levels and placement onstage may need to be adjusted, this will ensure that your channel is functional. This will apply to everyone as they finish setting up and are pre-dialed in. There is no need to be too exact about this part; there often will be some adjustments during the "balance check."

David Garfield—Keys
George Benson/Boz Scaggs
Natalie Cole/Smokey Robinson
Karizma/Los Lobotomies
www.creatchy.com

COURTESY OF DAVID HAPLEY

"At soundcheck, the first thing I do is make sure everything is in fact 'working'; that it's in the system. From there, I work on the stage sound and leave the mix to the engineer. Once the FOH engineer is happy, we're done! Whatever you do, don't go out front and badger the engineer in an empty room over the little stuff. It's a Pandora's box, and you don't want to open this up! The only requests I'll have is to keep me up in the mix since I'm leading a lot of the songs and melodies and don't start us off at full volume in the beginning. If you start off at the top, there's nowhere to go with the show. Keep us around 75 percent in the beginning; as the show goes along bring it up some, and toward the end take it up. It keeps the show dynamic.

When you're working with the monitor engineer, you have to keep in mind that you're not the only one onstage; you've got five or six other people onstage that need help as well. A lot of people seem to have no concept of this, and I think it's very important to show some consideration for the engineer and wait your turn. *When something goes wrong, don't freak out; try to keep a smile on your face and get through it.* When you're working with techs and roadies, try to have some respect for them. When something happens, I'll instantly react; but it may take a second or two for this to get picked up on, and it seems like an eternity. Just try to stay cool and not overreact or draw too much attention away from the show, but make sure you communicate what the problem is so it can be handled."

6. BALANCE YOUR STAGE LEVELS EVENLY

When everyone is set up and ready, play a quick few bars and check your stage levels. This is called a "balance check," and is where you determine your best location, focus, and balance. Sometimes this is difficult to do in a busy show: the engineer often wants to go right to soundcheck. There really is no need for PA levels until your stage levels are set. Ask for a quick minute to set stage levels before the engineer starts. Have someone stand out front about halfway back in the room and check to see if all the players are fairly balanced in volume *without the PA*. The drums, which are capable of levels over 115 dB, should be slightly louder than the instruments or just as loud, but you should balance everyone else equally. Everyone's perception of volume is different, so be flexible if you need to and listen from different spots in the room.

Don't just turn the quietest player up; you may have to turn the loudest player down a bit as well. Keep in mind that it doesn't have to be perfect, because that is impossible, but you don't want someone to be buried onstage. This only takes a minute; after a few bars of a typical song it should be easy to decide. Do a quick chorus from an old cover tune—you don't have to play anything from your set, unless you just want to practice it.

If turning the guitarist up makes her uncomfortable with her stage volume, have her push her cabinet back some. While it will matter very little to the balance out front, it will make a sizable difference onstage due to the "proximity effect." This also works in reverse; if the guitar needs to come down in volume, upstage her cabinet a little to compensate for some loss of volume.

For someone listening out front, the closer you are to the stage, the less accurate your perception of balances will be. The farther away you are, the more accurate your perception of the mix blend will be; *however*, your primary concern is the area where most of the audience will be. Fig. 6.1 shows how this balance will change from front to back and side to side. Once again, you should hear the drums slightly better in the center, especially when you are closer to the stage.

Sometimes it's not about the volume as much as it is about the tone. If an instrument is extremely bright, it will sound very loud. If it is particularly dark, it will sound muddy and indistinct. Often, it's here where most stage level mistakes are made. Since electric guitars and basses have the most control over their tones, these instruments should be matched with the drum kit. Everyone's taste is different, and this may be easier said than done and still keep everyone happy, but highly contrasting tones should be balanced to complementary settings. You don't want the guitar to sound like a bass, or vice-versa. Overly bright guitar sounds and heavy-bottomed bass tones are the most common mistakes by players. When each player is comfortable with their levels and tone, then you can move on to the next step. Since this extra procedure will add a few minutes to your soundcheck, your setup has to be quick.

Fig. 6.1.
Out front
balances

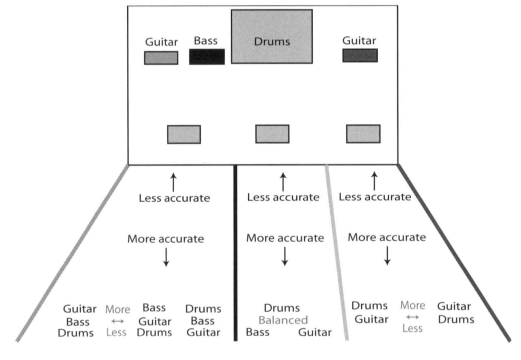

Glen Sobel—Drums
Elliott Yamin/Sixx A.M.
Beautiful Creatures/Impelliteri
P.I.T. Instructor
www.myspace.com/drummerglen

"I try to have my stands memory locked in place for quick setup. *Anything that can be done at home should be.* Not on stage during setup! It could be a "throw and go" situation where there is minimal time between bands. For the Ozzfest side-stage acts, sometimes the changeover time is 10 minutes; the band and crew need to work quickly and efficiently to set up on time.

Musicians should be prepared for less-than-stellar mixes onstage if they are an opening act or playing local gigs without the benefit of their own personnel. *As an opening act, a band is lucky to even get a soundcheck.* If it's a quick change or "throw and go" situation, the less complicated, the better. I wouldn't want too much in my monitor. For example, if it's a tight stage and the bass player's cabinet is close to or right next to me, I probably won't need much or any bass in my monitor mix. I'll ask the monitor engineer for some of myself in the monitor mix: kick, snare, and then toms, overheads, and hi-hat if those are available. Then I go to guitars, etc."

7. BRING UP THE MONITORS FIRST

If you have given the engineer(s) your sound and monitor cues, they should be already dialed in and ready to bring up at this point, beginning with the monitors. In chapter 5, these cue sheets and how to go about creating them were covered in detail. Now is where you actually get to put them to use.

Play another few bars of a song and check your monitors. Move around the stage to the places you like to be and listen for dead spots in those locations. There will be some dead spots on a larger stage, but don't try to fix them unless they are important spots. Simply avoid those areas as much as you can. The most important place for you to be concerned about is where you spend most of your time onstage. If you sing as well as play, you will need the spot where you sing to have enough vocals and where you play to have enough instrument. Make sure that the monitor is focused on that point before you ask for more monitor.

It's okay if your instrument level is a little bit low at that vocal spot, because you will be singing right there; when you are just playing, you can always step back closer to your amp. This is the third variable in the triangle: *your location within the zone.* And while drums and keys don't have this option because they are stationary, a keyboardist could place his vocal monitor on the side he hears best with and the keyboard monitor on the other side. From there, it's simply a matter of moving left to right to find the right balance. The middle is where you will place your vocal mic. Try to keep your monitor requests as simple as possible; don't ask for "all that and a bag chips" in your wedges. The more sounds you put in a mono wedge, the less you will be able to distinguish.

COURTESY OF REISEG & TAYLOR PHOTOGRAPHY

Mindi Abair—Sax
Concord Recording Artist
Duran Duran/Backstreet Boys
Lee RitenourMandy Moore
Adam Sandler/Keb' Mo
www.mindiabair.com

"I usually run soundcheck fairly tightly. I figure we have a lot to check in a little amount of time. I want to get it to the point where we've line-checked everything to make sure it's working, and then move to each member to get their monitor rockin'. *The better we sound and the better the mix is in our monitors, the more comfortable we'll be on stage and the better show we'll put on, guaranteed!* Once we get through the band, I'll ring out my microphone by singing different octaves and scales into it. I'll sound *t*'s and *puh*'s into it to simulate overloads at those frequencies. That'll show where the EQ is punched up and where it's too low. Always make sure your main mics are rung out before your band hits the stage, or it will be a concert of all distortion and feedback. No one wants that!

Last but not least, I walk around the house during soundcheck. I want to hear what the mix sounds like in the house. I want to hear what the band sounds like. *Usually there are huge variations in sonic quality from the front to the back of the room and from side to side.* I try to gain a happy medium of quality for the whole room with the sound man. I make sure I like the effects used. I make sure I like the bass-to-drum ratio, etc. I want to make sure that it's loud enough to get people moving and feeling the show, without making them hold their ears and become disengaged. If it's an acoustic show, make sure your instruments sound the way you want them to and have the right balance. If it's a rock show, make sure it rocks. The only way to know that you're achieving the sound you're going for is to walk offstage during soundcheck and make it's right.

Make sure during your show that you showcase who you are. Know what you have to offer, and feature it. Remember that you're there for the audience. Play to them . . . love them . . . don't ignore them. They paid to come see you."

8. CHECK FOR GROUND LOOPS AND FAULTS

Now is the time to listen for hum, buzzes, and weird stuff in your sound. Use a groundlift adapter (a three-prong to two-prong plug) to isolate ground faults. If there are any two-prong AC devices in your rig, make sure that they are not plugged in upside down or backwards. Sometimes, reversing these types of connections will fix the problem (or make it much worse). Use the same AC outlet for all your gear; this keeps everything on the same ground plane. There are exceptions to this, but only in rare cases. If you have worked on your tones, most of your ground problems should already have been solved.

9. USE A WINDSCREEN TO AVOID GETTING SHOCKED

Before you approach the mic, ground yourself with your guitar by touching the strings; then moisten your finger and touch the ball of the mic. If there is a ground fault, you will notice a small pop. Sure beats finding out with your lips! Sometimes there is little you can do about this; it means that there is a difference in the ground potential between the PA system AC power and the stage AC power that your amp is connected to. In some cases it could be your amp; try reversing the polarity of your on/off switch or ground lift. You can use one of those foam wind covers to keep from actually touching the mic. It changes your sound, so you may have to touch up the levels and EQs on that mic. The thinner the foam cover is, the less it affects the sound. As long as it keeps your lips from touching the mic, it will keep you from getting shocked.

10. REFOCUS YOUR CABINETS IF YOU NEED TO

It's time to fire up the mains. Most engineers will already have rough levels for the FOH, but you should give them a chance to work the mix. Play a verse and chorus of a loud song, and then play a verse and a chorus of a quieter song or one with different instruments. Everyone needs to know how the dynamics are going to work. Try to play your opening song last; this way everything should be as close to "right" as it can be. Sometimes the engineer will want to make some adjustments to your stage levels. This is the place for "out of the box" thinking. If your amps are kind of loud and overpowering the mix out front but you are comfortable onstage, try refocusing the cabinet so that it isn't pointed directly out front, but more toward you. The trick is to point it away from the sound engineer, but make it appear as if you actually adjusted the volume. Keep in mind that most pro sound engineers know this trick, so be prepared to actually turn down if you get called on it! Sometimes all you need is just a little angle to overcome a phasing anomaly. If needed, you can always take "a little volume off the top" if it has increased the levels too much.

11. USE EQ TO GET SLIGHT VOLUME CHANGES

Another method of volume control is to use the EQ instead of the actual volume level. By bringing down 100 Hz and 3.1 kHz just a little, you will achieve a similar effect to lowering the volume. The "equal loudness contour" is an effect of these frequencies becoming considerably louder when the volume is raised. When all you have is a three-band EQ, the high and low EQ adjustments work fine. By lowering *just* these frequencies a small amount, you can get a similar effect to turning down without actually turning the volume down. It will change your tone slightly, but it shouldn't be enough to cause a problem. A slight adjustment of the mids may offset any difference.

This also works in reverse. Let's say that the levels are set and everyone is happy where things are, but during the show you need a little more level. Instead of turning up the volume control, add just a little low end and high end to your amp. If you have to make a substantial adjustment, you'll have to adjust the volume level. But if all you need is a slight amount of boost, you can try to do it with EQ. It's another option to consider, but one you won't have if your EQ is pinned to the top! Try to keep your EQ balanced.

Using EQ to control your levels is a technique you should be aware of. If you are making a considerable adjustment to your stage levels, keep in mind that the EQ will probably need some compensation as well. The more level you add, the less "ELC" (Equal Loudness Contour) EQ you will need. While this technique is certainly not exact, it's reasonably close. The effect of ELC has been known for decades. You may notice that the ELC effect of output devices is very similar to the proximity effect of microphones. Why? They are identical processes in reverse. Studio engineers use this technique along with others to bring sounds up and down in the mix without adding too much actual level. You may have to play with the mid control at some point to rebalance your sound, but this is just another weapon in your arsenal.

COURTESY OF KEYVON BEHPOUR

Tollak Ollestad—Harmonica
Don Henley/Michael McDonald
Kenny Loggins/Jewel/Seal
www.tollak.com

"At soundchecks, I try to get my monitor mix as dialed in as I can. And when the room fills up, that can change a little bit. *Make sure you know where the monitor guy is located so you can make contact with them when you need to at show time.* You'll want to introduce yourself to them and create a good vibe, a principle that extends into being cool to everyone you work with! You'll find that people will be much more willing to help you when you need it, and it's saved me many times! It's important for both the stage and the FOH to sound great, *but once the show is going you have no control, so you just have to let it go and have fun.* If you think about it too much, you'll take yourself out of the show. You have to get in your comfort zone and be in the music. At soundcheck I want to get a feel for what's happening out front, so if there's something glaring I can take care of it, but most engineers are pretty savvy about things.

Regarding the mechanical aspect of your voice, make sure you get plenty of sleep and warm up; you can't just get up there and start singing. It doesn't have to be a long, elaborate warm-up, but don't just get up there cold. You can hear when someone does that! I have a particular philosophy that was handed down to me by my vocal mentor, George Peckham. He always said, "The mind is musical, not the body," meaning your voice doesn't just come from your throat; its true power comes from your mind. I've cultivated this attitude over the years, getting into a more relaxed mental space and just trusting that my voice will sound the way I want it to. It's essentially a Zen approach: stop making your voice happen, and let it happen. It's tricky, but the more you get the hang of this the more your voice will surprise you in a good way. You still have to take care of it; after all, it is a muscle and is subject to some fluctuations, but this approach creates more consistency and has ultimately been much more powerful than just relying on mechanical methods."

Alex DePue—Violin
Steve Vai/Chris Cagle
DePue de Hoyos
www.myspace.com/alexdepue

COURTESY OF MICHAEL MESKER

"At soundchecks, it's really important to eliminate the 2–4 kHz range from the violin channel as much as you can without compromising the FOH sound. I'll even go up to 8–16 kHz. So all those annoying frequencies that happen naturally without EQ have to be dealt with right away. The graphic EQ in my pickup system allows me to pull them if I need to. Between my EQ and the house system, I'm able to get a handle on most any adjustment I need to happen onstage.

For the most part, everything is important to me in the monitor mix. I like to hear everything so I can play off other people and not step on anyone when I'm in an improvisational role. I need to be able to find the space to say what I need say musically, so soundchecks can be a bit of a procedure. Once you have that dialed in with your own guys on your own system, the settings typically won't differ very much; maybe some adjustments for each room. I rarely concern myself with what's going on out front unless it's my own show. I've had the pleasure of working with some of the best FOH guys in the business, so I never have to worry about that."

12. LOG YOUR SETTINGS BEFORE AND AFTER THE SHOW

Okay, now everybody's relatively happy, and it's time to strike for the next soundcheck. Make sure that you record your settings and the locations of your equipment *after* you get offstage. If you aren't striking and are playing after the soundcheck, then write them down after the show. This is another handy place for a smartphone; just snap a picture!

If you *are* striking, take one of your stage plots and note any deviations from the plot as far as your locations are concerned. Each member should do this with his or her own sheet. Write your control settings down on the back of this stage plot. You will do this again once the show is over to see what changes you made during the show.

Keep up with these adjustments, and after a few times playing the venue, you should be able to walk in and nail it without much effort. Compare these notes with other shows you play and look for trends as well as differences. When you get to a show that gives you a line check only, you may be able to use these settings as a reference point.

13. BE CAREFUL WITH FANS ONSTAGE

Appearances aren't everything, and sometimes nonessential stage equipment can cause some unwanted side effects. A prime example of this would be fans. No, not your everloving dedicated followers, but those things with turning blades on them—*fans*. I know it can get pretty hot up there onstage; a fan blowing through your long hair not only cools you off, but looks really cool, too! There are some instances where this isn't a problem; i.e., when there's not a microphone involved. But the minute that a microphone has a fan blowing on it, you've got a problem. You can completely *ruin* a mix with one fan. If it's on a frontperson or is plainly visible, the engineer may be able to spot this problem quickly and get it resolved.

If it's on a drummer and isn't plainly visible, it may take a couple of songs with bad mixes to get to the root of the problem. If you are going to use a fan onstage, *be very careful* that you don't aim it anywhere toward a mic or across a mic. And use the smallest fan that will be effective. Two small fans set close by and aimed properly have fewer problems than a single-engine airplane propeller. You will be surprised at just how much "wash" can come from even small fans. The fan may need to be several feet away from a mic to not cause a problem; ask someone out front if you aren't sure. Sometimes you can tell from listening to the monitors; other times you can't.

14. PAY ATTENTION TO STAGE PROPS ONSTAGE

Bands often use props onstage as visual aids. You need to think about each stage prop you have and how it may affect your stage sound. What is it? Where is it? Will it block sound? Is it changing the way you are hearing things onstage? If it interferes with an instrument's amp, it may need to be relocated.

15. USE STAGE PROPS TO CONTROL YOUR ZONES

While your primary concern is whether a prop causes a sound problem, this very same issue can have a positive effect: a prop can be used to *intentionally* block a particularly troublesome sound from interfering in a sensitive area. Fig. 6.2 shows a stage prop that is blocking part of a guitar cabinet, preventing sound from bleeding into the lead vocalist's zone. While this is a nice trick in certain instances, the point is to understand what is happening and be ready to turn what normally would be a disadvantage into an advantage: Think outside the box!

Fig. 6.2.
Stage
blocking

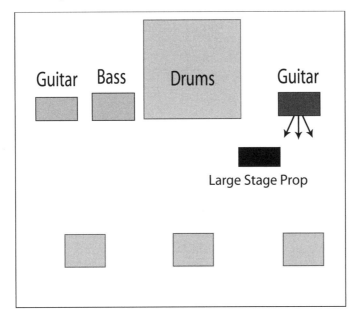

STAGE RESONANCE

One of the least considered aspects of stage sound is the stage itself; it can affect the overall sound of everything that is set upon it. You will need to pay attention to the low end balances. This will be discussed next in this chapter. Light wood frame stages are the noisiest. This is where you may have to really change your settings in order to prevent stage rumble from contaminating your mix, especially if the stage is "wobbly" or "bouncy"; it means that there is more opportunity for the low end to run wild onstage.

Bryan Bassett—Guitar
Foghat/Wild Cherry
Molly Hatchet
www.myspace.com/bryanpbassett

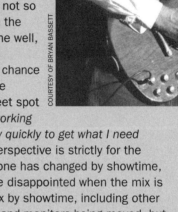

COURTESY OF BRYAN BASSETT

"At soundcheck, my objective is to get a good stage balance and satisfy our soundman from a FOH perspective. Most guitar players want to play a little louder than they should, so you need someone you can trust to tell you when it's too loud. The quieter you play on stage, the more you're in the PA. Unfortunately most players play loudly thinking they will be heard more, but it's really the exact opposite. You want a powerful sound onstage, but not so overpowering that you blow out the room or kill the people in the first five rows. That being said, my drummer needs to hear me well, so a little soundchecking goes a long way with me and him.

Soundcheck is more about giving the FOH soundman the chance to get a great mix so we can hit the stage running, but for me personally I can walk into a room and find my levels and sweet spot by the first half of the first song. *As long as my guitar rig is working correctly and set up right, I know I can make adjustments very quickly to get what I need onstage.* Everything else done during soundcheck from my perspective is strictly for the benefit of the sound engineer. Every soundcheck I've ever done has changed by showtime, so I don't get too overconcerned with them and then become disappointed when the mix is different at showtime. Many things can change a monitor mix by showtime, including other bands using the rig, monitor engineers losing their settings, and monitors being moved, but mostly it's the human bodies in the room.

When working with stage personnel, give respect to get respect; these guys are professionals. Treat them as pros and they'll act like pros and treat you as such. Don't be a whiner or a crybaby prima donna, and don't get on your guys in front of people outside the organization. Believe me, they will smile to your face but your rep as a musician will be trashed.

In my 40 years of playing onstage, I've noticed that while the level of production and equipment has changed considerably during that time, my approach to performing on it hasn't. I'm certainly more patient and focused on the music now . . . more mature, I guess, but a great show is still a great show—then and now!"

16. CHECK FOR STAGE RESONANCE

The sturdier the stage, the less it will resonate. It is also a wise idea to stomp on the stage *after* everything has been dialed in and all channels are up to see just how much is making its way to the PA system. You will hear it in the vocal monitors, but you are looking for feedback potential, so if a frequency range lingers excessively when you do this, you will definitely have a problem. There will generally be some resonance if you are stomping right next to the mic, but if it is very noticeable from several feet away, you may have to make some adjustments to the low end of your stage amps and possibly engage some low-pass filters on the console to keep stage rumble down. Here are some of the adjustments you should consider.

17. MAKE ADJUSTMENTS FOR NOISY STAGES

Bass Guitar. Not everyone likes the same bass sound, but everyone likes bass. Yet it's easy to get carried away with the low end, and higher volume levels make this even more of a problem. If you have rolled off most of the high end and upper mids, you may not be able to hear all the pitches and attacks correctly in your playing. Certain styles of players have particular "timbres" in their tone, but both the pitch and attack require some upper-range frequencies to be present to hear them. A way to know if you have entirely too much low end is if when you play a note, you can hear it resonate in everything onstage: the drums, the monitors, even the stage. The more resonant the stage, the more critical your low-end balances are. Always check your location and your focus before adjusting your volume and EQ balances.

Most stages are covered in carpet and it's hard to see their actual construction, but simply stomping on a stage should give you an idea of how it will behave. Doing this before you set up may change not only how you set up, but also how you dial in your tones. Let's take a look at some of the differences between stages.

Nick Menza—Drums
Megadeth/Marty Friedman
Deltanaut
www.menza.com

"I've always said, *If you can hear yourself really well, you're too loud, because you're not listening to the big picture.* I try to listen to the whole band in the house, not so much the monitors. I know the music so well that I could play it by myself, so I don't rely on monitors to do my job properly. Everything could go out and I'd still be able to play through the set. That's called being prepared. I try to disconnect from where I'm at and listen to the whole picture when I play.

You got to be prepared: having your stuff dialed in and being able to set it up, turn it on, and know that it's going to work. The more stuff you have in your rig, the more problems you're going to run into, and Murphy's just waiting to get a shot in—he's no joke! After you've done a few gigs, you should have an idea of what's going to work. Make it good and make it work wherever you go.

When you get into a situation where it's not sounding all that great, don't let it affect you. The audience is more concerned with how well you're playing. In a bad-sounding room, you can get caught up in it and start bashing away at your kit; and next thing you know, you're spent trying to make it work!"

Concrete floors will transfer less stage rumble than other types of stages, whether they are covered with carpet or not. Here, you could run a bit more low end than normal without a problem. There is a limit, however; low end transfers well in the air, too. But you would certainly be able to have more low end on a concrete floor than on a different type of stage. Heavy wood frame stages with padded carpet are popular for most permanent installations and also transfer a minimal amount of stage rumble, but there will be some.

Guitar and keyboard monitors should follow the same guidelines for bass guitar. It's easy to get carried away with your tone onstage: *If some is good, then more is better!* This is not always true. Don't think for a minute that you are mixing from the stage; too much will always be too much. Pay attention to location, focus, and balance before making any volume adjustments, and take stage resonance into consideration when you do. If the stage is very resonant, take some low end off your tone. Locating your cabinet farther away from the drums will allow you to keep most of it, but make sure you aren't moving it toward another microphone by doing so or you will simply be shifting the problem. This is true for bass guitar as well.

LINE CHECKING

There will be times, more often than you might think, when your band will only have time for a line check. Here are a few instances when you can expect one, regardless of what you may have been told:

1. Your band is first on the show billing. Typically, you are the least important band on the billing. If the headliner and supporting acts run late with their checks, yours may be bumped. Try to be a bit early to keep things honest, and make darn sure you aren't late. Often the opening and closing acts are the ones that get squeezed the most, because the ends are the best places to "trim" a show.

Sean McNabb—Bass
Montrose/Dokken/Quiet Riot
House of Lords
www.myspace.com/bassriff2

COURTESY OF MICHAEL HERBACH

"It depends a lot on the venue, but you have to tailor it to the room. If you're playing an arena, then obviously it's going to be kind of boomy, and you've got to EQ some low end out. If you're playing in a room with concrete, there's going to be a lot of high end, and you may want to add some lows. *You've got to learn how to improvise your settings and your tone.*

For music to be as good as it can be, everybody's got to be listening. If your tones are right and you're not competing for the space, and everybody's got their stuff set right, you're making music. And if people are listening, you're really making music. Guys who are just worried about being the loudest thing onstage, who don't want to hear anything else—that's not making music. Making music is musicians listening to one another; having the right sound that makes this big, beautiful painting.

You could spend your whole gig trying to get your mix right, but the fans don't know and they don't care; they want you to rock out! They don't want to see you trying to adjust your mix the whole set. It's never going to be perfect, and it always changes. If you do a soundcheck, it's going to change anyway with a lot of bands on the bill. You kind of learn after a while what you need and what you can get by with."

2. Technical problems with the house system. If a technical problem is affecting the performance of the system, measures must be taken to fix the problem. A soundcheck does not take priority over a problem; besides, a soundcheck would of very little benefit without solving the problem first anyway.

3. House policies may not provide soundchecks for everyone as a general rule. Every soundcheck takes about an hour (which doesn't mean that you can play for an hour!), so this can make soundchecking every band very expensive for the venue, as someone has to cover the extra hours worked by the engineers and staff who have to open the place up early. Smaller clubs with small Type II systems can often get by without doing soundchecks; however, it does make things a bit tougher on the engineer, who has to deal with the unknown all evening.

Line checking can be somewhat uncomfortable for some bands, especially if they are used to having some time to work on their sound both in rehearsals and soundchecks.

Paul Doty
Engineer and Lighting Designer
CEO, West Coast Sound & Light
www.wcsl.org

"My advice to bands is *control your stage volume!* Hint: You do not have ears at the level of your knees; however, the audience does. Turn it down or angle it away from the audience. Many pro setups actually have the *real* amps offstage in a controlled environment with dummy cabs onstage. Once again, I cannot stress enough the importance of quality, well-tuned instruments in the hands of accomplished musicians.

"I want everything in the monitors" just doesn't work. Amateur musicians do not understand that *the monitors are there to balance anything they can't already hear.* Drummers need to feel their kick, but if they can't already hear their snare, they need to retire and purchase a hearing aid, lol!

Mix cues, monitor cues, lighting cues, stage plots, and input lists will help the people you work with, but don't stop there: if you're working long-term with an engineer, they need to be a part of the process of building those documents. And *never molest or generally piss off your FOH engineer, your stage monitor mixer, or your cook.* Think about it.

Soundcheck is *not* rehearsal. On larger shows, you have a professional crew that someone is paying hundreds of dollars an hour for; they are not here to be your audience. If you need rehearsal time, do it after your soundcheck. Take the half hour to get it done right. Then, use whatever allotted time remaining to rehearse whatever you need to. Your engineers may not be saying anything, but I can guarantee they'll know you're amateurs if you don't understand the concept of a soundcheck."

18. USE SETTINGS FROM REHEARSALS FOR LINE CHECKS

Really, the only part that should be tough is getting a balance check. Since there is usually no time to get one during a line check, it's a wise idea to open with a song that allows you to do this. It needs to be something that comes in with one or two instruments and then builds. This not only gives each member an idea of where their level should be in relation to each other, but gives the engineer a chance to focus on dialing in one or two instruments at a time.

Even if you don't actually have a song that does this, an "intro" can be written specifically for this purpose. It can be used regardless of the set list since it really isn't an actual song, and is only needed for live shows. This isn't a terrible idea even when you do get a soundcheck. In any case, it is something to consider for a live show.

Step 1. Set up quickly. You will want to get as much time as possible, so do this just like you would for soundcheck. Have your stuff unpacked, pre-setup, and as close to the stage as you can without blocking the preceding bands' strike lanes. Drums and large keyboard rigs first, then all other instruments. Try to set up as you normally do for rehearsals and pay attention to the differences between the two areas. Compensate if you need to. Start with the locations and balances you use for rehearsal or for the last show. Chapter 5 showed you how to organize your show data and clock your settings for your gear, so you can use these settings specifically for this purpose.

Step 2. As soon as your gear is set up, tuned, and ready to go, ask for a line check. If the engineer is still busy setting up mics for other instruments, you may have to wait until he or she is completely done before you do this. Start with the settings you had from the last show or rehearsal.

Trevor Thornton—Drums
Asia/Saxon/Nelson
Michael Lee Firkins
www.myspace.com/theseventhhourmusic

COURTESY OF ROBERT M. KNIGHT

"A much larger venue will require a much larger monitor system. It's like having your own PA and engineer to yourself. I didn't like having monitors on both sides of me; they ended up canceling each other out. I couldn't hear them! The nice thing about having a large monitor system is you can EQ the kit to sound very sweet and powerful. It really inspires you to play.

If doing a large gig with a monitor engineer, be nice to them. Learn their name and be very polite. (It goes without saying that you are nice to everyone—be extra nice!) This person has your sound at their fingertips. They can give you a great gig or a terrible one. I would even go as far as to ask if you can buy them a drink. It's worth the effort.

In some cases, the gig will only afford you the chance to line check, and this means really no soundcheck at all; they are just making sure the mics work and everyone is coming through the PA. *In this event, make sure you can hear your kick, the bass, and the vocal.* You will always hear the guitarist . . . even when you don't want to! There are also in-ear monitoring systems, but the idea of not hearing anything acoustically is strange to me; you would be relying 100 percent on the monitor engineer for even your own drum sound—cymbals too."

Louis Metoyer—Guitar
4 Non-Blondes/Stanley Clarke
Terence Trent D'Arby
New Edition
www.myspace.com/louismetoyer

COURTESY OF MCNULTY

"Act professional no matter where your gig is. Don't jam with the music before your show. Most people who jam with the jukebox play the wrong notes or aren't even in tune with the darn thing, making your band sound like amateurs. Besides, nobody's impressed that you know the jukebox tunes anyway. Come out strong like a concert! The sonic change from the preshow to the live show is huge, so don't diminish its impact. You don't get a second chance to make a first impression. Use your advantage wisely.

Your performance should be 150 percent at all times. Regardless if I'm performing at Madison Square Garden or a local bar, my performance output is always the same. If you keep your personal standards high, then you will elevate your bandmates as well!

When you're on tour, check with your stage manager to find out which city would be best for an extended soundcheck. Some shows are closer together, so the setup time should be quicker for the crew, giving you extra time to work on parts or new songs all together. *When there's a long haul between cities, try to have a quick soundcheck so your crew can eat, take a nap, or relax before the doors open.* This is in the best interest of everyone. It's called teamwork, people!"

19. CHECK YOUR RIG CAREFULLY BEFORE THE SHOW

Step 3. There often isn't much time between the line check and the start of the show, but make the best use of it while you can. Check your settings, channel switches, footpedals, cables, tuning, and anything else that could be a problem before you find out the hard way. Drummers should check their retainers and adjustment screws and make sure their stick bag is ready.

20. THE FIRST TWO SONGS ARE YOUR SOUNDCHECK

Line checks serve one purpose: They make sure that everything plugged into the PA system is working correctly; they do very little for the band. In all actuality, *your first couple of songs are your soundcheck*. Don't get upset; that's just how things are with a line check. If you have a difficult song, this might not be the place to try to pull it off; get your stage sound right first. Now you can see the importance of an "intro" piece that was intentionally written for this purpose. It doesn't have to be boring and it doesn't have to be very long. It just needs to be long enough to get a balance check onstage and sounds dialed in out front.

21. MAKE ADJUSTMENTS CONSERVATIVELY

Showtime. Once the show begins, the engineer is scrambling to get the mix under control. The band is getting acquainted with what they have for a stage sound, and it's a little chaotic for a few verses. By the end of the first song, each member should have an idea of what they need to be comfortable. Communicate with your band for a brief moment and get a single idea of what everyone needs, instead of having four people ask for something at the same time. If you need to make adjustments to your stage levels, do so conservatively. If everyone were to make a substantial change after the first song, the engineer would be scrambling *again* to get the mix under control. It may take a song or two to get it all right, but do so in moderate steps, not giant leaps, or you risk overcompensating and making it worse.

22. DON'T ALWAYS TRUST AUDIENCE OPINIONS

Many times I have noticed that band members will ask people in the audience how things are sounding. They often ask someone they trust, who knows the sound of their band. This may seem like the right thing to do, but usually these dedicated fans are right up close to the stage and not in a good place to hear the house PA system. "Not enough vocals," "drums were weak," or "couldn't hear the guitar" are some of the responses you will get from these trusted souls. While that may have been true from their vantage point, it was hardly the case from 10 or 15 feet farther back. If you want an opinion from someone you trust, have them take a listen from the halfway point in the room. You can still get some stage volume, but you are getting a better blend of the PA system. Since different frequencies are coming from different cabinets, it takes some distance for them to blend. Halfway back in the center of the room will often be the best spot to make judgment calls, but be sure to check the sides as well. The very back of the room would also be acceptable; the closer to the stage you get, the less accurate your perception will be.

dUg Pinnick—Vocals/Bass
King's X/Living Colour
The Mob/Poundhound
www.kingsxrocks.com

COURTESY OF DUG PINNICK

"Since we're a three-piece band, our soundchecks are easy and quick. We've been together long enough to have this part down. I mix the monitors from the stage, and we have our own FOH guy who we give full control over the mix; we just play and let him deal with it, lol! We usually do one or two songs that have enough vocals for our engineer to get a bearing on where the tones are. "Born to Be Loved" is a song that has everything, and we can do that one in our sleep; it's long enough to give everybody time to get comfortable. Our real objective at soundcheck is to make sure everything is good for the engineer and it's all working right; we've been lucky to have great engineers who can get this done pretty quickly. Ty and I both have some pretty good tones to give to the house, so it's really just a matter of getting the drums to sound great. Once we get that, the mix comes up really easy. At soundchecks, sometimes I'll have to mix Jerry's drums a bit lower, because we come out with more attitude and heart when we play and his drums will be a couple dB louder. We're feeding off the energy of the audience, so this is a natural thing for most bands.

Occasionally, there's a stage where the low end can be funny. In some of the odd-sounding rooms, you can feel it with the in-ears, and I have a 10-band EQ on my ears so I can compensate for this. Move a couple faders on the graph, and problem solved! Some stages can sound pretty bad, but we rely on each other and just get through it and smile!"

23. GET OFFSTAGE QUICKLY

It doesn't matter if it is a soundcheck or a show: whenever you're done, *get your stuff off the stage!* That doesn't mean take your cymbals down one at the time and bag them up, drag your drum cases over and put your drums in them; *it means strike your kit and do all that offstage.* You need to have the same zeal for getting off the stage that you should have when getting on it. When there's only about 15 minutes scheduled between soundchecks and shows, what do you think happens when you take 10 minutes to get out of the way? When you show up early for a gig, and the band before you drags their feet getting offstage, you will understand why you should do this. Sound engineers and stage managers everywhere will thank you.

Pull the mics and get your gear to the staging area as quickly as you can. The next band is watching your band to see if this is happening; if not, you may not get to play another show with them, especially if they are the headliner. You can do all your disassembly and case everything up from the staging area.

24. PACK YOUR GEAR UP OFFSTAGE

Once your gear is offstage, then grab your cases and start packing it all up. If you have an inventory list for that night, now would be the time to check it. If you need to mark your post-show amp settings, do so now. If you need to mark your stage plot with updated equipment locations, you've got time to do that. Just be darn sure that you aren't trying to do all this while a band is waiting to set up. Once you're offstage, you can take your time and check everything. It's much nicer to pack your stuff up without a gun to your head, so to speak. You also stand a much better chance of keeping up with your gear this way.

COURTESY OF CLAUDIA ROSE

Ira Black—Guitar
Vicious Rumors/Lizzy Borden
Metal Church
www.irablack.com

"*I have a backup plan for almost everything I do, especially live performances.* When you are touring, the environment changes with every show, so out of necessity you will have to come up with the quick fix or bare bones of what you can operate with. As an example, when I experience technical problems with cords (I have a lot of cords in my setup), I have backup cords for everything. I will unplug the send and return for the effects loop, but disengage it only a quarter inch to see if the cord from the guitar to the amp is working properly. If so, I will play the rest of the show with no effects. *This is where ability overrides reliance on your equipment.*

Also, you should always have backup parts for your equipment, and as much as you can predict an unlikely situation—prepare for it! From fuses, strings, drumsticks, drum bolts, drum keys, and microphones to bringing your own powered monitors (if possible). Things like batteries, cords, cymbal stands, guitar stands, backup instruments, Super Glue, tools for instruments, and lots of duct tape will surely be needed!"

COURTESY OF NEIL ZLOZOWER

Ed Roth—Keys
Coolio/Rob Halford
Christine W/ Glen Hughes
Bombastic Meatbats
http://onlinekeyboardsessions.com

"What makes a great soundcheck is a good balance onstage, players that listen, an attentive monitor engineer who is constantly checking everyone's mixes in his cue wedge, players that don't have earplugs in the whole gig, and time to play through some tunes. If you are not comfortable on stage, you will not play well.

I do so many different projects that I almost always use cheat sheets. *For tempos, sing the chorus/hook of the song in your head.* Don't think about the intro for tempo, it's about the song. If you don't have a good tour manager, or one at all in these joyful economic times, make lists and notes. Save your e-mails so you can look up things in your phone if you need schedules, hotel info, etc."

Pawel Maciwoda—Bass
The Scorpions/Genitorturers
www.myspace.com/stirwater

COURTESY OF MACIEJ RUDZINSKI

"In the beginning, what counts the most is the sound and the groove from your fingers; then you have endless possibilities with the combination of the amps and guitars as well the strings. To me, simplicity is best.

Both Fender and Music Man have unique tones that are very different from each other. Fender has this great midrange growl and Music Man has an absolutely metallic aggressiveness, so I have to use them both.

I use 8×10 Ampeg cabs and Ampeg heads (usually the Classic or SVT 4 Pro), and I have no problem hearing myself onstage. If you have techs to help you drag this heavy stuff around, *get them!*

It's important to get a good, clear sound out to the PA system. Direct signal is always good, because if the line from the amp mic goes down, you're down as well. I also notice that too much low end from my amp will actually give me less clearness on stage, and sound guys will automatically turn me down. So watch for that low end. Go for the midrange instead!"

IN CONCLUSION

Allow yourself the opportunity to succeed by preparing for your show ahead of time, showing up early, and moving quickly. "Go for what you know," to quote Pat Travers. Start with your rehearsal settings and make adjustments when you need to. Every stage has zones, and you must learn to control your zone by using Location, Focus, and Balance to adjust both your personal equipment and the house equipment. If you have worked on your tones and refined your setup at rehearsals, you should be able to do this without any problem. Soundchecking properly is the summation of all the techniques and principles you have learned both in this book and on your own. If you take the time to understand the ideas and principles in this book, you will have many tools and options to work with when a problem arises. Not all of the answers can be put on a page, but the principles of Location, Focus, and Balance will solve almost any situation that becomes an issue. Anything that is not solvable with these principles can be discussed on www. rockinyourstagesound.com.

Let's have a look at what has been covered in this chapter:

1. Get There Early
2. Have a Look Around
3. Get Set Up as Quickly as Possible
4. Start with Your Rehearsal Settings
5. Adjust Your Placement and Levels for the Stage
6. Balance Your Stage Levels Evenly
7. Bring Up the Monitors First
8. Check for Ground Loops and Faults
9. Use a Windscreen to Avoid Getting Shocked
10. Refocus Your Cabinets If You Need To
11. Use EQ to Get Slight Volume Changes

Jon Butcher—Vocals/Guitar
Jon Butcher Axis
Barefoot Servants/Johanna Wild
www.jonbutcher.com

COURTESY OF JON BUTCHER

"In a good soundcheck, I make sure that everyone I'm playing with has the same comfort level; that their equipment is sounding good and they can hear themselves like they need to. Then I make sure we go over the most dynamic points in the show so that the engineer has no surprises there. He needs to hear the loudest moment and the softest. Once that is taken care of I really don't need to sit around and play; I'm done. My priority is to create a comfortable environment for the guys onstage and the techs we're working with. When it happens, I know this show is going to be great! *It's not about sitting out front with your wireless, making sure every nuance is there; it's all about creating a mental comfort zone.* Anything other than this really isn't important for a soundcheck.

Most of the lighting cues have all been worked out on the computer for big shows, and there are people who take care of all that. I try to stay focused on soundcheck. I've found that professional courtesy will carry the date every time. I treat people in a very respectful way; I say please and thank you. I'm respectful to people I've just met, because I don't know their history; they might be the greatest LD in history! I'll come down and introduce myself to the stage manager and the FOH guy; you want to make sure that those two people like you!"

Back of stage

| GTR > | < GTR | BASS | Drum Riser | BASS | GTR > | < GTR |

12-31-01 Saturday   10:30pm-12:00 pm

The Watering Hole 19654 Camelback Dr, Phoenix AZ-Guy Dude/602-333-7777

381 Miles/60 mph avg= 6.4 hours

8:00am Load Up from Reherarsal space

9:00am En Route

3:20pm Arrive at Venue

4:00pm Load in and setup

5:00pm Soundcheck

5:30pm Set Strike

6:00pm Meal, Showers Provided-Dress for show

9:00pm Set up Promo and Merchandise

10:15pm Set up for show

10:30pm Showtime

12:00pm Set Strike and Load out

12:30pm Promotion and PR

1:00am Load out Merchandise Finalize Business

2:00pm Hotel Check in

Take Los Angeles freeway 10 East all the way to Phoenix Az
Exit North on Central Ave, go approx 2 miles
Turn Right on Camelback Rd, go approx 1/2 mile
The Watering Hole on right, drive to the back of club

1 meal, 2 drinks, 1 guest per band member
Dressing Room with shower
(1) 3' x 6' merch table Club takes 20% of all merch sales
Opener/Joe Schmoe -- Support/Wasted Breath -- Closing/Last Chance Band

A Complete Review

Dave Foreman—Guitar/Bass
Snoop Dogg/Christina Aguilera
Jay Z/Rihanna/Boyz II Men

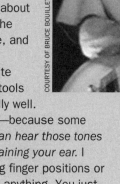

COURTESY OF BRUCE BOUILLET

"My advice to young musicians is to get in tune with the style of music you want to play. This will speed up your ability to learn and increase your willingness to practice harder. If you're trying to learn something you're not interested in, you may not put the time in that would take you to the next level. Once you get your direction figured out, learn all you can about it and know it inside out. Just make sure while you're doing this that you're working on your rhythm and timings; *without this it will never feel right, even when you're playing the right notes.* Dynamics are very important too. It's not just about playing loud or soft, it's about creating tension in the song. The tension creates a vibe that's more important than the volume, and it's about how you use your hands.

Anything can be music: You can listen to a construction site and hear music from the sounds of the hammers and power tools pounding out rhythms; you can lock with that if you listen really well. If you can hear the tone of a cricket and not just the chirping—because some crickets are bigger than others and it sets off tones—*if you can hear those tones as if the cricket were your sound, then you're on your way to training your ear.* I learned how to play through broken strings onstage by shifting finger positions or hand positions, but you have to think very quickly to not miss anything. You just have to reach within yourself and really listen."

WORKING THE SYSTEM

This is a very short chapter, as most of the individual concepts have already been presented to you. Here, we will skim through the previous chapters one at a time and see how they all work together. Each chapter was written with a purpose and a connection to the next chapter, so be sure you have thoroughly digested them before trying to make sense of it all. You may not get everything all at once, but work through the items you understand and go back through the chapters if you have questions that remain unanswered. Some solutions will have to come from within yourself, as you are the only person who will know when your problem has been solved. I couldn't possibly put the answer to every problem in this book, even if I were foolish enough to think I had them all. I do think that the key to finding your solutions lies within the covers of this book, but you will have to read and understand your tools for problem solving. Remember, go to www.rockinyourstagesound.com for help.

Your Tone is where it all begins, and this greatly affects everything that comes afterward in the scheme of the mix. It has to be your best. Don't confuse *best* with *loudest*; volume and tone are not the same. You should set your sound up to have a great tone and the ability to be louder or softer when needed. Eliminate anything that will compromise your stage sound, but keep in mind that your stage sound itself is a compromise. You shouldn't sacrifice everyone else just for your stage sound. Be sure to have personal monitors for anything you need to hear onstage, and set them at reasonable levels so that both you and your bandmates can hear them onstage.

Since these devices are also part of your tone, they should sound as good as they can onstage, and learning how to make them sound great is essential. Always remember that the engineer can turn you up, but s/he can't turn you down.

Setting Up is your secret weapon to put the control of your sound back in your hands. It is here that the battle is won or lost. Most of your solutions will reside within chapter 2, because this features the part of the show that you control the most. The engineers will generally have to work with what you give them in regard to setup. If you can give them a balanced stage where everyone sounds great and can hear themselves, they can focus on making your band sound better, rather than just fixing the problems created by an inadequate or problematic setup. Too many times I have seen bands become their own worst enemies by creating problems and expecting others to fix them. "This is how we do it" is not an excuse for self-inflicted wounds. There will be a few limitations at times, but you have the tools to make compromises: Location, Focus, and Balance! Keep your setups simple and quick, or you may waste time creating more problems than you have time to fix! Rehearsals are more than just working on songs; they are also for working on your show. Many problems begin and end at rehearsals. If you set up badly at practice, you will set up badly at shows or be very uncomfortable with your performance. Always try to set up for rehearsals as you would for performances, and vice-versa; you will be able to whittle away at small problems until you have enough solutions to work with.

Monitor Systems is the area that you will have the least control over. You should ask as little of your monitors as you possibly can. The simpler the monitor mix, the more control you actually have over your sound. Monitors are not there to become the mix; ask only for what you *need*, not what you think you want. Remember that the more sounds you put in them, the less you will be able to hear any of them. This happens to be one of the areas where the sound engineer has the most control, and depending on them heavily will often leave you disappointed. The best way to take control of your stage sound is to use your own personal stage monitor gear as much as possible.

Todd and Troy Garner—Vocals
Lenny Kravitz (bkg)
The Seventh Hour (lead)
www.myspace.com/theseventhhourmusic

Troy: "You have to know deep inside your heart that you have what it takes to be in this business. Right now the industry is changing, so there's no room for mediocre crap. If you're going to contribute to the music business, you have to come out and give it all of your soul and bring back the love for the music. There's so much lip-syncing and artificial tracks, and I think it needs to be *live*, not *Memorex!*"

Todd: "With music comes a passion, and that brings about a true commitment to being the best you can and giving it all you've got. It's not about who the next boy band is or who's got the coolest look; these guys come and go. *The bands that have stood the test of time are the ones who really put their heart into everything they did!*"

COURTESY OF DERON REED

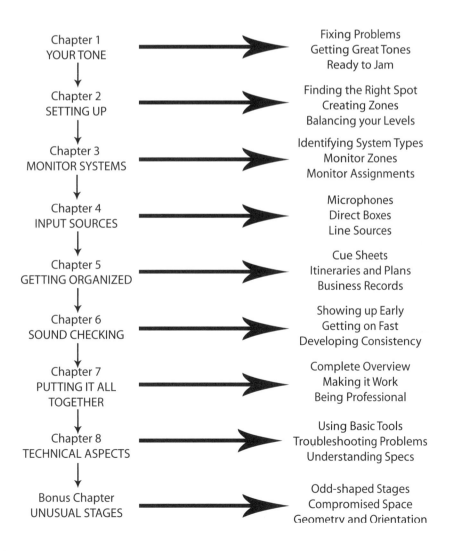

Chapter 1 YOUR TONE	Fixing Problems / Getting Great Tones / Ready to Jam
Chapter 2 SETTING UP	Finding the Right Spot / Creating Zones / Balancing your Levels
Chapter 3 MONITOR SYSTEMS	Identifying System Types / Monitor Zones / Monitor Assignments
Chapter 4 INPUT SOURCES	Microphones / Direct Boxes / Line Sources
Chapter 5 GETTING ORGANIZED	Cue Sheets / Itineraries and Plans / Business Records
Chapter 6 SOUND CHECKING	Showing up Early / Getting on Fast / Developing Consistency
Chapter 7 PUTTING IT ALL TOGETHER	Complete Overview / Making it Work / Being Professional
Chapter 8 TECHNICAL ASPECTS	Using Basic Tools / Troubleshooting Problems / Understanding Specs
Bonus Chapter UNUSUAL STAGES	Odd-shaped Stages / Compromised Space / Geometry and Orientation

Fig. 7.1. Working the system

Input Sources are sometimes at your discretion and will be another area that you can control. If something is really important to the mix, make sure that you have provided an input for that to go to the monitors and mains as quickly and correctly as you can. Don't count on clubs to have everything you need; this is where you take control and bring the special items that will set your sound apart. Chapter 4 will not teach you how to run sound, but it will show you some options to getting your sound into the mix.

You need to consider how things will be miked, how to get line signals into the console, and when it is likely that you will need to provide sources for them. Be aware of most club system's limitations and stay well within them, because you won't get a 32-channel mix everywhere you go. Not only does every additional channel add noise to the mix, but every source takes time to dial in and assign to monitors. The equipment has to be loaded in, set up, wired in, dialed in, assigned, and mixed. Then it has to be unhooked, torn down, loaded out, and kept up with. You can actually tear down and setup *two or three times* for every show!

If you think about it, you have to tear it down and load it up from rehearsal or home, set it up for the soundcheck, tear it down (even if it's a limited breakdown), set it up again for the show, tear it down again, and load it up, transport it, and set it up again at rehearsal or home. The more you have to set up, the more work this becomes. Keep your needs to the essentials. It's easy to see why you should be organized and have a show plan with this much extra work involved.

Getting Organized should be done long before you get to the stage. It is here where you will be able to visualize and document your blueprint for excellence. By organizing your show on paper, you will have partially committed it to memory. By having your preferences listed on paper, you will be able to transmit them to others who could help make them happen. Our ability to communicate is what sets us apart from the vegetation that populates this planet! Having these cue sheets won't eliminate all questions and may even bring up a few additional questions, but they will keep you from having to go over every single detail in your show and provide the engineer and lighting techs with something they can refer to. It's always better to plan to have a great show instead of reacting to an unsatisfactory one.

COURTESY OF ALEX SOLCA

Mike Hansen—Drums
Tribe After Tribe/George Lynch
Souls of We/Leif Garrett
The Pointer Sisters/Paula Abdul
www.myspace.com/cymbalcrasher1

"Stay true to yourself and play what makes you happy. If you're not on top of your game, you may lose that 'opportunity' in life that sometimes only comes once or maybe not do as well as you could have otherwise. Be a good businessman. Play your instrument as much as you can and learn as many styles as possible. Think of it as a color palette: the more colors you have, the more you can offer. And don't just focus on the primary colors, have some secondary colors. The more you've got, the more you can give! You never know when you have to pull a rabbit out of the hat."

Soundchecking is where you will be able to make your final adjustments before you perform. It is here that all your preparation begins to pay off and you can be confident that you have the tools to take your stage sound to the next level. If your initial game plan isn't working as you had expected, you can examine the problem and make an informed decision. Always remember that soundcheck is more about getting the stage sound right *before* getting the FOH sound right. If your stage sound is great, then your FOH mix will be even better. Sometimes soundcheck will bring out a problem that can be fixed before showtime; if not, then you have to make a choice and stand with it until you can solve the problem.

Technical Aspects will help you transcend the common mistakes and technical challenges that handicap almost everyone who has ever been a musician. Some learn by trial and error, and some never learn at all. Some are afraid to take chances and always feel like there is more to be had. Here is a chance to see mistakes before they happen and to handle common issues when they occur. At some point this chapter will save you many times the price of this book in repairs or unnecessary equipment.

Tollak Ollestad—Harmonica
Don Henley/Michael McDonald
Kenny Loggins/Jewel/Seal
www.tollak.com

COURTESY OF KEYVON BEHPOUR

"I'd like to talk about 'overplaying,' which 90 percent of harmonica players do. Harmonica players are generally featured as soloists for specific sections, but inexperienced players tend to fill and solo nonstop through the set. *Nothing will turn you into Typhoid Mary or Mario faster among your musical colleagues than the inability to leave space and to lay out until it's really appropriate to play.*

Listen to great harp players playing along with singers and hear how tastefully they fill or play a little rhythm behind them. You'll see how much more desirable you can make yourself to bands when you develop this kind of musicality in your playing. As with all instruments, the great players have the ability to hear what they're playing as a part of the whole and are not just living in their own little bubble hearing only what they're playing. *That's what makes a band truly a great band: all the parts working together to make the whole better.* I can't stress this enough; it doesn't matter how many chops you develop, this sensibility is what separates great players from average players, and it's what makes you a much more valuable commodity to any band or artist that's considering hiring you.

As far as why you're playing music, everyone starts out wanting to be a big star, but in the end it's a greater source of misery than anything: it really needs to be about the joy of playing music and being grateful that you have a gift that most people don't have. Playing with big names is nice, but the real prize lies in the fact that you have a gift and you can share that with the audience. If you really keep that close to you, you'll be able to ride the waves of success—and there's going to be waves; it's all part of the journey! If you're only concerned about success and how you look to other people, those waves are going to beat the hell out of you!"

Matt Cross
Systems Engineer
West Coast Sound & Light

WORKING WITH SOUND ENGINEERS

This is one of the most important things you can learn to make your show better. If an engineer feels that his efforts are being appreciated and his experience valued, you will get more cooperation than you would otherwise. *Let's examine the type of person it takes to be a sound engineer.* Each engineer has had a different path leading them to where they are. Some have been schooled, others are self-taught. Most have worked very hard to understand the many elements of a live show. These systems are not toys (well, sometimes they are!) and a great deal of trust has been placed upon them to take care of these systems and operate them correctly.

Engineers are often responsible not only for making sure that the sound is up to the standards of the venue, but also for keeping the show on schedule. They are responsible if any part of the system is blown or damaged. Sometimes the priorities of the club or venue are completely different from the priorities of the bands. If it's too loud or sounds bad, you can empty a club out quickly. The bands just want to come in and *rock the place*! These two objectives are not exactly the same. Most engineers are in the precarious position of having to keep the club *and* the bands happy. Who's paying his wage? The club? Guess who wins? And if a band comes in with an attitude, guess who loses? It's not that engineers don't give a damn; it's that there are quite a few forces at work in live shows that have to be balanced against each other. How you approach them may shift that balance. There is a tremendous difference between honest respect and insincere "bum-smooching." Here are some things you should assume *before* you approach an engineer.

▶**An engineer is there because they are the best person available for that gig on that night.** In almost every case, this will be the truth. Try to get hired as an engineer and you will find out just how picky these places can be!

▶**An engineer knows his stage better than you do.** Once again, this will almost always be true, unless you were the former sound engineer for this club and they are brand new.

▶**An engineer's reputation is at stake as much as your band's.** No engineer *ever* wants to listen to a poor mix, much less be the cause of it. They will always do their best *with what they have and what you give them.*

▶**An engineer does not work for you.** These guys work long hours in a noisy environment with a lot of impatient people for fairly slim compensation. They have to work *with* you, but they don't work *for* you.

▶**Engineers do their job because they love what they do, not because of the money.** While this is almost always true, you'd be surprised how far a $20 bill will get you. The engineers on higher-profile gigs may like to see a little more, but it's usually worth it!

Get these things in your head before you even set foot in the door. If you are not impressed with the sound of the venue when you get there, refer to #3 above. Take a minute to listen to the band, walk up close to the stage, and check out the stage sound. Look around and see if you can spot some mistakes the band might be making. What would you need to do differently? Don't immediately assume that a bad sound is the direct fault of the engineer; they may have had some help.

If you walk in and it sounds *awesome*, do exactly the same thing as above, but with the idea of learning what *is* working in the room. There will always be something to learn every place you go, and pretty much every time you play. Next, there are few things you *never* want to assume about an engineer.

►**The engineer is your roadie.** *Wrong!* However long it takes you to get set up will come out of *your* time, not his. If he does grab something or offer a hand, be grateful, because he is under *no* obligation to do so. Generally, when you do get some help, it's in regard to getting your stuff *off* the stage!

►**The engineer will remember your verbal requests.** Not likely. Did you put together a cue sheet for her? Even if both the sound and light cues are simple, having this sheet will remind her after the show has started and the adrenaline has kicked in. Yes; she may remember a couple of key requests, but many will go unheeded if you pummel her with too many verbal details.

►**Since your band is headlining, your band should sound better.** While this has been known to happen in arenas and at concert-level events, if you are not a rock star, *don't act like one!* Most engineers give every band their best mix. You have to give them your best. If your bands sounds better, it's because your band is having a better night. And always remember that the term *better* is very subjective!

Bjorn Englen—Bass
Soul Sign/Yngwie Malmsteen
Robin McAuley/Quiet Riot
http://bjornenglen.com

COURTESY OF CARVIN; USED WITH PERMISSION

"If you're a hired gun, you want to leave your ego at the door. If you can do that, you'll be amazed at how much respect you'll get back. If you show that you care and are happy supporting the band as an artist, it becomes fun. It has been easy working with Yngwie because it was very clear long before I started working with him that he is always the boss. This doesn't make it harder to play with him; in fact, even the first time I jammed with him it felt very natural, which is great, because you always want to remember why you're doing this: because it's fun!!

One of the things you want to remember is that most of the personnel you work with are doing their best, and if you're nice and communicate with them, then you can get a lot accomplished, even with guys that aren't that experienced. Be friendly, speak clearly, let them know what you need, and you'll find that they'll go out of their way for you. Pick your personnel carefully when you go out on the road, because you want everyone to be competent and reliable, but you also need the personalities to work together. If you're working with outside guys, make sure that you cut a deal with the venues to get good help—it's money well spent. This is a wise idea, especially if there's a complicated setup or a lot of instrument changes. It can easily make your show very tough trying to be your own tech."

►**The engineer remembers everything about your last show.** Not gonna happen. He may remember your band, hopefully in a good way. He may remember some of the more unique elements of your show, but rarely will he remember enough for you to forgo your stage plots/input list, sound/lighting cues, and monitor cue sheet. Comments like "Remember what we did last time?" will often be met with a "you gotta be kidding me" look, unless it was just one of those unforgettable moments!

►**You can win an argument with an engineer.** Impossible. You only lose his cooperation in most instances. Occasionally, there will be a point that the engineer feels very strongly about; refer to #2 from the previous list of things you should assume about an engineer.

Things to consider before talking with the engineer: Before you get to the show, you should think about what kind of night it's going to be. Where, when, and who is playing that night may affect not only the engineer's demeanor, but yours as well. Here are some things that may change the course of a normal evening.

How many bands are playing that night? Is this a normal schedule for the venue? One extra band may really tighten things up. If your band is on later in the show and it begins to get behind, time will have to be made up somewhere. Make sure you don't waste any time, and be prepared to shorten your set. Are any of the bands very large? Normal four- and five-piece bands are routine for most stages, but extensive keyboards, percussion, and brass/reed sections can slow down the normal schedule. If there are several acts with these types of setups, it can be even more time consuming.

These issues can really affect your engineer's stress level. Everybody deals with stress differently, and even this can vary from night to night with the same person. If you come in and notice a bit of chaos, go out of your way to not be another stress point.

Is there a national act headlining? Expect some disarray and a few disadvantages. National acts sometimes won't strike their stage, leaving your band with less-than-optimum stage privileges. They may not relinquish console and monitor channels either, leaving you with a compromised mix. These types of shows *have* to run on schedule. Not only is time a factor, but there is more pressure on the engineer from everyone. Management, celebrities, and even the opening acts are all trying to make the show a success from *their* standpoint. This can have a noticeable effect on engineers when they are being pulled in several directions at once. Everyone is expecting more when there's actually less to work with. Other things that can affect a show are weather, traffic, PA system issues, and one band with an attitude. Don't make it two!

Georg Voros—Drums
eVoid/Black Star Liner
Jimmy James and the Vagabonds
The Stu Page Band
www.georgvoros.com

"In retrospect, most stage techs have been on the same page and focused on achieving the best result, which is a great sound. Be agreeable and cool with everyone concerned, as the people responsible wield a lot of power over the end result. And if you do experience the odd occasion where you work with somebody who is difficult or maybe not switched on, then be diplomatic and do the best you can.

For drummers and specifically acoustic kit drummers, the challenge of reinforcing the sound of our instruments electronically can often prove to be difficult. In my book *Rhythm of the Head*, I wrote that *the more control we have over our sound in a live situation, the better the end result will be.* There are limits to what we can do, as the sound that we want to hear and what we may achieve onstage are not always faithfully reproduced to the audience. This is an aspect of live sound we have no control over and should learn to accept. But *if we can be masters of the immediate sound we are hearing, this will ensure we at least have more good gigs than bad ones.* If it all comes together and the people responsible for the sound out front reproduce what we'd like the audience to hear, this is the ultimate goal in live sound!"

WORKING WITH STAGE MANAGERS

As the name implies, the stage manager is in charge of keeping things moving onstage. Stage managers make sure that everything is ready for the next band and that everyone is ready to go. They may not always set up, but they try to make sure that bands are moving in that direction. They prevent bands from hanging around after their soundcheck or show, and they direct the next band into place. You can't have everybody onstage all at once, so the stage manager is the one who makes sure things happen in the correct sequence. The current band needs to get offstage first before the next band can set up. If the last band is slow getting off the stage and the next band starts loading their gear onstage, it turns into a traffic jam.

In smaller shows, the engineer is often the stage manager as well. Larger shows will have a dedicated individual. Larger bands may have their own stage manager who may or may not coordinate the entire show, but they will at least be in charge of managing the band they are working for and will coordinate with the house stage manager or production manager. If they see you dragging your feet, you may get some unwelcome help getting off the stage! In either case, the stage manager is *the man*! Now that we have covered the job description of a stage manager, let's look at what his job *isn't*.

▶ **The stage manager is not your roadie.** I do see quite a few of them grab some gear and help out, but they are surely not your butler or the "water boy." They

205

have a job to do, and locating items you've left at home isn't it, but they will often help out when they can.

▶**The stage manager will not pass your cue sheets out.** Their job description involves handling their stage responsibilities. They *may* direct you to the sound and light technicians, but they will not be your runner. Whoever is setting up your mics and wiring in your inputs may be the right person to hand over sound-related cue sheets to.

▶**The exception to the above is rare.** If the stage manager is also the engineer or light tech, *then* you can hand them the appropriate cue sheet(s).

The truth of the matter is that your cue sheets should go to the right people well in advance of your setup. Otherwise you are wasting setup time. Always respect the stage manager as a professional, not some flunky who can't run sound or lights. It takes a strong personality to be a stage manager, and respect goes a long way in this business. It might make a difference when your band needs some help onstage.

COURTESY OF BRUCE BOUILLET

Bruce Bouillet—Guitar
Racer X/The Scream/DC 10
Epidemic/Bottom Dwellerz
Grammy-Winning Producer/Engineer
www.myspace.com/brucebouillet

"Consistency on the road is essential. *If you're consistent onstage, you're one step closer to having a perfect show every night.* That's what people pay money to see; they came to see your best—bring it! I saw Joe Satriani do this night after night. After 11 years of touring, his show was flawless. There may have been a lick or two that changed, but every night, his show was tight, smooth, and completely without panic. *So if you've got problems in rehearsal, that's the place to fix them.* Don't go out and play until you resolve them.

As far as the stage goes, never sweat the small stuff. Very few people catch little problems; they came to enjoy a great show. There's always a handful that will catch things, but unless you have to stop the show, very few people will be bothered by it. What I've learned from some of the better players is that no matter what, there's always a way to get the job done even when the gear isn't so great. Their attitude is 'Let's go mash!' because it is not about the car; it's about the driver. If you're stuck on an amp that's not yours, just get up there and drive it like you stole it!"

IN CONCLUSION

There is a certain Zen to sound; its energy can't be touched, but it can be felt. For some, visualizing sound as being light will help, for it is directional, with varying intensity and color. The similarities between the two are striking, and for light to be effective, it should be direct light, as "shadows" will darken your intended target. This is one of the reasons why your stage sound can be "muddy": reflective, unfocused sound. For others, it may be the 5.1 Surround Sound Theory that really turns on the light in their head. Having a place for everything and everything in its place may mean much more to some people than others. Focus, location, and balance are the tools you use to clear up your sound in both cases. Ask yourself these questions before you make any adjustments:

▶**Is the sound source *located* correctly?** You need to examine it to see if its location is adequate. Would physically moving it forward or backward or left or right help? Would that cause a different problem?

▶**Is the source *focused* correctly?** Sometimes a simple angle adjustment or slight tilt will do the trick. Even if it doesn't completely solve the problem, it should make additional measures less severe.

▶**Are other sound sources *located* and *focused* correctly?** Making adjustments to the loudest sound onstage will often bring additional adjustments into a workable range. Are your monitor cues accurate? Is the overall level sufficient? Are you standing in a dead spot? Are you too loud for the monitors? These are all things you should ask yourself before turning the level up.

▶**Is the source *balanced* correctly?** After you have made the three previous adjustments and still have not completely solved the problem, now you can safely reach for the level control. Your adjustments should be much less if you have properly focused, located, and balanced all of the sources onstage.

Once you have thoroughly answered these questions in your head, many solutions will become crystal clear. Your first choices should come from the physical aspects of stage sound that you are in direct control of, as the simplest answer is usually the best! Looking for an electronic solution to these problems is like trying to solve one problem with another . . . and we all know how that turns out. That being said, there is a limit as to how many physical solutions can be attempted without creating other problems, and some electronic solutions will be necessary for certain aspects of your stage sound.

The title of this chapter may imply that it is possible to make sense of everything, but it's not going to happen like that. Your area of expertise and level of understanding will determine which is right for you. While there are many solutions to individual problems in this book, the fact is that there will often be some sort of a compromise. In fixing one problem, you may create another one; it's up to you to decide which will be the lesser of two evils when those circumstances arise. You will have to actively seek solutions for the many challenges in your path; if not, you will wind up being the pavement for someone else who does. Always remember that most of your sound is in your hands, and what you do onstage is vital to what comes across to the audience. You are not there to make the sound engineer sound good, the engineer is there to make *you* sound good! You can't completely ignore his or her requests, so you should always try to understand *why* an adjustment is being requested.

When you're asked to turn down, see if you can make a "counter-adjustment" to keep yourself comfortable. Upstage the amp, relocate to the crossfired position, add a hotshot, or do anything else that will give you the levels you need without having to use the volume control.

Don't skimp on being organized, either. It's impossible to get organized all at once, so start with the basics and find out what really works for you before you complicate things uncontrollably. Having cue sheets will allow you to quickly communicate to others what you are looking for in your show. There is no way to be perfectly exact with these cues, because everything is subject to interpretation. Putting in the specifics will take the guesswork out of most situations. You have to remember that a sound engineer is an artist too. Each person will have a different ear for tones and balances and a completely different set of eyes with which to spot solutions. Most engineers take great pride in a killer mix, but you must be careful that you don't let them destroy your stage mix to get theirs. Take control of your stage sound, and most engineers will make adjustments to make it work. If your stage sound is reasonable and balanced, their job will be much easier. Remember to visit www.rockinyourstagesound.com for updates and additional information from other musicians participating in the forums.

COURTESY OF JAMES KOTTAK

James Kottak—Drums
The Scorpions/The Cult
Montrose/Kingdom Come
Warrant/Kottak
www.jameskottak.com

"For young players, my advice is once you start, don't stop! It only gets better the longer you do it. If you get frustrated in the beginning, don't worry about it—everybody does. Go get AC/DC's "Black in Black" and play along with it for a few weeks . . . seriously! Once you learn that, everything else is cake. *After you get a handle on what you're doing, play every show like it's your last.* Sounds kind of dorky, but you set the bar a little higher than normal. I just want to rock 'n' roll forever!"

dUg Pinnick—Vocals/Bass
King's X/Living Colour
The Mob/Poundhound
www.kingsxrocks.com

"When you're on the road, try to eat right and get plenty of sleep so you can have the extra energy for the stage. I always try to eat right, but it's really important on the road, where it's hard to do.

We're pretty easy when working with our techs. If something happens, we just look at them and laugh . . . there's no blaming anyone or riding on them. They're usually more upset than we are! We know they take their job seriously, so we don't have to add drama to the situation. We know they'll fix it. Occasionally, something will happen in a show where I can't stop; I may yell at them, but it's nothing personal, and after the show it's all forgotten; let's get a drink and have some fun.

Don't be discouraged if you do not 'make it,' because you made it when you first picked up that instrument; you made it when you first walked on stage and played for people; and you made it when people actually liked your show. 'Making it' isn't about getting a record deal, it does not mean selling millions of records and the world knowing who you are. *'Making it' means that you get to do what you love doing and make a living at it for the rest of your life, regardless of your level of success."*

COURTESY OF DUG PINNICK

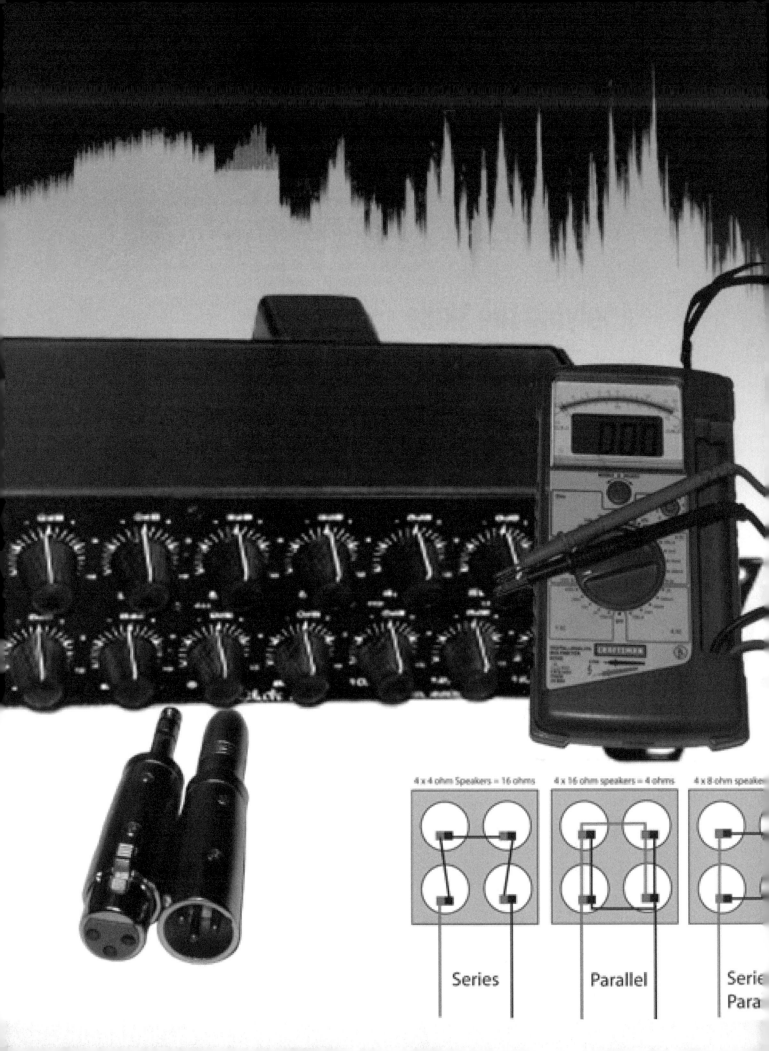

4 x 4 ohm Speakers = 16 ohms   4 x 16 ohm speakers = 4 ohms   4 x 8 ohm speake

Series   Parallel   Serie
                                                     Para

Applying the Skills
You Need to Succeed

TECHNICAL ASPECTS

Musicians are highly creative people; most of their talents are intuitive and come naturally. The technology that projects that talent is not. Simply having the right equipment doesn't guarantee a great sound; it has to be connected, located, and operated correctly, and requires specific knowledge of physics and electronics. There are many fine points that could have distracted you from the main points of the earlier chapters, so some of this information was incorporated into this chapter is to inform you of some of the more common technical challenges you will face as a musician. It is also here to help you with applying some of the radical approaches in this book that will allow you to get the most out of your tone. A solid foundation of basic technical knowledge will save you time and money, not to mention that it will be the key to a more consistent stage sound. Even if some of these aspects don't apply to your instrument, take the time to browse through them; it may come in handy when a band member is having some difficulties. These technical aspects are given in a certain order, because some of the later aspects require knowledge of the previous ones. It would be helpful if you read through all of them, as there is much more than what appears on the front page. Let's have a quick look at how it all interacts.

Volt-Ohm Meter

Since electricity is invisible, you need some way to see it, and a volt-ohm meter is your electronic eyes. You need it to do the following:

Test Cables. Cables are often the most common problem and should be your first checkpoint. Having a cable tester helps, but is not necessary when you know how to use a volt-ohm meter.

Test Speakers. While speaker problems are not as common as cable problems, they do occur, and can have some really adverse consequences. When there is more than one speaker in a cabinet, you need to know which one is the problem.

Check Fuses. Many times a fuse can be visually inspected, but you can be fooled by appearances when it doesn't look damaged.

Creative Applications. Without a basic understanding of electronic principles and a means by which to check them, you will not be able to solve problems and create solutions. You don't have to be an engineer to get the right signal to the right device.

All of this begins with volt-ohm meter!

1. LEARN TO OPERATE A VOLT-OHM METER

A volt-ohm meter is one of the handiest devices ever made for electronics. Nothing could be more important to learn to use. Without this very important device, you will be forever handicapped in your ability to find problems. Despite its various settings, you will probably use only one or two for 99 percent of what you need to know. No one is asking you to tear down amps and repair them, but you will need to know if the speakers are working or what impedance your cabinet is. You can check cables, pickups, power supplies, batteries, and even extension cords. Being able to use a volt-ohm meter will allow you to find problems, even if you can't fix them.

Until you find the problem, you won't be able to do anything at all about it. If your amp stops working, how will you know if the amp is blown, the speakers are blown, or the speaker cord is bad?

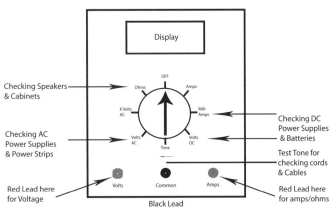

Fig. 8.1. Volt-ohm meter settings

Once you have established the correct setting for your speaker, mark it on your meter. This setting can be used for almost all your ohm testing needs. Fig. 8.1 shows a volt-ohm meter and its settings. When checking DC voltages and amperes, make sure the leads are terminated correctly, or you will blow a fuse inside your volt-ohm meter. (I bet you didn't even know it had one!) Somewhere inside the meter—it may be in the battery den or inside the unit case itself—there should be a small fuse that protects the device from damage in case the wrong setting is used or if the leads inadvertently touch the wrong connection. If this happens, the unit will be dead until the fuse is replaced. Have a look and get a couple of spare fuses before you need one. A blown fuse resembles a dead battery, with the difference being that one minute the volt-ohm meter works just fine; the next minute it's a goner.

2. LEARN HOW TO TEST IMPEDANCE

Testing Speakers. If you are having a problem with a speaker, look for the impedance marking on the speaker that tells you what the impedance is *supposed* to be. Disconnect the speaker from everything else and set your meter to read ohms in one of the lower settings—200 ohms or below. Using too high a range will not give you an accurate reading. Using too low a range will not help you, either. Since speakers are in the lowest range, this won't be an issue; for pickups it is. Touch both the positive and negative leads to their respective terminals on the speaker and check your reading. While it really doesn't matter if they are reversed, you should get in the habit of "polarizing" your tests. It will matter when working with DC volts/amps. A 16-ohm speaker should read around 14 ohms. An 8-ohm speaker should read around 6 ohms. A 4-ohm speaker should read around 3 ohms. This happens because the ohm meter itself has impedance, and is reading both itself and the speaker.

There will usually be a quick static noise when the volt-ohm meter contacts both terminals. This tells you that it is operational in addition to the volt-ohm meter reading. If the reading is *completely* different from the speaker's rated ohmage, you may be losing your coil. If there is no reading at all, the speaker is dead—call the morgue! But before you panic and toss it out, double-check the settings on your volt-ohm meter and verify that the device isn't working. Touch the two leads together to verify the meter; it should read "0." If your meter has a calibration adjustment, this is where you set it for "0."

If your reading is close, but the speaker sounds harsh, is intermittent at low levels, or crackles on the peaks, there may be a voice coil problem. If you have access to the cone, you can check for coil-rub by lightly pushing on the cone evenly. It should feel completely free with no scratchiness or friction; there will be some resistance, but it should be smooth. If there is some scrubbing, rubbing, or scratchiness, expect some problems down the road. Dropping a speaker can warp the coil and cause misalignment, leading to eventual enamel wear and coil failure. Thermal exposure can cause the coil to swell. One of the indications of a swollen voice coil is that the speaker cuts out at very low volumes; there isn't enough energy to overcome the resistance of a damaged coil. Rough handling can cause the coil to crack or split. It works, but it rattles badly.

But as long as the speaker is still working and sounds okay, use it. If not, replace it. My experience is that re-cones are never quite as good as the factory specs, but they do work. It's very difficult to do a precision alignment by hand.

If your entire cabinet is a problem, set your volt-ohm meter as instructed above and plug a known working speaker cable into it. Touch the leads to the tip and sleeve of the cable and check your reading. You can put the black or red lead on either the tip or the sleeve; just make sure the leads are touching the plug and not each other. The reading should match the impedance on your cabinet. In most cases, the cabinet will indicate what the impedance is when it leaves the factory. *This is something you should know* (see Fig. 8.2).

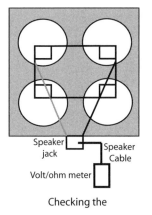

Speaker jack / Speaker Cable / Volt/ohm meter

Checking the

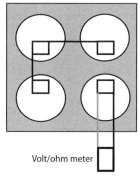

Volt/ohm meter

Checking one

Fig. 8.2. Testing speakers

3. LEARN HOW TO TEST CABLES

Set your volt-ohm meter to just about any ohm setting you want, then touch the probes to each cable end: tip to tip, sleeve to sleeve. You can also use the "continuity" setting, which simply beeps when the circuit is connected. You must test all conductors individually.

XLR mic cables are a bit tricky: one end appears to be reversed, but is correct. Fig. 8.3 shows why, as they line up when facing each other. It's not easy to test the male end of an XLR cable as the housing is in the way. Each connection (#1 to #1; #2 to #2, etc.) should show a 0-ohm (or very low) reading on the meter; however, this only indicates that you have conduction. It will not show if the connection is noisy or unshielded, or if there is a cross-connection. Now, touch one terminal on one side and a different terminal on the other side. You should get no reading at all. If you do get a reading, check to make sure that it is a different terminal, and check the others for no reading. This will tell you that none of the connections are touching each other. If you can, wiggle an end while you check them; this could reveal an intermittent or damaged cable. (This is not easy to do when your hands are full.)

Fig. 8.3. Testing XLR cables

Facing the connection

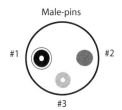

Female-holes

#2   #1

#3

Male-pins

#1   #2

#3

Facing each other

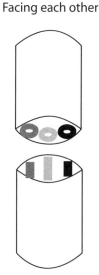

4. LEARN HOW TO CHECK FUSES

Most medium- and high-powered amps come with fuses. Some will have several fuses of different ratings. Don't wait until you have a problem to buy a couple of spares for each type. If you suspect a problem with your amp, power it down and *unplug it* from the wall; don't take any chances. With the amp totally disconnected from the AC power source, pull the fuse and have a look. Is it burnt? Can you see the filament clearly? A quick visual inspection can tell you if it's a goner, but it will take a meter to say whether it is working. Since fuses can be deceptive and you have to be certain, put the meter on it just to be sure. Use any ohm setting you like. You just need to see that it is conducting current. If it's working, check the next fuse. Most tube amps will have at least two fuses:

▶**Mains fuse**. This keeps the incoming AC power from destroying your amp. While it's rare that you will accidentally plug in to a 220V receptacle, it happens!

▶**Output fuse**. This fuse is here to save your amp in case something internal goes wrong, which is usually the case. Incorrect ohmage settings, blown grid-screen resistors, bad tubes, or spilled beer can really wreak havoc with amps. Your power light will still be on, but there will be no sound.

Some amps use small breakers instead. There is a difference: breakers are slower and don't always protect your amp properly. The primary reason people use them is that some protection is better than none, and you don't need to replace a breaker when it trips. It can be tricky to tell if there's a problem with these as well, so you actually have to get them to trip and then reset them if you are suspicious of a breaker problem. Most breakers are found in solid-state amps. Tube amps generally require the fail-safe aspect of a fuse, as breakers don't always trip.

5. UNDERSTAND OHM'S PRINCIPLES

If you are a guitarist, bassist, or own a PA system of any kind, you should have a basic understanding of how changing the impedance of a device will affect that unit. This is true for anything that has an amp or a speaker. There are probably more ways to run something wrong than to run it correctly, so you have to be sure that you know what you are doing when you set something up. When working with your own gear, this usually isn't a problem; when you are using someone else's equipment, you must be sure!

OHMS

An ohm is a unit of resistance between two points of a circuit. In the case of a speaker, it is this resistance that causes it to move when an amp drives it with current. The lower the resistance, the easier it is to move. In the case of an amp, the lower the resistance (impedance), the easier it is to *blow*! Often amps will run extremely hot before going "thermal."

There is a carefully designed balance between the amp and the speaker that allows them to both work effectively within each other's range. Since we aren't building amps here, we will be looking at speakers and cabinets, and you will probably change the workings of the speakers before you change the specs of the amp.

There are two ways to change impedance when you add more cabinets/speakers, depending on whether you connect them in series or in parallel. However, it is important to know that when you add a speaker or a cabinet, you will change the impedance of the load.

Serial Wiring. Fig. 8.4 shows a serial connection. The positive source of the amp is run to the positive terminal of the first speaker, and then the negative terminal of the first speaker is run to the positive terminal of the second speaker. The negative terminal of the second speaker is then returned to the negative source of the amp. This forms a single path of current that passes directly from one speaker to the next.

The resistance of both speakers will be added together, since it is a single current path. If they were both 8-ohm speakers, then your total load would be 16 ohms. Should one of these speakers fail, *all* signal would be lost due to the fact that the circuit has been broken. Note that the negative terminal of speaker 1 is run to the positive terminal of speaker 2. This is "phase correct" wiring. (When thinking of serial connections, keep batteries in mind: they run from the positive terminal on one battery to the negative of the next, and form a *series*.) If the negative terminal of speaker 1 were run to the negative terminal

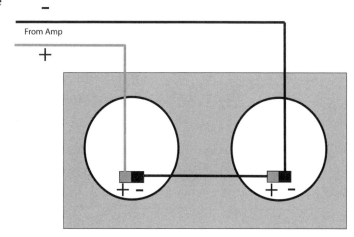

From Amp

Fig. 8.4.
Serial wiring

of speaker 2, then the speakers would be "out of phase," and would cancel each other out. They would sound funny like this because one speaker would be pushing out, and the other would be pulling in. It would greatly decrease your levels and sound very nasal and weird. Phasing is where most speaker wiring mistakes are made. Pay close attention to any wiring and its polarity before disconnecting it.

Parallel Wiring. Parallel wiring means there are multiple signal paths. Fig. 8.5 shows an example of this type of wiring with two speakers. As you can see, there are *two* signal paths. The amp's positive source is running to *both* speakers' positive terminals, and both speakers' negative terminals are run back to the amp's negative source. *Having two paths means that the ohmage load is now divided instead of added.* Two 8-ohm speakers run in parallel would have a total load of 4 ohms. Should one of the speakers fail, the amp would have a secondary path and still work, but the load would go back to 8 ohms. Note that both of the speakers are wired "phase correct." If one were reversed, the impedance would not change, but the phase would. Again, this would sound funny, because one speaker would be pushing out while the other speaker was pulling in. You really have to pay attention to polarity when wiring *anything*.

When running any combination of speakers, you need to know two simple fractional formulas to figure the total load:

Serial wiring formula: ohms/1 + ohms/1 = total ohms/1

So if you had four 4-ohm speakers in a cabinet run in series, the formula would look like this:

4 ohms/1 + 4 ohms/1 + 4 ohms/1 + 4 ohms/1 = 16 ohms/1

You divide the top by the bottom to get 16 ohms.

Parallel wiring formula: 1/ohms + 1/ohms = total ohms

So if you had four 16-ohm speakers in a cabinet run in parallel, the formula would look like this:

1/16 + 1/16 + 1/16 + 1/16 = 4/16 =4

Divide the bottom by the top to get 4 ohms.

Fig. 8.5.
Parallel
wiring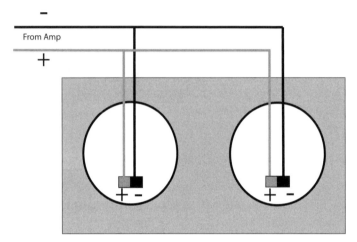

Series/Parallel Wiring. As the name would suggest, this is a combination of both types, and requires three or more speakers. This is how most four-speaker cabinets are wired. Two pairs of 8-ohm speakers are wired in series to form a pair of 16-ohm loads, and then paralleled together for a total load of 8 ohms. Fig. 8.6 shows an example of all three types of wiring for the same 4×12 cabinet. The full formula for series/parallel wiring looks like this:

Series/parallel wiring formula: (ohms/1 + ohms/1 = A) (ohms/1 + ohms/1= B) (1/A + 1/B = total load)

This is rather tedious for most typical wiring calculations, but will yield precise results when working with speakers of different ohms. When all the speakers are of the same ohmage, the formula below will simplify things somewhat:

(ohms/1 + ohms/1 = subtotal) × ½ = total load (8/1 + 8/1 = 16) × ½ = 8 ohms

This gives you 16 ohms per pair. Then when both pairs are paralleled together, you arrive back at 8 ohms.

As with speaker pairs, two cabinets can also be wired in series or parallel; however, a special harness must be constructed to create a "serial" connection between the two cabinets. In this case, I suggest that you keep it simple and run parallel connections when using two cabinets. It would be much simpler to rewire or reload each cabinet to meet your ohm specs.

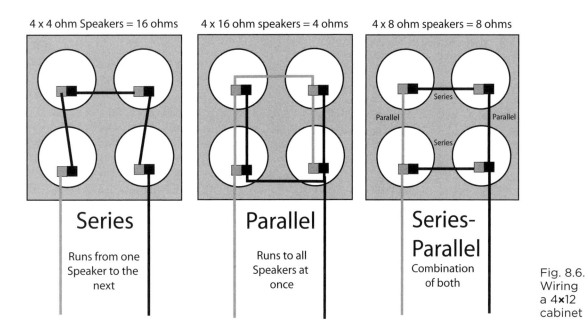

4 x 4 ohm Speakers = 16 ohms   4 x 16 ohm speakers = 4 ohms   4 x 8 ohm speakers = 8 ohms

Series
Runs from one Speaker to the next

Parallel
Runs to all Speakers at once

Series-Parallel
Combination of both

Fig. 8.6. Wiring a 4×12 cabinet

Finally, the last couple of things to remember about speakers and cabinets in general is that regardless of how they are wired, be it in series, parallel, or both, each speaker will always operate at its rated impedance. If you run an 8-ohm speaker across an amp set for 4 ohms, it will still run at 8 ohms. The amp will also run at 8 ohms, but at a reduced power level.

Mixing speakers of different ohms will not cause them to operate at the same volume. If you were to replace a 16-ohm speaker with a 4-ohm speaker, they would not operate at the same volume. The 4-ohm speaker would effectively be four times as efficient, and the 16-ohm speaker might not even be noticeable. This is one of the primary reasons for matching impedances within a cabinet—parity. This means that all of the speakers operate at an equal efficiency.

6. ALWAYS USE THE CORRECT IMPEDANCE
As you might suspect, a 16-ohm speaker has twice as much resistance as an 8-ohm speaker. This means that the amp has half the wattage at 16 ohms as it does at 8 ohms, and twice as much wattage at 4 ohms. This is only true for solid-state amps. They have only one output transformer tap. For a tube amp running as high as 700V across its power grid, it would go into meltdown very quickly; therefore, separate transformer windings are used to keep the amp within its operating range for each specific load.

This is why quite a few tube amps have three output transformer taps. They can have settings for 4, 8, and 16 ohms. Some old amps, like a Fender, are tapped for 4 ohms and won't be hurt by running a higher load, but can be damaged by running a lower load. Running a higher ohmage will never hurt a tube amp, but it will certainly be noticeably inefficient. However, some people like that sound. A tube amp will sound different at various ohmage ratings. Usually, the lower ohmages will produce a slightly more distorted sound and the amp will definitely run a bit hotter. They will not produce additional wattage by running lower impedances, because the transformer has compensated for the change in resistance across the output section. However, if you are adding an additional cabinet to cause the decrease in impedance, the mechanical aspects of two cabinets will certainly increase your volume!

SOLID-STATE AMPS
These amps are real workhorses. They are preferred when clean, reliable power is needed. They will take a fair amount of abuse and rarely complain, but they aren't as warm and

friendly sounding as tube amps. They require very little maintenance other than blowing out the dust from the inside and maybe cleaning a fan filter.

Solid-state amps have a wider range of operation than tube amps, so a variety of loads can be run without having to make changes to the output section of the amp. While most are nominally rated at 8 ohms, they can often be run at 4 and 16 ohms as well. It's not that the amp's wattage will remain the same, as it will become more efficient across a lower impedance and less efficient across a higher impedance. All amps are designed to have some resistance in the circuit.

It is important to note that the principles we are currently examining are in reference to a *mono* amp. You should understand what happens to a single amp before you consider the implications of a stereo amp and its various possibilities. While a lower impedance will increase an amp's potential, one of the effects of running at 4 ohms is that the amp is running hotter and will have a bit more distortion. The increased power will allow you to run lower input levels, and often this will offset the increased distortion specs.

Another effect of running lower impedances is that the amp will be a little less reliable. This is because it is working harder, and the thermal aspects have increased. This can be a problem when operating in really hot areas with no ventilation. If your solid-state amp blows a breaker or fuse in a hot area, you have two choices: add more ventilation, or increase the impedance. Make sure you know what the load limitations of your amp are. Some modern amps will run as low as 2 ohms, but *be sure* before you load them. Expect them to need considerable ventilation to operate properly, because blowing hot air on them won't work.

Tube Amps

These animals sound awesome, but they can be a bit cranky at times. They like clean voltage, fresh tubes, and specific loads, but will reward you with warm tones and singing feedback (the good kind!). Tube amps are usually rated at less output wattage, but require more AC power than their solid-state cousins. They require a bit of preventative maintenance to keep them sounding great. Output tubes should be replaced after six months of regular use.

Bad tubes will not only sound weak, but can also damage your amp. Since it is a gradual occurrence, most people don't notice bad tubes until they sound really bad; however, if you notice that the low end is soggy and weak, it is probably time to change them. Just make sure there isn't something in your signal chain causing this. Preamp tubes generally last for years; don't change one until it goes bad. If you notice "bad" feedback, excessive ringing, and noise, it is time to look into it.

With your guitar unplugged from the amp, powered up, and the controls set to normal levels, gently tap on each tube. If one of them responds loudly to your taps, it may be on its way south. If it is a multichannel amp, change channels and repeat until you have gone all the way through your rig. You will want to keep in mind that the V1 tube (the very first preamp tube) will always sound the noisiest, because all other tubes are amplifying its signal as well. So don't panic if you hear this tube make some noise, only if it's really bad.

It is very rare that a clean channel will go microphonic. If you aren't sure about a particular tube, swap it with another like tube from a different socket. Use the correct tube to swap with. Try using the clean channel tube in the drive channel tube socket. When you do find a bad tube, get a couple of replacements: not every new tube is tested for microphonics, and they all sound a bit different. When one tube goes bad, others may also be on their way out.

Tube amps will have fuses more often than breakers. Check your amp to see what kind and how many fuses it has. These specs will usually be listed next to the fuse holders. Get a few backups for each type. You may not need them for quite a while, but when you do, you'll need them right then. Regardless of what kind of amp you use, make sure that you are running it properly and have the right load across its output. Remember, you can always adjust the load by changing the wiring of the cabinet when you want to add more cabinets to your rig.

7. USE THE CORRECT TYPE OF CABLE

The Difference Between "Speaker Cords" and "Instrument Cables." It's not really a surprise that these two get mixed up. While they look very similar, they are not! Speaker cords are designed to handle much higher voltages and currents than instrument cables. They require a comparatively heavier-gauge wire and are *never* shielded from interference. Since they are located behind any amplification, there is no possibility of interference. Also, their higher voltage will reject any other signals, especially low-level RFI. You need a certain gauge wire for a specific wattage. The size will need to be increased for longer runs due to the accumulated resistance.

Instrument cables, on the other hand, should be of a smaller size and should *always* be shielded from interference. They are located *before* any amplification, and any noise they pick up will be subsequently amplified. Since their voltage range is very small, larger gauges affect the quality of the signal with capacitance. An amplifier can be damaged by running a small instrument cable as a speaker cord; it will cause you to run the settings higher than you normally would, and it will never sound "crisp" and "tight." While you will certainly get some sound out of your cabinet, it isn't always going to be the sound you are looking for. When selecting an instrument cable, use the shortest length possible. I suggest you use "oxygen-free" cable, which has been purged with nitrogen during the manufacturing process. The outside of the copper wire oxidizes first, where electricity prefers to travel—outside of the conductor. A quality cable should last quite a while, but if it isn't oxygen-free, its tone will degrade over time due to corrosive oxygen being trapped inside the coating. If you've ever stripped an old wire and seen green copper, you'll know what I'm talking about. Fig. 8.7 shows a table of recommended wire gauges for different wattages and lengths.

Wattage	Length	Minimum Gauge
50 watts	5'0 or less	18 ga.
50 watts	25'0 or less	18 ga
50 watts	50'0 or less	16 ga
50 watts	100'0 or more	14 ga
100 watts	5'0 or less	16 ga
100 watts	25'0 or less	16 ga
100 watts	50'0 or less	14 ga
100 watts	100'0 or more	12 ga
200 watts	5'0 or less	14 ga
200 watts	25'0 or less	14 ga
200 watts	50'0 or less	12 ga
200 watts	100'0 or more	10 ga
400 watts	5'0 or less	14 ga
400 watts	25'0 or less	12 ga
400 watts	50'0 or less	12 ga
400 watts	100'0 or more	10 ga
1000 watts	5'0 or less	12 ga
1000 watts	25'0 or less	12 ga
1000 watts	50'0 or less	10 ga
1000 watts	100'0 or more	8 ga

Fig. 8.7. Recommended wire gauges

8. UNDERSTAND THE DIFFERENCE BETWEEN BALANCED AND UNBALANCED CONNECTIONS

Balanced Cables. Microphone cables are balanced cables with three conductors. All three conductors are required for the cable to work properly. The way these cables work to keep noise out is really very simple: They feature an extra conductor that is out of phase with the original positive conductor, and when the signal reaches its destination, its polarity is reversed (thereby making it a positive signal conductor with a now-negative noise signal) and added to the positive conductor. Any noise picked up along the way is canceled, because it is common to both conductors, one of which now has been reversed. I realize this can be confusing to most people, so Fig. 8.8A shows what is happening to the noise. This is a clever concept that was developed by Bell Telephone many years ago. When you consider how many miles a land line has to travel to reach its destination, it's a miracle you can hear anything at all.

Fig. 8.8A.
Balanced
signals

Balancing Transformer

Hot and Cold are twisted
to pickup noise equally

Balancing Transformer

+

+

Positive Phase-Hot

Negative Phase -Cold

Ground - Shield

−

−

The positive signal is split
into 0 degrees and 180
degrees out of phase

The noise that is picked
up is common to both
phases

The Negative Cold AND noise
is reversed 180 degrees and
combined with Positive-Hot
All common noise is cancelled

Balanced cables will work with only two conductors if they are the right two combinations (ground-hot and ground-cold); otherwise they just stop working when the ground is out. You may not notice that the "cold" or "hot" is not working when using a short cable, but if you were to run a microphone snake many yards to a console, it would be extremely noisy and sound weak. If for some reason you notice that your mic is noisy, try a new cable and see if this helps. If it takes care of the problem, replace the bad cable. Checking with a volt-ohm meter will confirm or deny any suspicion of this. Simply verify that all three connections are reaching the opposite end without touching each other.

Hot Pin Designation. Another point to consider when using any three-pin XLR balanced devices is the "hot pin" designation. While most devices are wired "pin 2 hot," some of the older units aren't. This will invert the phase relationship of that device with the rest of your pin 2 hot units. Since these devices reverse the phase again on an XLR output, you may never even notice that your signal has reversed its phase *twice* and is now correct. However, there are some cases where your connections change and don't automatically reverse the phase. You can correct this by intentionally wiring a cable out of phase. Reversing the pin 2 and pin 3 on *only one side* will take care of this (see Fig 8.8B).

Fig. 8.8B.
Phasing
balanced
signals

Facing the connection

Facing each other

#1   #2

#2   #1

#3

#3

Male-pins

Correctly phasing a Pin 3 Hot device
Reverse one side only!

Female-holes

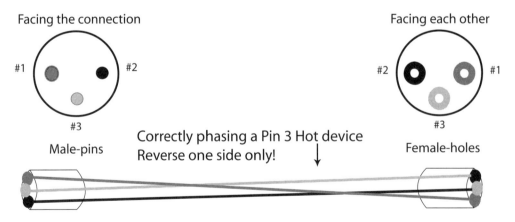

If you do this on both sides of the same cord, you will be right back where you started; out of phase but on different leads. However, if you choose to correct the phase going into the unit, *you must also correct the phase coming out of the unit.* The only way to tell if your device is pin 2 hot (as it should be) or pin 3 hot (where the trouble begins) is to look on the back of the unit. There should be an input wiring diagram or hot-pin designation.

Checking the manufacturer's specs online will help if you can't get to the unit itself or if it just doesn't say. There will be very few times that musicians will ever set up a system that has this problem, but it is always a point to consider when setting up any PA or monitor system. Fig. 8.8C shows some examples of how this affects your signal.

TRS balanced cables look very similar to ¼-inch unbalanced cables except that they have a tip, a ring, and a sleeve. They look exactly like a stereo ¼-inch plug. That doesn't necessarily mean that you can use a "stereo" cable. Many cheap "stereo cables"

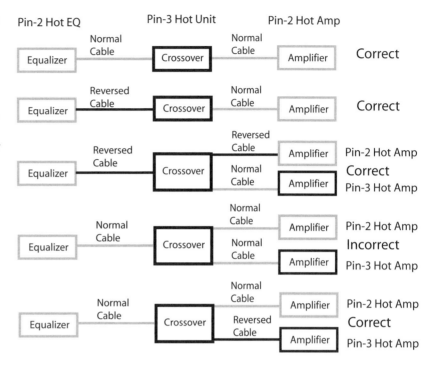

Fig. 8.8C. Pin 3 hot devices

are designed for headphones and are typically unshielded. For a balanced line to work properly, it must be wired and shielded correctly. In a TRS cable, the tip is hot, the ring is cold, and the sleeve is ground, unless the device specifies otherwise. TRS ends can be soldered to any XLR cable; you just have to make sure that the terminations are correct for each application. Also remember that the XLR end will need a female jack for output connections and a male jack for input connections. The TRS cable is always male.

As we just covered, all adapter cables should be correctly terminated, and any cable with an XLR end should be designated either pin 2 or pin 3 hot. While most TRS cables are universally tip hot, it is the XLR end that has to be correctly specified. Fig. 8.8D gives three examples.

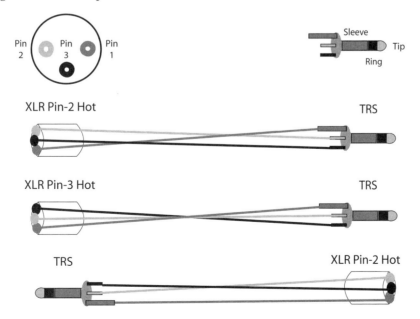

Fig. 8.8D. Terminating adapters

Unbalanced Cables. Unbalanced cables are usually the guitar-jack type with a ¼-inch tip/sleeve configuration. These cables should be shielded, but will not prevent noise and signal degradation over long runs. They are particularly sensitive to the AC voltage hum that can occur when audio cables and AC are run parallel to each other in close proximity. All low-level audio is. I know that sometimes it is necessary to run both audio cables and AC to the same destination, so you need to keep them at least a foot apart, preferably 1½ feet apart.

You can *cross* AC power cables with audio cables and vice-versa, but *only at a 90 degree angle!* The reason you can't run them parallel is that the high-voltage AC will "induct" its 60-cycle hum into the low-voltage audio lines that are on their way to be amplified. Inductance is a normal electrical phenomenon and is used in many aspects of electronics; this just happens to be one of its *bad* habits. Fig. 8.9 shows the proper way to run AC cords and input cables.

Fig. 8.9. Running A/C cords and input cables

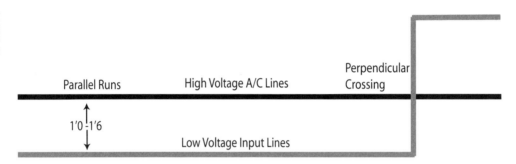

Parallel Runs   High Voltage A/C Lines   Perpendicular Crossing

1'0 - 1'6

Low Voltage Input Lines

Keep input cables at least 1'0 from high-voltage AC cords 1'6 (18") is optimum

Cross high-voltage cords at a 90 degree angle ONLY! The short distance of the crossing will not induct hum Either can cross at a 90 degree

9. LEARN HOW TO MAKE A HOTSHOT

In chapter 2, there is a brief description of a "hotshot." Essentially, it is a monitor floor wedge that has been converted into an instrument wedge cabinet for unobtrusive placement onstage. Using a hotshot will put sound directly where you need it without elevating your stage levels. In this chapter, we will go into more detail about this type of alternative speaker cabinet. Before you begin, you should examine a few things to determine what will be right for you.

Selecting the Right Wedge. What will be the purpose of the hotshot? Is it for guitar or bass? Will it be used for the other side of the stage or for your own personal wedge? Will it be very close or placed a short distance away? *What, why,* and *where* are your determining factors when selecting the right wedge.

Guitar. I wouldn't recommend anything but a 12-inch cabinet for guitar. It seems to have the right frequency range for guitar tone. It's also a pretty common choice for monitor wedges. Both guitar and voice are fairly close in timbre. If the wedge is for you to listen to and you like a lot of guitar, go with a 2×12 cabinet. If you only need a little and it will be close to you, you could use a 1×12 without a problem. If it is farther away, you will probably want to use a 2×12 wedge.

Bass. I think most bass players would prefer the sound of a 15-inch wedge to a 10-inch or 12-inch wedge, but that doesn't mean that you couldn't use the smaller speakers. It's a matter of preference. The 15-inch speaker has better bass response and should be placed *away* from mic stands or it will leak low-end rumble into the microphone. You probably won't find a 2×15 monitor wedge; besides being bulky and quite heavy, it would have too much bass for its intended use as a normal vocal wedge, which is why one wouldn't be easily available. The same goes for 18-inch floor wedges. You will probably have to settle for a 1×15 wedge or build your own. Unless you are a decent carpenter, you'd be better off converting a floor wedge. The time and energy required would be better spent on your band!

Selecting the Right Impedance and Wattage. Once you have decided on a single or double speaker cabinet and its size, you will need to find the right speakers to load it with. Now is the time to evaluate your amp and determine what impedance will be best suited for it. Most amps will only run 4, 8, or 16 ohms, and you will be "splitting" your load by adding another cabinet in parallel. To get your amp to run 8 ohms, *both* your cabinet and the hotshot *must* be 16-ohm loads. To get your amp to run 4 ohms, both must be 8-ohm loads. You wouldn't want to add a 16-ohm hotshot to an 8-ohm amp cabinet; you'd wind up at 12 ohms. It would be best to match your present cabinet (as long as it's 8 ohms or more). This will save having to change the impedance of your cabinet. Don't try any serial wiring techniques here; losing one load would cause you to lose both. Keep them parallel!

Wattages can't be forgotten, either; use speakers that match the wattage of the other cabinet, or in the case of using *just* a hotshot, you need a total wattage that matches the amp's rating. Hotshots aren't quite as loud as most conventional cabinets, so you may be tempted to push them a bit and overrun the wattage rating. It's a good idea to keep the wattage and impedance of your hotshot similar to your amp's cabinet: *matched efficiency*. The two cabinets will behave in a similar fashion, which makes setting your amp much easier rather than compromising the tone of each to make both work. Fig. 8.10 shows a table for selecting speaker ohmage and wattage.

Amp wattge	Cab Watt/ohm	Hotshot ohmage one speaker	Hotshot Watt/Ohms two speakers	Set amp for
50 watt amp	50 watt @ 8 ohms	50 watt @ 8 ohms	25 watts @ 16 ohms X 2 Parallel wired	4 Ohms
100 watt amp	100 watt @ 16 ohms	100 watt @ 16 ohms	50 watts @ 8 ohms X 2 Series wired	8 Ohms
100 watt amp	100 watt @ 4 ohms Rewire for 16 ohms	100 watt @ 16 ohms	50 watts @ 8 ohms X 2 Series wired	8 Ohms
400 watt bass amp	400 watt @ 8 ohms	200 watt @ 8 ohms	100 watts @ 16 ohms X 2 Parallel wired	8 Ohms

Fig. 8.10. Selecting loads and ratings for hotshots

Rewiring Your Wedges. Most floor wedges were designed with vocals in mind, and feature passive crossovers and tweeters in the wiring. Tweeters aren't needed for guitar, and even though they are handy for bass, your levels will probably destroy them. You are running your amp directly to them with a fair amount of wattage behind it.

Most players "drive" their amps so the speakers can get that "tone," and this will tear up crossovers and tweeters. You don't want to physically remove them, or you will compromise the cabinet porting. In some cases, the cone tweeters will "sympathetically" resonate without being wired in—it won't be much, but it will be some enhancement.

You want to "electronically" remove them *and* the crossover that runs them. Wire them directly to both inputs. Fig. 8.11 gives an example for wiring up a hotshot with one speaker. Having two inputs will give you a backup in case one is damaged or you need to double them. For those who would like to use a two-speaker hotshot, refer to the table above for impedance and wattage specs.

Fig. 8.11.
Wiring up
hotshots

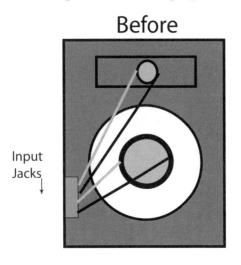

Remove Input jack,
crossover assembly
and all wiring

Replace crossover assembly
with dual input jacks on a
flat non-conductive plate
Replace Speaker correctly

Wire speaker directly
to dual input jacks Do
Not remove horn or
tweeter

Since using two speakers changes the final load, refer to Fig. 8.12 for two different ways to approach this. If your hotshot is too loud when your amp cabinet is running where you like it, you could place an attenuator in the path and reduce the volume to a comfortable level. See "Learn How to Use an Attenuator," below.

Fig. 8.12.
Wiring up a
two-speaker
hotshot

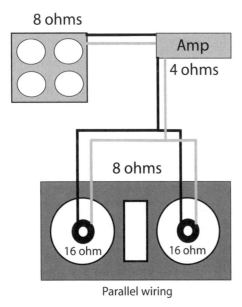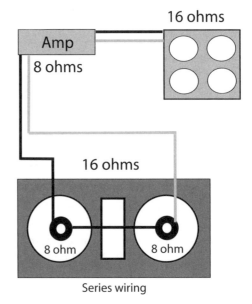

Hotrodding Your Hotshot. For more adventurous and electronically inclined individuals, hotshots don't *have* to be simple passive speaker wedges. They can be run by an entirely different amp, giving you full control over the volume, EQ, and even effects. Many players use two amps with completely different tones. In some cases these amps are switched between the two sounds; in other cases, they are run together as one sound. This hotrodding technique is a more radical version of the same idea. The emphasis is on getting your sound in a more practical spot. Consider the time it would take to set up two separate amp rigs and dial them in. While this is not the most practical solution, it may turn out to be the *only* solution to some problems. Fig. 8.13 gives an example of hotrodding a hotshot.

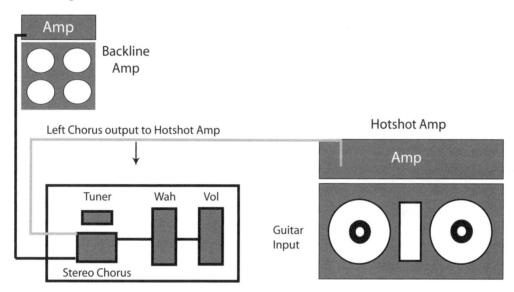

Fig. 8.13. Hotrodding a hotshot

10. LEARN HOW TO USE AN ATTENUATOR

What the devil is an attenuator? It's a passive high-power volume control. This device is generally used to overdrive an amp to get that "cranked up" tone while giving you control over the volume level. Quite a few guitarists use them on old non-master Marshalls and vintage Fenders for this purpose. Usually a medium-size unit, a good attenuator is not cheap. It requires no AC power and will only *reduce* volume.

An attenuator is used *after* the amplification process instead of during or before it. It is run between the amp's output and the speaker cabinet. Because it comes after the power stage of the amp, it can handle some fairly high wattage. For this reason, it has to be quite a bit sturdier than your normal "volume control." Note that an attenuator will make your amp sound different.

Attenuators can have a few other tricks up their sleeves as well, although their task will be the same. For example, if you had two cabinets in different locations and you wanted to control the volume of one but not the other, you could patch in an attenuator (see Fig. 8.14 examples A and B). This is also how you can adjust the level of a hotshot or crossfired cabinet if it is too loud. An attenuator also works great on the far-side cabinet in a doubled configuration. The player on the other side can easily adjust the level of your sound in his zone without affecting the level in your zone.

An attenuator is quite simple to use, but you need to consider the ohm settings when using it. Where it is placed in the configuration is important in how you set the impedance on the attenuator. See Fig. 8.14 for how you would set it for one cabinet, two cabinets, or one of two cabinets.

When using one cabinet, set the attenuator for the same load as the cabinet. When using it for two cabinets together, as in Fig. 8.14 Example C, set it for the total load of both cabinets. If you are running two 16-ohm cabinets, you would need to set the attenuator for 8 ohms, because that is the "total load" when the two are paralleled together. When using it for one of two cabinets, like a hotshot or cross-stage cabinet, then place it *after* the first cabinet and *before* the second cabinet.

You would set it for the "total load" of the single cabinet, not the combined ohmage of both. If there is ever any doubt, put a volt-ohm meter on the load and that will tell you all you need to know. Always remember to check your final ohm load and set your amp for the correct impedance setting. Since most amps have two output jacks on the back, you could run one directly to a cabinet and the other directly to the attenuator, keeping in mind that they will still parallel together at the amp.

Fig. 8.14. Wiring up attenuators

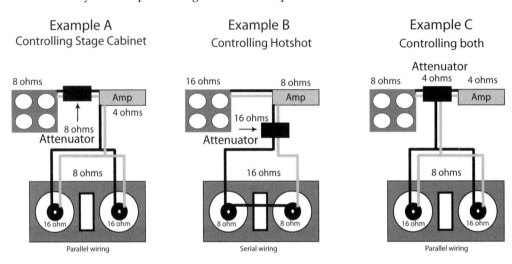

Example A
Controlling Stage Cabinet

Example B
Controlling Hotshot

Example C
Controlling both

11. UNDERSTAND UNITY GAIN

Understanding Unity Gain and Gain Structure. Most signal-processing devices are designed to operate at a "line level" of 0 dBV. *Unity gain* is a term used for the gain setting in which an audio device neither *adds nor subtracts* any gain from the signal being sent to it, independent of its actual function. 0 dBV doesn't mean no signal; it is just the point of reference on the voltage scale for unity gain. Anything above 0 dBV *adds* level to the incoming signal. Anything below 0 dBV *subtracts* level from the incoming signal. This is a very important setting when you have several units wired in succession. If each device added a couple dBV to the signal, then you could easily distort the devices toward the end of the signal chain. Unity gain is simply a point of reference between two units.

If each device subtracted a couple dBV, then you could be forced to drive the input stage into distortion to make up for the gain lost at each stage. Since each device is designed to operate at 0 dBV cleanly and provide the maximum amount of adjustment at that point, unity gain provides a point of reference when setting up systems. On a properly set up system, you would be able to run full, clean volume from the mixer and *know* that all devices were running full, clean volume as well. This will give you the maximum amount of headroom and efficiency in each device and through your entire system. If you ran the mixer above a certain point, then all devices would "clip," so you would be able to tell from the mixer when you were about to start clipping. Fig. 8.15 shows a typical gain structure configuration. All of this has been simplified to help you grasp the concept of unity gain, but there are some things you should be aware of when setting up multiple devices in succession.

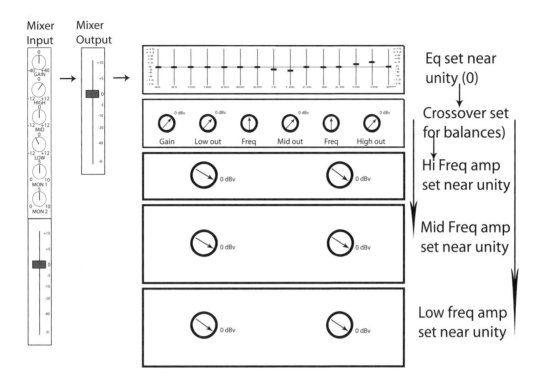

Fig. 8.15. Typical gain structure configuration

Matching Operating Levels. Not all devices are created equal. Professional gear operates at +4 dBV. Semi-pro devices usually operate at –10 dBV, although they still are showing a 0 dBV unity gain level. There is a considerable difference between the signal levels of these devices. The theory of unity gain discussed above goes out the window when operating levels are mismatched; however, most devices have a "makeup" gain adjustment that will allow you to add enough gain to the input or subtract enough from it to compensate for this at the price of added noise. Fig. 8.16 gives an example of mismatched operating levels.

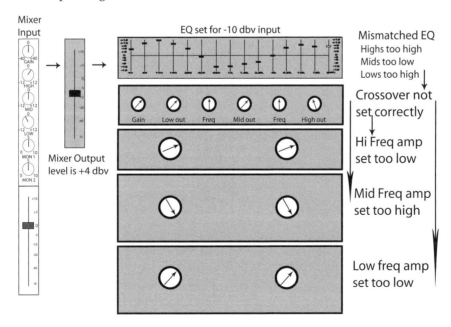

Fig. 8.16. Mismatched gain structures

In Fig. 8.15, all devices have matched operating levels. In Fig. 8.16, a –10 dBV EQ is being used on an otherwise +4 dBV device chain. There are also many common mistakes shown in this example. The mixer output is reduced to match the EQ's input level, and the EQ's output is raised to match the crossover's input level. I really don't recommend running a system this way. There seems to be a huge disparity in the quality of pro and semi-pro devices, and you could compromise your sound by using both in your signal chain. That doesn't mean you should buy all cheap crap just to keep your system matched, but should you buy a pro piece of gear, don't expect it to perform at a pro level if the rest of your system isn't pro quality. A pro piece of gear won't operate and sound better until the whole system has been upgraded. A signal chain is only as strong as its weakest link.

12. CORRECTLY TERMINATE ALL CONNECTIONS

Phase Relationships. The term *phase* can have a multitude of meanings. It can refer to an acoustical or electrical occurrence. For the purposes of the book, we will be discussing several aspects of phase. All electronic signals are AC, or alternate current, meaning they alternate between positive and negative waveforms. It takes *two* identical but opposite wave pulses to form a single waveform. *Polarity* refers to the particular direction at a certain point. Here are some examples:

►When signal is applied to a speaker, the positive form of the wave that is applied to the positive terminal of the speaker from the positive terminal of the amp will cause the speaker to push outward. To complete the waveform, the equal but opposite negative form will cause the speaker to pull inward. This is what happens when the wiring is correctly polarized. If the positive terminal of the amp were applied to the negative terminal of the speaker, then the positive form of the wave would then cause the speaker to pull inward as if it were negative. This actually makes very little difference to your perception if there are no other speakers for this output *or* they are all wired to matching polarity. However, if you have *two* speakers and one of them is reversed in polarity, or out of phase, then one speaker would be pushing while the other speaker is pulling. The result would be acoustic cancellation, and would be noticeably weird sounding, especially if the speakers were in the same cabinet. The sound would be seriously lacking in definition and volume. This is why it is *so* important to keep your polarity correct when wiring cables and speakers.

►When a sound reaches a microphone, the compression and rarefaction that makes up an acoustic sound wave causes the microphone to vibrate back and forth. The rarefaction wave causes the microphone diaphragm to move in one direction, while the equal but opposite compression wave causes it to move in the other direction.

Typically, the compression wave will produce a positive voltage at the positive terminal of the microphone output. If the positive terminal of the microphone is connected to the positive terminal of the console input, you will have a coherent connection, and the positive signal will be positive from the microphone all the way to the console. If the positive terminal of the microphone is connected to the negative terminal of the console, as in an improperly wired cable, then a positive wave from the mic will produce a negative wave at the console.

Once again, this would have very little effect on your perception of the sound *by itself.* However, if *two* microphones are picking up the same sound, being equal in loudness and opposite in polarity, the result would be "electronic" cancellation, and the sound would seem to disappear! Unlike speakers being out of phase in two different physical spaces, electronic signals of opposite polarity occupy the same electronic path and mathematically cancel each other out. Even though we are discussing alternating current, each current alternates in different directions, therefore they cancel each other out each time they alternate, because they are being summed. Now you can understand why it is so important to make sure that all of your input and output connections are wired in phase. There is *much* more to consider when discussing phase relationships, but these examples should illustrate how improper polarity can adversely affect your signal. You should get in the habit of *always* correctly terminating your connections properly, both AC and (especially) DC. DC, or direct current, absolutely has to be terminated correctly. Not only will a DC device not work, but you could damage it by incorrectly terminating it.

13. LEARN HOW TO CALCULATE DELAY TIMES

Calculating accurate delay times is a trick used by pretty much every professional recording studio in the world. A few delay units will let you "tap" in delay times, and I can't tell you how convenient that is! Delays sound much more musical when they are timed to the relevant tempos of the music they are accompanying.

Perfect quarter notes seem to be the delay that most people hear in their head when they envision an echo. I admit that this feels right most of the time, but it can get a bit predictable. Once you know how to calculate delay times, you will look at them as a very creative avenue. The secret of timing delays is to calculate the quarter-note timing of the song, as this is the starting point for other mathematical time divisions. You will need to know the bpm (beats per minute) tempo of the tune. This is a "per minute" measurement, but the delay times are given in a "per second" measurement. You will have to find a common denominator for both. One is given in minutes and the other is given in milliseconds:

$$60,000/bpm = milliseconds\ per\ beat$$

There are 60 seconds in a minute, and 1,000 milliseconds (ms) in a second. That makes 60,000 ms in a minute, which is the same calculation that your song tempo is given in.

$$60,000/bpm = 1\ beat$$

Here is a *very* easy example that illustrates how this works. You have a slow song that comes out to 60 bpm. Your formula would look like this:

$$60,000/60 = 1,000\ ms\ per\ beat,\ or\ a\ perfect\ quarter\ note$$

A song with a tempo of 120 bpm would be 500 ms per beat. If you want eighth-note delays, then you can divide the quarter-note figure in half, and so on. Here is a general guideline for delay times:

Long delay = half note

Medium delay = quarter note

Short delay = eighth note

Slapback = 32nd note

Double = 128th note

While most people just play with the delay time until they like something, starting with these time divisions will allow you to hear a musical delay time before you decide to play around with it. A dual delay produces a different delay for each side, giving your sound a sense of time and space. To get delays that don't coincide or step on each other, you can use a modified version of this formula to space the delays out musically. Figure your desired delay time; in this case, quarter notes. Then calculate the eighth-note time and add it to the quarter-note length of one side. This will be your secondary delay's time. It will sit nicely between the repeats of your primary delay and give a side-to-side bounce in stereo. It's not a "ping-pong" delay, but it's similar. It's a bit more full-sounding because the delays overlap. This can also be done in "half time" for a tighter delay sound.

Singers will use this formula more than anyone else, but it comes in handy for keyboardists and guitarists as well. It will save you hours searching for delay times by giving you a logical starting point.

Calculating BPM. Most people who write music rarely do so to a clock; inspiration strikes and they just go with the flow. Sometimes it starts with a riff, other times it's a melody or a beat, and then it's off to the races! One thing never changes in music: It has a tempo, even if it changes!

14. LEARN HOW TO CALCULATE TEMPO

Calculating tempos is an important production skill. It's not one that you will use every day, but when you need to, you should be able to calculate tempo. Delay times are one example; studio click tracks are another. There are really only a couple of ways to do this, and you need a drum machine or calibrated metronome and a good understanding of tempo. While most 4/4 songs are fairly simple, polyrhythms and odd meters can be deceptive. Calculations aren't reserved just for delay tempos; it's a skill you need to have in your musical arsenal for consistency.

Metronome. Finding tempos is simply a trial-and-error process. With the song in mind, adjust the metronome to what is in your head. Check it by playing to the metronome, and keep making adjustments until it's right. When you finally get through the song completely and you are comfortable with it, *write it down*! The real challenge is getting tempos to synchronize once you've made an adjustment; essentially you have to restart the song or part over to the new adjustment. Electronic metronomes are easier than mechanical ones for this purpose. You simply restart the new tempo adjustment on a new beat during the song. You will be able to find the correct tempo either way.

Drum machine tempos are a bit more involved. With most drum machines, sequencers, and software programs, you have the option of setting the tempo from the "master" tempo adjustment or the individual "program/pattern" tempo. If you are simply using the device to figure the tempo, then either way will work. If you are actually programming the song, its arrangement and count-offs, then it may be better to do so from the actual program/pattern. This way other songs will come up as you had programmed them. Changing the master tempo would change them all. If you are programming tempos into each pattern or song, then you can adjust the master tempo without having to go to each individual program to make any subsequent adjustments.

Set an empty pattern with a click and adjust the tempo until it matches the song in your head. Check it by playing with it and making adjustments until it's right, just like with a metronome.

Odd meters could use some help by placing a slightly louder click or a different sound on the 1 downbeat. This gives you an audio cue point with which to figure measures and arrangements. If you had a song in 7/8, this would emphasize the start of a new measure. This definitely requires a drum machine/sequencer-type device.

Using 7/8 timing as an example, set your empty "pattern" or "program" to a seven-beat length and adjust it like you would a standard 4/4 song, but make that first beat either louder or a completely different sound. Occasionally you will find that your tempo is actually a different timing than you had originally thought, and you will have to make a "time division" or "signature" change.

If adding or subtracting a beat to the length makes the pattern work, then you would actually be adjusting the first number of the time signature. If your tempo still isn't working because it's between adjustments, like a 15/16 time signature would be, then you will need to double the *length and tempo* of your current settings and try again until the length and tempo matches what's in your head. Keep in mind that you'll be counting in half time. Most drum machines will allow you to set the click on any time division you need. Machines and programs typically will not drop half a beat, which is why you need to double the tempo and length to fool the machine into thinking like you do; however, it is really exactly the opposite: you have to think like the machine! This may seem a little odd at first, especially if most of the song is a straight-ahead tune and only a lick at the end breaks the form, but it works. It may affect the way you have to program the rest of the song, which is normally in a conventional timing.

If you find that your song is polyrhythmic, meaning it has multiple time signatures and changes, you should use the largest common denominator for all of your patterns. If your changes went to 7/8, then your 4/4 parts should be programmed in 8/8 so that all you need to do is drop a single beat in the pattern to make them work together. This prevents you from having to program in tempo changes with the time signature changes.

Fortunately, most people who hear these timings in their heads understand tempo fairly well, but that doesn't necessarily mean that they understand programming very well. This should help you out when a song gets a bit tricky. It can be a lot of work just to figure out a tempo, but it makes you understand *exactly* what you are doing with a song and removes any "randomness" that can go awry onstage during a performance. You will find yourself going after some odd and complex signatures!

15. UNDERSTAND PRODUCT SPECS

Product specs are very useful measurements that allow someone to decide if a product is suitable for a particular purpose. They are also deceptive marketing tools in the hands of clever marketers. *A budget amp can appear to have similar specs to a very expensive amp if you loosen up the tolerances enough!* Since there is no "absolute" standard for general specs, leaving out an important figure or adjusting the testing criteria can make a lesser product appear to be adequate. Knowing what these figures mean and understanding the techniques used to generate them will allow you to make informed decisions about your purchases. While there a few common specs for almost all equipment, each type of product has a different function and requires a measurement for that application. There are also many different ways to test products, and it is here where you can be misled. We're going to take a look at some of these specs so you aren't fooled quite as easily.

Tolerances. When comparing specs from different products, you may see a similar graph between the two, but if the tolerances are different you won't get an accurate comparison. Tolerances are the amount of deviation that is "acceptable" to the test criteria. They often appear as a +/– dB value. Having a ±1 dB tolerance means that there can be a difference of 2 dB between any two points on the graph. One frequency could be 1 dB *more* than the graph, while another frequency could be 1 dB *less* than the graph. Having a ±3 dB tolerance means that it could deviate as much as 6 dB! This is a considerable amount of difference! In fact, it's a difference that may render the specs worthless for the device. If you don't see a tolerance value for a spec, it's hardly worth the paper it's written on. This "tolerance" is also used to smooth out graphs and make the product look flatter than it really is. A perfectly flat graph is almost impossible in real-world comparisons. In some cases, multiple units are tested and "averaged" for a smoother response curve, as few will have the same deviations in the same places.

Wattage. Another spec that can be deceptive is wattage: Let's say you are looking at 200W amps for your PA system, and one of them says "rated at 4 ohms" and the other says "rated at 8 ohms," but they are both 200W amps. Earlier in the chapter, we looked at impedance, so we can say that the 200W amp "rated at 4 ohms" will be about 100W when pushing an 8-ohm load. You have to be careful about this spec to *know* what ohm rating they are using to figure the wattage. If you were buying a 200W amp hoping to get 400W at 4 ohms, you'd be pretty upset when you realized this. This would also be true if the rating was in "bridged mode," as quite a few companies do this to double their rating specs. Another aspect to consider is that most of these ratings are for "both channels driven," and the spec would actually be less if the identical signals were not sent to both channels simultaneously with identical loads. In most "bipolar" amps, inductance is used to maximize the output by running each side of the amp out of phase with the other. This not only increases the amount of power produced by the transformer, but it also brings down adjacent channel crosstalk specs. One side of the amp is pushing while the other is pulling. If each side was in phase with the other, you would need a transformer twice the size to handle the larger voltage swings needed in each direction, *or* separate transformers. This is one of the methods that design engineers use to cut corners. It has three benefits: it's lighter, smaller, and cheaper; however, it has two distinct drawbacks: You can't run different loads on each channel, and when only one channel is driven, it runs at less than the rated power. Running a bipolar amp at two different ohmages will stress the transformer; the side with the higher load resistance on it will "drag" the voltage swing for the other side and eventually burn the transformer out. Running only one side of a bipolar amp will not give you the rated voltage swing that you are looking for because the idle side is "dragging" the active side; however, your chances of blowing the transformer are less likely unless you are running a very low ohmage at a high wattage. The way around this is to run the amp in bridged mode when only one channel is being used, provided it can handle the load.

Mono-bloc amplifiers have individual transformers for each side or are simply a single-channel amp. You can run them at any ohmage you like within spec without regard for the other side, because the two channels are not interdependent. They are *heavy* and *expensive*, almost to the point where it's more practical to run a bipolar amp in bridged mode. Bridging will double the rated single-channel wattage, but will not allow you to run the lower-ohm loads.

Bridging an amp will only allow you to run *twice* the lowest-rated impedance for the amp. The bottom line on wattage is that it is directly related to the ohmage. Be sure you understand these important facts about solid-state amps before you make a snap decision on buying one.

Signal-to-Noise Ratio. This spec is almost always present in electronic devices due to the inherent "self-noise" that is generated by the internal components. Signal-to-noise ratios are given in a –dB figure, with the rated maximum *clean* output level being 0 dB on the scale and the –dB figure being the amount of noise that will be present when all inputs are removed. If a device's specs stated that its signal-to-noise ratio was –97 dB, then when you set your device at its maximum operating range at unity gain and removed all inputs, there would be a residual amount of noise that is 97 dB *less* than unity level. When you are comparing devices and their specs seem similar, look at the signal-to-noise ratio and you may be able to spot the difference. The higher the negative number, the quieter the sound, in all cases. With mixing consoles, individual channels can build up noise *very quickly*! Add effects and some compression, and you will be hearing hiss before you know it on a cheap device with poor specs. Even a difference of 1 dB less signal to noise can make a noticeable difference between two units if you consider the implications of a 32-channel console. On a full PA system, there can be as many as nine devices in the signal chain— *keep it clean!*

Adjacent channel crosstalk is another spec closely related to signal-to-noise ratio. This spec is again given in negative form, with one channel being run at a nominal output level and the other channel being measured for "leakage" into the unused channel that is set for nominal output. The rating will reflect the crosstalk under this condition. You would be surprised at just how much leakage actually occurs, but since there is not enough of a difference to be directly perceptible by the human ear, it is often not much of a problem. When you are only running a couple of channels on a small console, this will matter very little. When you are running a 40-input console and using all the channels, you *will* notice a difference on a board with lower specs. The sound will seem to lose "clarity."

Slew rate is a term for the speed at which a signal travels from the front of the input through all the electronics to the output. Most people think that this is instantaneous, but it is not. It takes a very small amount of time, usually in the millionths of a second, but it is still measurable. When many units are wired in a signal chain, it can start to add up slightly. It's really not enough to create any perceptible delay, but this slight delay can "color" the sound and create distortion. The faster the signal "slews" through the system, the less chances of coloration and distortion. Different types of devices have different typical rates, so don't try to compare power amp slew rates with mic pre slew rates. Use similar devices when making comparisons. This is just another spec you can use to determine the suitability of a product.

Fluorescent Lights. Ah yes, the nasty zapping of a fluorescent light buzzing in your system is quite irritating. It's like a high-frequency version of 60-cycle hum. Yes, it is 60 cycles, but it is a "burst" of frequencies at 60 cycles that gives it its nasty "zapping" sound. What is happening is that the "ballast" capacitor is charging and discharging at 60 cycles, creating what you perceive as *noise*. By now, you have the idea: *don't use fluorescent lights with any audio equipment*. If there is another power outlet *and* it's on a different AC leg, you *might* not have a problem. If it causes any noise, *remove it*. Even light dimmers can do this. Other high- and medium-voltage devices may very well cause your AC power to be noisy as well. Some motorized stage props can induce noise while in operation. Take the time to check the operation of them *during* rehearsals and also with a full PA or monitors set up, and listen for noise while they are being used. Even if there is some noise, it may not be enough to cause too much of a problem if the effect is really needed.

IN CONCLUSION

Life is very progressive, so your stage show should be too. Nobody can possibly know everything, so when a problem arises, *go after it*. The Internet has a wealth of information on stage sound. Some of it is BS, but you really don't know until you actually try it out. Take the time to look into the equipment you own and evaluate its maintenance and troubleshooting procedures. Spend some time looking into the PA systems and monitor systems that you work with. Problems will find you all on their own; the solutions will not! When problems arise, make a note of them. Be as detailed as you can, then when you have time, seek answers for them. You will be surprised at how many of the answers are interrelated, and once you have a found a few, you will start finding more. Even dumb luck will hand you a few freebies! Go to www.rockinyourstagesound.com for any technical questions. I'll be more than happy to help!

Let's have a look at what we have covered in this chapter:

1. Learn to Operate a Volt-Ohm Meter
2. Learn How to Test Impedance
3. Learn How to Test Cables
4. Learn How to Check Fuses
5. Understand Ohm's Principles
6. Always Use the Correct Impedance
7. Use the Correct Type of Cable
8. Understand the Difference Between Balanced and Unbalanced Connections
9. Learn How to Make a Hotshot
10. Learn How to Use an Attenuator
11. Understand Unity Gain
12. Correctly Terminate All Connections
13. Learn How to Calculate Delay Times
14. Learn How to Calculate Tempo
15. Understand Product Specs

GLOSSARY OF AUDIO TERMS

808: One of the stock kick drums on a Roland TR-808 drum machine; highly popular in loops. It is a pure 80 Hz sine wave with a short 10 kHz attack. It's the long *boom* you hear in most hip-hop and rap.

909: This is the same as an 808, except it is a very short sound.

A/B Box: A simple switching unit that changes the direction or destination of a signal. It can change either the input or the output of any two devices.

Analog: A nondigital, unquantized, linear form.

Attenuator: A device that is wired between the amp and speaker that reduces the volume of the speaker without affecting the volume of the amp.

Aux: An abbreviation for auxiliary.

Auxiliary: A send or an additional output. It provides an additional mix.

Axis: Directly in line with a microphone or speaker diaphragm. Also directly in line with a sound source.

Backline: The amps/cabinets/drums that reside at the back of the stage and the most basic equipment a band would need.

Balanced: A balanced signal; usually a 3-pin input, output, or cable. *Balanced* can also mean equality between one or more subjects. A balanced line has a positive (+) signal, a negative (–) signal, and a ground. When noise is introduced into the cable, it is "common" to both the positive and negative signals. When the negative signal is reversed in polarity (making the signal positive and the noise negative) and added to the original positive signal with the positive noise, the signal is reinforced and the noise is cancelled. This is called CMR, or Common Mode Rejection.

Bipolar Circuit: When a power amp has two amps in different phases, with one amp pulling current while the other amp is pushing current. It takes both a push and a pull of the transformer to reach a full voltage swing of the amp.

Bleed: What happens when a sound is loud enough to "leak" into a mic placed on another sound.

Bs: Abbreviation for bass guitar.

Bus: A path that allows you to route multiple signals to one output.

Cancellation: What happens when two identical waves of opposite polarity combine to cancel each other out. A simple example is +6V + –6V = 0V. Cancellation can be either "physical sound waves" or "electronic signals."

Changeover: A set change; removing one set and replacing it with another.

Coloration: The effect when a piece of equipment is added to a signal path. Also the effect that one device may have on another when they interact.

Compressor: An audio device that turns down the input by a certain percentage when it reaches a defined level. Similar to a limiter, but not as aggressive.

CMR: Common mode rejection . The process of reversing the negative signal of a balanced line and summing it with the positive signal, thereby canceling the noise that is common to both signals. A balanced output requires that a negative signal is produced from the primary output in order for this to happen.

Cyclic: Moving in cycles. Being cyclic means that the end product will affect the source, which in turn will affect the end result in proportion to its effect. *Feedback* is an example of cyclic redundancy.

DI: Abbreviation for direct input. Typically a DI is a direct box that allows you to plug a non-XLR input into a mixing console.

Downstage: Toward the back of the stage.

Element: Another term for a microphone diaphragm.

Equal Loudness Contour: The effect of certain frequencies becoming louder or softer than others when the overall level is raised or lowered. 100 Hz and 3.1 kHz will become noticeably louder when the volume is raised and noticeably quieter when the volume is lowered. It is similar to the "proximity effect" on a microphone.

Feedback: Squeal, howl, or hum due to an input device receiving the output signal of itself. A form of *cyclic redundancy*.

FOH: Front of House. Usually refers to the main PA system and its engineer. This is what the audience is listening to.

Gtr: Abbreviation for guitar.

Hi-Z: High-impedance. Unbalanced 2-pin connections and cables.

LEDs: A term I use for Large Element Dynamic microphones.

LECs: A term I use for Large Element Condenser mics.

Limiter: An audio device that prevents a signal from exceeding a certain level.

Linear: Literally meaning "in a straight line," it can also mean smooth and even; e.g., a 10 percent increase of a control produces a 10 percent increase in level at all points. See *Log*.

Line check: An abbreviated soundcheck in which individual signals are checked for gain, level, and EQ settings.

Log: *Logarithmic*, or a nonlinear exponential characteristic; e.g., a 10 percent increase of a control at one point produces a 15 percent level increase at another point; or the same 10 percent increase of a control produces a 7 percent level increase at another point. A "log" generally has a specific chart value for this change.

Lo-Z: Low–impedance; normally a balanced 3-pin or 3-conductor connector. Lo-Z is typically 1 kilo-ohm or less.

Mains: The main PA speaker system.

MEDs: A term I use for Medium Element Dynamic microphones.

Mic: An abbreviation for microphone.

Microphonics: When a component or piece of equipment becomes sensitive to environmental noises. Ringing, feedback, coloration, and distortion can happen when something goes microphonic.

Modular: A system comprised of individual parts or sections.

Mono: Abbreviation for monaural, or one sound. Mono can be one channel, multiple channels summed into one mix, or the panned center of a stereo mix.

Mons: Abbreviation for monitors.

Ohmage: Amount of resistance in a signal path.

Pan: Abbreviation for *panorama*, meaning L/R placement in a stereo mix.

Phase: Used when a signal or voltage is traveling in a particular direction, either positive or negative.

Pink Noise: A term for an equal balance of all frequencies in the form of a test signal.

PLA: Prime Listening Area. In every venue, there is a spot where the blend of the PA system and the stage is balanced. The PLA is the location where everything is properly focused and sounds its best. This area varies from system to system, and is highly specific. Practically speaking, this area is where the majority of the audience is located.

Polarity: The positive or negative direction of voltage or a phase relationship.

Pre-EQ: A signal that has received its input before any EQ and is therefore not affected by any subsequent EQ.

Pre-Fader: A signal that receives its input before any output fader and is therefore not affected by subsequent fader adjustments.

Polarize: To designate a specific polarity to an electronic device, either positive or negative.

Proximity Effect: The increased low-frequency and upper-midrange boost that happens when a mic is placed close to a sound source. Similar to the Equal Loudness Contour. This phenomenon must be considered when "close miking" a signal.

Rejection: The tendency of a mic to not pick up noise from the back and/or sides of the element.

RFI: Radio frequency interference. Sounds such as radio signals, hiss, and white noise.

SECs: A term I use for Small Element Condenser mics.

Snake: A remote input box connected to a mixer.

Sonic Space: The area in which a sound can dissipate without being reflected or encroached upon by other sounds.

Soundcheck: A band's full setup and test mix. When stage levels, monitor levels, gains, EQs, and effects are all adjusted for a proper mix. Often these settings are logged and saved for showtime when they are recalled.

Specs: Abbreviation for specifications.

SPL: Sound pressure level; refers to the decibel level at a point of reference.

Stage Left: The left side of the stage when facing the crowd from onstage; the right side of the stage when facing the stage from the audience.

Stage Right: The right side of the stage when facing the crowd from onstage; the left side of the stage when facing the stage from the audience.

Staging: A location for equipment when loading on or off the stage.

Staging area: A staging area can be near the stage, but out of sight.

Strike: To remove from the visible stage area.

Subgroup: A mix bus that is used for summing a number of inputs before going to the master outputs; a way to premix drums, vocals, etc.

Teardown: To remove and pack away equipment after a show.

Thermal: Relating to heat. If something goes "thermal," it means that it has overheated and malfunctioned.

Transducer: A device that transforms one form of energy into another; e.g., acoustic energy into electrical energy. Microphones, speakers, and pickups are all transducers.

Upstage: Toward the front of the stage.

Wedge: A term typically used for floor monitors due to their "wedge-like" appearance.

White Noise: The typical hiss sound, which contains a random balance of frequencies.

XLR: The 3-pin connectors used in most balanced, low-impedance systems.

Zones: A term used in this book to illustrate the relationship between stage setups and monitors.

Unusual Stages and Other Oddities: Dealing with Some of the Strange Situations Bands Often Face

Topics covered online include:

▶Triangle Stages
▶Wedge Stages
▶Diamond Stages
▶Island Stages
▶Compromised Stages
▶Unbalanced Rooms
▶Classifying Unusual Stage Types
▶Stage Geometry
▶Stage Orientation
▶Using Location, Focus, and Balance
▶Stage/PA Coordination

UNUSUAL STAGES AND OTHER ODDITIES

While researching stage setups for this book, I noticed some really strange-shaped stages, weird PA setups, and a few other conditions that made me wonder, "What were they thinking?" It's not unusual for a bar or club to add a stage as an afterthought, sometimes with even less consideration as to PA system aspects. It's all about compromise. In almost every case, it's an issue of money: What does it cost to make a stage, and how much can I make from having bands play? This philosophy can create some highly unusual conditions for bands to deal with.

Most of the techniques in chapter 2 were meant for conventional stages and cover a lot of ground as far as technique is concerned, but there are a few odd types of stages that are quite similar in their design flaws and can serve as useful examples of how to approach these situations. While it was very tempting to include these oddities in chapter 2, I felt it would be much more comprehensive after covering conventional stage approaches and monitors. The techniques used in this chapter are meant as starting points and are very subjective to the needs of each individual band. While not an exact science, these examples can serve as a starting point for many uncommon band setups. As always, Location, Focus, and Balance will be your primary tools.

The Logic: Odd-shaped stages and unbalanced rooms present a challenge not only to the band that is setting up, but also to the engineer who has to mix them. Many times these strange stages create large gaps in the PA system coverage due to the PA cabinets being placed very far apart or by being off-center of the area where people prefer to be located. It is here where correct sound source placement begins to matter. And while it is not your job to "mix" from the stage, some considerations should be made to not overemphasize these imbalances.

THIS REST OF "UNUSUAL STAGES" IS AVAILABLE ONLY AT WWW.ROCKINYOURSTAGESOUND.COM

Why? This is one of the most unusual pieces ever written for live sound, and the situations described in this material aren't everyday occurrences for most bands. I can assure you that you will see some strange stages. While most of you will run into something very similar at times, this material will only become relevant when it happens. Now that you have fully read and understand the contents of this book, check out the situations I decribe on the website, and you'll be aware when you confront them.

While I have based some of these examples on the real-life venues I have dealt with, the examples may not resemble what you will see in your part of the world. The web content makes it easier to reference and discuss. (I expect it to be a much talked-about addition to the book!) The forums on the site will allow you to interact with other readers who have had similar experiences, ask direct questions, and submit your own unusual stage situations. The content of the piece is subjective and primarily meant to be suggestions. There will no doubt be many varying opinions as to the right way to approach some situations. This material will help to get the ball rolling!

So go ahead and work your way through the book, and "Unusual Stages and Other Oddities" will be available when you need it on www.rockinyourstagesound.com. It will become much easier to understand now that you've read this book.

DENNIS NEIL

ABOUT THE AUTHOR

Rob Gainey is a musician and engineer with 30 years of experience on both sides of the mixing console. As the house engineer for Hollywood's Troubadour and Coconut Teaszer, Rob has mixed sound and monitors and stage managed for bands including Mötley Crüe, The Wallflowers, No Doubt, Weezer, Incubus, System of a Down, Coal Chamber, Tom Jones, Christian Death, The Wild Colonials, Bighead Todd and the Monsters, Leatherwolf, Dirty Looks, Rhino Bucket, The Proclaimers, Corrosion of Conformity, World War III, The Riverdogs, Drown, House of Pain, Mitch Perry and many other prominent artists.

Rob has also worked as a freelance engineer at Hollywood clubs including The Whisky a Go Go, The Roxy, The House of Blues Sunset Strip, Club Lingerie, The Roxbury, Mancini's, FM Station, The Palace, The Galaxy Theatre, and The Key Club.

Rob is currently CEO of Ultrasonex Corporation, dealing with the many aspects of audio including studio and live sound, vintage guitar and gear appraisals, and Jurassic Cabs® stage cabinets. Rob is available for freelance sound, PA system design and installation, seminars, and stage setup instruction. For information please contact him at www.rockinyourstagesound.com or www.jurassiccabs.com.

INDEX